Basic Thinking

On Beginning at the Beginning in Thinking about Social and Economic Problems

Wilmer MacNair

University Press of America, Inc.
Lanham • New York • London

Chapter 1

What Basic Thinking is

Basic thinking is thinking that begins at the beginning. It, like any thinking, is concerned with events, with what happens, and it wants to understand these events. But it does so in a special way. Basic thinking strives to get back to a beginning, to a point of origin where the first causes of what is happening are to be found. It is not content to look only at the surface of events or at the obvious "buttons" which, when pushed, make things happen. Rather, basic thinking intends to begin analysis with the first and basic causes and to proceed from there.

As an example, imagine a person who is working very hard in order to get important things done. As he works and struggles, he has a bad feeling that makes continuing his work difficult. That feeling, he learns, has a name. It is called "being tired." The person then discovers, or someone advises him, that drinking strong coffee will make the feeling go away. Delighted to have learned this, he pours a cup every time the feeling comes upon him. The coffee is the "button" that he pushes. In time, however, someone advises him that he has not noted the root of his problem. The root, the adviser suggests, is fatigue; its cause is excessive or prolonged exertion, and its cure is sleep. What a wonderful discovery! Sleep deals with the beginning cause of the problem, and for this reason affords a far better solution than repeated doses of caffeine. And the person will find he fares better when he takes up that practice.

By itself, this example seems silly. Everyone knows about fatigue and rest. But there are cases that are not so silly, such as the economy, unemployment, poverty, and the like. Here also, there are problems, and here also, people suggest solutions to the problems. But often the solutions are like those cups of coffee: they might help, at least a little bit and in the short term, but they provide no long-term solutions. Among them are "free trade," "managed competition" health care, enacting "tough" anti-crime legislation and others. These may (and may not) make us--or some of us--feel better for a while, but for real and long-lasting solutions, we need to look elsewhere.

Thinking is, of course, always about something. We have a problem or a pain; something is not right with us, and we focus our reflections upon our unhappiness. Perhaps there are things we feel we need but do not have. Without these things, life is drab or full of anguish. It certainly is not as good as it should be. Or we may have things we do not want--burdens lie on our shoulders, and obstacles stand in our way. When confronted with these lacks and burdens, the first thing we tend to do is reflect upon them. We *think*. In due course we may want to do something, but reflection comes first. We have to image or define what it is that bothers us. The project which this book undertakes is to begin such thinking--at the beginning.

This book labels thinking that is *not* basic as "usual thinking." It is the kind of thinking in which people engage most frequently. In contrast to basic thinking, usual thinking begins with "surface" events, those that are in the middle between the beginning and the end. People usually start their thinking at this mental place. When they do, their thought processes proceed along familiar courses; it is a comfortable terrain in which they simply continue to think.

People commonly think in terms of money and ideas associated with it, such as the concepts of debts, being able or not able to "afford" things, exchange rates and the like. Such thinking is by its nature usual rather than basic. To think "money" is to land in the middle of the process of thinking and to move from that point. Actually, money is an abstruse and difficult concept. If it were not for the fact that we have thought in terms of money all of our lives, we would find it difficult to do so. We would not readily envisage our world as the give and take of money as we do. Money does not, we may note, satisfy any need or afford any pleasure. By itself, it is nothing. Things, not money, fill our empty spots and make us feel good. The state of being fascinated, or perhaps even mesmerized, with money that grips people in our society and dominates their minds provides a good example of usual thinking. It is by its nature mistaken thinking. The thesis of this book is that we, as people concerned about the world, need to get back to the beginning. We need to talk about how we organize to get from nature the things that we want (production) and how to get those things to the people who will use or consume them (distribution).

Also, this discussion has to do with "us." When people do basic thinking, they are thinking as members of a community. Each person is a participant in a very large "we." This "we" can be a group of any kind: a tribe, community, region, or nation. And the group invariably suffers problems. Troubles of various kinds beset it, and these difficulties are those of the group as such. The members of the group think of the problems as being "ours"--as community problems. The group as a whole addresses its problems in terms of a unified plurality--the troubles belong to "us", and "we" must think about what "we" will do to solve them. It is similar to what people do when they discuss politics. The focus of attention in "talking politics" is not on an individual and what he can do independently to make his own life better, but on what "we" can do to make "our" lives better.

Certainly, any individual has problems that are uniquely his, and he does things himself to solve them. But at that point, basic thinking is not an option for him. He must begin in the middle because he *is* in the middle. He finds himself in a situation, and he must decide how to make the best of it. He is surrounded by things, by specific lacks and obstacles. He did not choose his present dilemmas; he was, rather, thrust into the midst of them. Finding himself there, he must now try to manipulate what is at hand in order to make his bed a comfortable one.

So this discussion is concerned with a "we," not an "I." It is clear that all human groups and the world as a whole do have trouble. Right here, we Americans, together with the rest of the world, are not doing well. Things are bad in our cities, our nation, and our world. People are hurting; they are beset by lacks, pains, and anxieties. A sadness afflicts people, striking them at all levels of society. And worse, it is a sadness that is difficult to identify. No one can name it or label it, much less indicate what its origins, causes, and cures might be. People can express only that things are not going well. They hurt.

Pain encompasses many aspects of human existence. When people do not have what they need to make them happy, they are distressed. There is a lack or an empty space that is painful. Because of this, they feel that life would be good and pleasant if they just had more--

of something. Yet the word "have" here is a bit fuzzy. It clearly means that things are available to someone, or that he has access to them. But this access can take more than one form. It can mean owning a thing, either grasping it in one's hand or having a deed to title to it. In this case access is exclusive. Or access can mean having the right to use something alongside others who also may use it. In this case, there is shared access. Regardless whether the access is exclusive or shared, people are hurting because life, in its unkindness, has not provided them what they think they need and deserve.

Even if some have enough--or a lot--at the moment, they remain anxious about the future. They sense, even if they cannot articulate the matter, that the ground beneath them is slippery and that all of the having-of-things could collapse as one day yields to another. Humans love security, but security is never more than partial. For instance, every time the newspapers report that thousands of workers are being laid off, businesses are failing, or corporations are reorganizing, people wonder if they too will soon come under the ax.

As people see it, all of the different kinds of "have's," combined with anxiety about the future, are like a whirl-pool pulling everyone into one central point, which is *money*. No one seems to have enough of it. Whatever the amount is, it is not sufficient. That is the nice thing--or perhaps the awful thing--about money; there is no such thing as "enough." The only sufficient amount is an amount greater than that which a person presently has. Certainly, he thinks, money in greater abundance would enable him to do all and to have all that he wants, and it would also set up protection for the future. Or at least so he thinks, since his reflections have not been chastened by the runaway inflation that people elsewhere have experienced.

Closely associated with the pain of not having is the shame of not being respected or honored. We hurt because other people do not esteem us to the degree to which we feel they should. We have a problem as individuals and as members of a group. The people who fail to honor us, those who negatively stereotype us, are difficult to identify. These people include a distant and awesome "they" which exists out on the horizon. They are like the tall buildings which form a city skyline, having eyes that gaze at us. Under the force of this stare, we become certain *things*; we are labeled as "successful" or "unsuccessful," "in style" or "out of style." But among people is also the much smaller group of those with whom we are more familiar and intimate. These too look at us and either give us respect and affection or do not. The term "people," by its nature, embraces both those who are many and distant and those who are few and close. We want positive regard from both. When we fail to get it, we hurt.

"Having" and being respected, though seemingly different, are actually similar. Although the former connotes material issues and the latter suggest emotional matters, the two cannot be separated. "Having" and being respected go together. Certainly there are people who have little but are still respected (Baptist ministers, for example), and people who have much but are given little honor (such as gangsters). Nevertheless, having things usually brings respect and not having things brings humiliation. Poverty means both having to make do without and being denied dignity. On the other hand, a wealthy person whom people disdain for any reason vindicates himself with his money. When the wealthy and talented pianist Liberace was told that some spoke ill of him, he reportedly said, "I cried all the way to the bank." His remark, presumably, was a definitive and effective rebuff to his detractors. Money and honor do not necessarily go together, but people usually link the two. Gaining respect and having money are tied up closely together in people's experience--and in their reflection on that experience.

Once the hurting is identified, questions about why hurting occurs and what causes it arise. Some may find that the causes and reasons inhere in their own personal choices. These people assume that they have not worked well enough or hard enough, or that they have made bad decisions about their educations and careers. Others may perceive themselves as neurotic and thus forced into an interior, psychological unhappiness. In contrast, others many see the causes of their distress as residing in the external environment, something over which they have little or no control. Perhaps they have unpleasant co-workers, or bosses who do not appreciate their efforts and enjoy making life difficult for them. Going farther into the "out there," many people see the causes of their pain in the larger realms of society--economics and politics. Members of minority groups feel victimized by discrimination; the dominant group feels threatened by the minorities; the unemployed are haunted by the lack of jobs, or of good jobs, and the heavily taxed feel burdened by governmental greed and by whatever or whomever they can blame for that greed, such as welfare cheaters ("baby producers"), bureaucratic inefficiency, the military, and so on. Members of various groups feel threatened by

others whom they take to be their foes, which can be drug dealers, big
business, government bureaucracy, corrupt politicians, the Chinese,
Black people, White people, males, feminists, liberals, conservatives,
and the list goes on. For example, just recently, some in Brazil
blamed street children for the country's economic difficulties.[1] Some
of these "out there" explanations are, of course, fanciful. Others merit
further inquiry. In some cases, people have valid reasons to affix
blame as they do, while in other cases, distressed people point their
fingers at certain causes simply because they do not know where else
to point. Their objective, in every case, is to account for the hurt.

This book is about such efforts. It attempts to explain why all is
not well in the world and why we humans suffer as we do. The
discussion centers on explaining things basically, by engaging in basic
thinking. Thus, the book begins the process of thinking--at the
beginning.

Beginning in the Middle

Well, how else could one begin to think? One could begin in the
middle as is done in usual thinking. This is the way people think
most of the time. Usual thinking is the kind of thinking that seems
normal and respectable. When one engages in it, he seems able to
express his thoughts readily and gain assent from those around him.
Heads nod; listeners gesture in agreement; and others, also beginning
in the middle, add further comments to what the individual has
expressed. An air of dignity and seeming wisdom pervades the whole
process, and everyone present feels that matters have been discussed.
In actuality, for matters to be properly discussed, it is necessary to
begin at the beginning.

Consider the following analogy. A person is setting out on a trip.
He has a thousand miles to go to reach his destination. To get there
quickly, he simply gets in his car and goes. He drives and drives.
But after traveling five hundred miles, he realizes that he ought to pay
some attention to what route he is following and to whether it leads
to his destination. Since he paid no attention to this problem initially,
what results is very much a matter of chance. If he is lucky, the route
he has been traveling will lead him to his goal, his city of Oz. He
will have five hundred fewer miles to go than he had at the
beginning; he can subtract the miles he has driven from the total
length of the trip. However, if he is unlucky, he has traveled five

hundred miles in the wrong direction. He now has fifteen hundred miles to travel in order to reach his goal; he must add the five hundred miles he has driven to the length of the trip. However, chances are that he has traveled at an angle, neither straight towards nor completely about face from his destination. Thus, he must add or subtract a distance less than five hundred miles to or from the total distance. The probability that he had to add or subtract is fifty-fifty; he really would have done well to look at the map before departing.

When reflecting upon the causes of pain and hurt, the individual who engages in ordinary thinking, and who begins in the middle, is like the man who sets out without first consulting a map. In such thinking, setting out without first looking at a map and without paying attention to which route leads to where one wishes to go is called *making assumptions*. People commonly base their thinking upon certain assumptions, without questioning those assumptions or even being aware of them. They certainly do not consider alternative assumptions they could have made. A person just makes them or, we could say, has them made for him.

In the United States, there exists a certain public discourse, a set of things being said and regarded by all and sundry as normal to say. Moving within this realm of talk, people simply take for granted many understandings of the world. Because they do so without critically examining their starting-points, whether the assumptions are good, bad, or indifferent becomes a matter of pure chance. People could be lucky and think the right thing, but this is not likely, given the high-voltage complexity of the world. It is much more common that they think the wrong thing, and are even unaware of having reasoned on the basis of assumptions that are doubtful and to which there are alternatives. The task for us as people who wish to understand things rightly, therefore, is first to acknowledge that we are in the middle of the process of thinking and then to find our way back to the beginning.

The Case of America's "Need to Compete"

Since the 1980s and early 1990s, people have often asserted that America has a serious problem about competing in international market places. While Americans produce all kinds of goods, the country does not do well selling them. The Japanese and other producers have proved to be better at persuading buyers to purchase their products. Sale of American goods has lagged both at home and abroad. For example, though the United States is the land of the automobile, at least one fourth of the automobiles sold in the country are foreign, whether manufactured abroad or put together in foreign factories on American soil. And automobile buyers throughout the rest of the world show marked preference for Japanese and European vehicles. In a free market economy, competition is the name of the game, and the American players are not doing at all well at playing it.

The reasons for the weakness of the American sales are twofold. First, American products are believed to be of inferior quality. Second, American manufacturers charge higher prices, either because they desire profits or because costs are higher. Labor costs significantly figure into the equation, since American employers pay workers higher wages than employers in non-European countries.

To improve America's ability to compete, observers propose several measures. One of the most prominent among them puts the emphasis on education. The argument here is that Americans are ill-trained at all levels from kindergarten to the university, and that improving instruction should have priority in our national agenda. Better education, it is said, will generate better workers. These workers will work more efficiently, and will produce products which are better and/or which may be offered at lower prices and which will therefore fare better in global competition.

Also among the suggestions for improving America's competitive edge are devices which reduce the costs of production. The most significant of these costs is labor. Some strategies by which labor costs may be made more economical include inducing workers to settle for lower wages, establishing plant sites in areas where people accept low wages, and building plants outside of the United States in countries where laborers work for a fraction of what it takes to satisfy the American laborer. Also, since labor costs do not consist only of wages but also of features of the work site that make the working day safe and pleasant, money can be saved by reducing expenditures on these items. Further, things which corporations are required to do to protect the environment are an expensive part of production. Getting environmental legislation repealed or not adhering to environmental laws can reduce costs for corporations.

When we look at these efforts to improve education and reduce costs of production, we would normally think that there are reasons for them. Activities are *interpreted* in ways that are appropriate in view of their contents. If, for example, a man appears at a lady's door with flowers in his hand, we think he wishes the lady's favor. If another man is running frantically, we assume he needs to get somewhere in a hurry, and so on. The activity suggests, so to speak, an interpretation of itself, though of course there are cases where more than one interpretation is reasonable.

Efforts to compete in the global market suggest that it is very important to the people involved to ship goods abroad, or, as we say, to export. And this in turn suggests an interpretation. It suggests that we Americans have a *need to import*. It implies that there are things which we want, but which we cannot or do not produce, or that we do not produce in sufficient quantity. To have them, therefore, we must obtain them from other countries. These other countries, however, are not going to give us coffee, bananas, petroleum or tin out of the goodness of their hearts. They will deliver these items to us only as an exchange, as payment, in effect, for what we give them. Since we want what they have to give, therefore, we mobilize to send them things that they want but do not or cannot produce. These would be, of course, goods that we Americans are able to produce in excess and which would be useless to us unless exchanged for something else. The value of surplus television sets is that we can change them into bananas and coffee. These are items that, like television, make life worth living. We need, that is, to import some things and to the end of doing so, we export some things.

Important about this interpretation--and it is only an interpretation- -of competitive behavior is that the need to import is primary. It is, indeed, the only true need. The effort to export--to sell our products-- is simply a means to that end. Exporting has no value in itself, but instead makes it possible to import. We produce as well as sell such items as farm machines because we want things that others can give us. We want to participate in an international divisions of labor, one in which we trade with peoples who have specialties complementary to ours.

The reasons for this complementarity are twofold. First, there are the climate and the resources that certain nations have and which others do not have. The United States has petroleum, but not in the quantity in which it is found in the Near East, Mexico and elsewhere. Americans grow oranges, but in limited supply, and there are virtually no bananas or coffee grown north of the Rio Grande. Second, there are the capital goods that certain nations have in their possession while others do not. The world's poorer nations cannot just decide one day that they will manufacture trucks, tractors, and computers. Even if they acquire the requisite knowledge by sending students to American or European universities, they do not have the necessary apparatus. They may acquire it one day, but they do not have it now. Just, then, as we think that the man with the flowers wishes to elicit a romantic interest in the lady he visits, we will naturally assume that a nation that frantically undertakes to exports goods has a great desire to import goods.

Competition appears on the scene because there is a problem about who trades with whom, and who, therefore, has the opportunity to produce a surplus of one thing and so to acquire the thing which he lacks. In trade as in love, "it takes two to tango." A group cannot trade unless it has another group with which to trade, and to do so, it has to make the goods it produces attractive to that other group. Because it is often one of several groups which seeks to do just that, however, making the goods attractive is not enough. It has to make them *more* attractive than the same goods produced by another group--it has to compete. For example, if America produces a large number of television sets when what it needs is coffee, the country would most likely seek to induce Brazilians to trade coffee for sets. But if the Brazilians prefer Japanese televisions, Americans may be left with a surplus of television sets and a shortage of coffee.

Competition involves not only customers abroad but also America's domestic clientele. Since manufacturers in other countries make and sell the same goods that are in demand in America, they seek to make their sales to Americans living in America. Thus, American corporations compete with foreign producers for customers here in the United States, just as they try to outdo their rivals seeking buyers elsewhere in the world.

There properly should be no problem concerning this. Presumably, the Japanese or the Italians seek customers in the United States for the same reasons we seek them in regions outside our borders. They want something from us, and to get it, they are willing to give something to us. Every item bought from a foreign producer rather than his American competitor, therefore, should be matched by an item produced in America but sold elsewhere in the world. If an American buys a Japanese car, that purchase should be coupled with an item of similar value which is produced in the United States but sold either to Japan or to a country that also trades with Japan. The trade can be direct, product-for-product, or it can take place in a circle. In any case, if some residents of the United States prefer Toyotas to Chevrolets, General Motors may have a problem, but the United States as a whole does not. Even if a General Motors employee loses his job because of the allure of Japanese vehicles, he could presumably go to work for whatever company produces the matching items to be sold abroad. After all, the Japanese do not send those cars here because they love us and want us to have their cars. They presumably are out for "number one" just as Americans are.

Stated in simpler form, this means that because the United States specializes in what it produces, competition becomes necessary. Because Americans must export in order to import what they want, they must make their products attractive in quality and/or in price so that others will want to receive them and so send things to America. Important to observe here is that having such trading partners is in a precise sense the same thing as a farmer possessing land. The person who wishes to farm cannot do so unless he has land. He may be able-bodied and willing to work; he may know how to farm, but all of that is to no avail if he has no land. He cannot go to work and produce. Similarly, anyone who specializes cannot go to work and so acquire and enjoy goods unless he has a relationship with complementary producers.

The above explanation of trade is all based on assumptions. The fact that corporations seek to export would seem to suggest that there is the wish to import. The fact that it seems to suggest this, however, does not mean that it is of necessity true.

The Real Reason for the Quest for Markets

Despite being reasonable, the belief that Americans export in order to import is *not* correct. It is true that there are things America wants from other countries, but these are marginal relative to the volume of exports aspired to in this country. America does not produce bananas and coffee, and so must import these items if the American lifestyle is to be maintained. The nation does produce oranges, vegetables, timber, and petroleum, but not in sufficient quantity; and so it is necessary to import varying proportions of these items from elsewhere. We Americans have to induce people in other parts of the world to send us what we need, and in order to do this, we must send them things which are surplus for us but desirable for them. We must export in order to import. But does this explain why we wish to export goods in mammoth volume? The answer is no.

The amount Americans wish to export is more than that required to trade for what we want to import. To say this, one must of course have a table of equivalences. It is not simply obvious that a certain quantity of one thing is the same in value as a certain quantity of something else. When Moses came down from the Mountain, he did not bring with him a formula for determining how many bananas to trade for a farm tractor or how much coffee to exchange for a specified quantity of antibiotics. No divine table of equivalences is available, and there is no true market which could determine what is fair and right. There is always something arbitrary about saying what should be traded for what. But using any standard that is in some degree acceptable, Americans have more of a wish to export than they do to import.

Just which Americans have this wish is not immediately apparent. Certainly, it is not all Americans, or Americans as a community. The nation's people need to import because they want coffee and other items that have to be obtained that way. They need to export because that is a prerequisite to importing--for that and no other reason. Such is not the case, however, with certain Americans. Corporations that produce more of a product than they can sell in the United States have, in a pure and simple sense, a need to export. They must sell their surplus abroad or not sell it, in which case they would have just as well not produced it. It would be a non-good to them.

These corporations are the ones who have a need to export, and it is they that benefit from shipping goods elsewhere. The community as a whole does not. It, indeed, cannot, since America already produces enough to take care of its own needs in all but a few areas. It cannot benefit by importing clothing, "high-tech" apparatus and other items because it already has them or has the ability to produce them. If a glass is full, one cannot make it more full by pouring more in. If a nation has a full complement of goods, it cannot become richer by adding goods to the store.

The conclusion, then, is that the much-heralded need to compete better and to export is not a need of America as such, nor do Americans in general benefit from doing so. Rather, it is certain corporations that are wealthier because of finding markets elsewhere in the world. And they are wealthier in the specific sense that they are able to lay claim to a larger proportion of the goods and services available in the country. They do not add to that store; they merely garner more of it for themselves.

Of course, the picture is more complicated, and the results of exporting are different under different circumstances. Exporting could benefit the community as a whole in a Keynesian way by bringing in more money. This money then serves to keep exchanges within the country going--to stimulate the economy, as is said. Or, the "more" that is claimed by the exporting corporations could result in an increase in production. Just as water seeps into a place from which water has been removed, a claim on luxury goods by corporate executives made wealthy by exporting could create holes in the total mass of production that are then filled in by an increase in output. In this sense, the wealthy claiming more might *not* result in others having less.

Basically, however, the need to export is the need of certain Americans, not of all Americans. Its result is that certain corporations, their stock holders, and their employees increase what they have. Depending on circumstances, they may become wealthier at the expense of other Americans, or because of an increase in production, they may become wealthier without affecting others. In either case, they will be laying claim to more of the store of goods and to a larger proportion of that store.

Thus, when the United States takes up the banner "We must compete," Americans set out on a journey, but we begin it from a point that is in the middle. We have already traveled, intellectually, what would have been half of the distance if we had been going in the right direction. That is, in our effort to understand what is going on and to prescribe what to do, we would be halfway to our destination *if* we had made the correct assumptions. However, we have made the wrong assumptions. We are not engaging in true trade but in a project by which some Americans enrich themselves, very likely at the expense of others.

Desire as the True Beginning

In order to move in the right direction, toward true understanding, is necessary to find a true and fundamental beginning point. This point is a *wish*. It is the wish that people have about their existence, the condition that they want or require if they are to call life "good."

This condition may be marked by pleasure: "the good life" is one in which there is more pleasure than pain, a net profit of pleasure, so to speak. Or, the key word might be fulfillment. People wish to engage in projects that "fill" life and in that way make it good; the good life is one in which a person realizes himself. Or it may be blessedness that people want. They want to do what is good and right and so to cover life with a glow that dispels all that is negative or despairing. The wish, then, has different names. It can be for pleasure, fulfillment or blessedness. But all have in common that they pertain to the wish that people have regarding their existence.

Of all the terms and phrases cited, "happiness" is probably the word which best sums up what the wish is. Happiness can result from various experiences depending upon the individual's perceptions of life. The word "happiness" suggests that the individual experiences pleasure in a *gestalt* or pattern rather than in a single experience. It pertains both to what a person *does* and to what happens *to him*. Happiness evokes an image of the family person who enjoys a good marriage and felicitous relationships with his children, relatives, neighbors, and friends, and of the individual who is active in fulfilling the responsibilities of career, family, and perhaps community. An individual who meets these responsibilities and experiences these pleasures is "happy."

Obviously, much is required for a person to be happy. The requisites fall into two categories: the need for *things* and the need for *personal relationships*. The word "things," used broadly, includes items which people consume or "use up", as with food, and those that they use over and over again, as with plates and spoons. It also includes goods which only owners may use, as with houses and cars, and others to which they have shared access, as with roads and parks. Among the things, many are physical objects, called "goods," while others are actions, generally termed "services." Both goods and services afford pleasure or convenience, but they are also associated with dignity and honor. The very fact of possession or access gives a person rank or membership in a group; it marks him as "one of" a worthy or sacred company of people and may set him apart as an individual of special eminence or rank. By virtue of owning something or having a right to use it, a person has a name and is "somebody."

The realm of personal relationships is clearly independent of the sphere of things. What people have to do to get things is very different from that which is required of them to enjoy good personal relations. The latter, at varying levels of intimacy, has a lot to do with a person's happiness. While most would not argue that people who have good marriages and relationships in general can be supremely happy even in deep poverty, such people are certainly happier that those in poverty who do not have good relationships. And the poor with favorable links to family and friends may compare well with the wealthy whose relationships are full of hostility and recrimination. The typical relationships among the wealthy may not be as terrifying as those of the television series *Dallas* of the 1980s, but they may be bad enough to annul the virtues of possessing things in abundance. These wealthy people may be "comfortable in their misery," but it is misery nonetheless. Important as personal relations are, they are not the concern of this discussion. The subject here is human happiness to the extent that it is determined by things, by goods, and by services. Although one must acknowledge that personal relations have a lot to do with individual happiness, this discussion limits itself to how things affect happiness.

The Objects that People Want

What, then, are the *things* that people need to be happy? There is the familiar triad of food, clothing and shelter. These, clearly, are the objects that we need. Food is the only absolute necessity, but our wish for the other two is enough to earn them the title "necessities." About that, few will argue. In addition, economist Kenneth Galbraith has argued that there is a fourth necessity--an orderly environment.[2] His argument embraces both the societal notion of a moral consensus which constrains people to act in accordance with rules, and the political concept of order being imposed by police and the whole criminal justice system. Galbraith believes that this order is a necessity just as are the three components of the basic triad. Indeed, without order, individuals do not have anything, since "possession" is a state of affairs in which people respect the obligation to keep their hands off of what belongs to others. Thus, without order, people cannot possess or "have" anything. In contrast to the triad, public order is by its nature a community matter. Each person may be able to own his own house, but he cannot own a piece of an orderly environment. Either everyone in the community has such an environment, or no one has it. The community provides order, and the community possesses and enjoys that order.

Adding order does not, however, create an exhaustive list. Clearly, there are other things we want. Automobiles, televisions, medicines, and vacations are only a few examples of the many things which add a certain grace to our short lives on Earth. Reducing this multiplicity of other things to an intelligible list involves placing these things into broad categories. The other things we and all people want fall into the following four classifications:

*T*ransportation (private cars, public buses);
*E*ducation (schools, libraries, books);
*R*ecreation (parks, "shows," vacations, sports);
*M*edical Care (doctors, health care professionals, medicines).

The first letters of each item form the word TERM. This acronym makes the categories easy to remember. Each of them subdivides into smaller classifications. Note that not every item which falls under TERM is necessary for everyone. Residents of some cities do not need cars, while others may not have access to buses. Personal preference can also make some things useless and other things necessary. In any case, the list defines the things most individuals feel that they must have to be happy. "Having" refers both to owning goods such as cars and having access to things such as public parks. Thus, necessities include food, clothing, shelter, order, and TERM.

Battle with Nature, Battle with Society

People get the things they need for happiness by *producing*. Defined broadly, producing covers a wide range of activities. Were we alone with just a few others in a forest 25,000 years ago, we would simply find some of the necessities. We could live in caves, pick fruits from trees, and hunt such animals as we were able in order to get food and skins. We would be engaged in "hunting and gathering." Nature would be our factory, and we would be availing ourselves of its bounty. In due course we might begin to do things to the goods which we find with a view to fashioning them to our liking. In this case, we would be working or, as we say, *producing*. Yet even so we would be acting on an "each man for himself" basis. There would be no division of labor except within families or small bands. In other words, we would be living and producing in a parallel relation with each other rather than in a cooperative one. Each person or each small group would produce only for itself and would consume only what it produces.

Significant about this state of affairs is that production is entirely a *battle or a negotiation with nature*. By their labor, people seek to induce nature to yield what it has to offer. And nature, doing its part, resists in some ways and yields in others. Coming to terms with nature's patterns of yielding and resisting becomes the material aspect of human culture; it is the *knowledge* necessary for survival. Inevitably, human relations, or the ways in which people cooperate with each other in forcing nature to make concessions, also becomes part of that knowledge. In this ancient forest setting, human relations are family relations in which personal or customary bonding obscures any exchange feature of the relations.

Of course, contemporary Americans do not live in such a forest; in any case, the supply of things such independent activity could afford us would be, to say the least, mediocre. Living in a hut or at best a cabin, wearing skins or crude fibers, and living on a monotonous diet would be our lot, with very few bits and pieces of TERM available. Far from enjoying the prospect of such rudimentary living, most people do not even want to go back to the way our ancestors lived a scant few centuries ago. They are too fond of the amenities which modern industry affords them. For example, an American's list of things that make life good might include, among other things, a three bedroom brick home with two pine-scented bathrooms equipped with flushing toilets and hot and cold running water. The temperature inside the home must be constant no matter what the weather outside might be. A microwave which cooks dinner and a TV and music center which provide divers entertainments are only a few of the home's furnishings. Behind the house, on the green lawn cut by a power mower, is a barbecue pit and a boat for summer vacation. The garage has two cars in it which, like the bathroom towels, are marked "his" and "hers." When the children reach a certain age the automobile fleet increases to three, four, or more. All of these things and more are what most Americans consider necessary to live a good life. Whoever seriously suggests that people should seek the good life with fewer or different things urges a view of life even more radical than that suggested in this book.

This, or any alternate list, clearly reveals that the things needed for the good life cannot be acquired by people producing these necessities entirely, or almost entirely, for themselves. In order to obtain these things, individuals have to *specialize* and, as a community, develop a *division of labor*. The necessary knowledge and skill and the required facilities and apparatus come into view only by dividing the work and letting each person do a small part of the total task, while he exchanges what he produces for what others have produced. Indeed, any one worker does a tiny part of the larger task, and each large task is mutually articulated with others to form a vast system of exchange. This production system is the womb from which issues the three bedroom brick home together with all that goes with it.

Yet there is a catch to all of this. For now, the negotiation with nature is not the only demand placed upon humans. Previously, humans had to battle nature with muscle and mind and force it to grant its benefits. If the early humans met nature's terms and matched its power, they got what they wanted. The struggle of life was a struggle with nature. This is no longer the case. The matching of wits and strength with nature continues, but humans do it with far greater success than before. (That is why modern people can have pine-scented "full" bathrooms.) But now, a new adversary challenges the victory. Wit and strength now have to turn and deal with a foe approaching from another direction like an enemy suddenly entering the battlefield. The new adversary is society and the exigencies of cooperation and exchange. To get what we want in this new theater, contemporary society must confront a possible failure in cooperation and find ways to overcome it.

Contemporary people work in various fields with specialized tasks. Each individual hopes to take what he produces but does not need, thrust it forth into the world, and receive it back in a new form, as a galaxy of goods that will satisfy his needs and make him happy. This does not happen automatically, any more than a farmer can throw apple seeds on the ground and expect to get apple pie without further ado. Arrangements have to be worked out for all of the necessary tasks to be performed. Each of the many things desired must be produced by someone. Goods that are of no use in themselves but which may be used to produce things that are useful (tools) must be created out of raw materials. These raw materials must be put into the hands of workers who use them to generate things people may consume. Once all these tasks have been performed, the resulting fruits of labor must be distributed. The goods have to be moved from the production site to a location where the people who will use or consume them can obtain them. And further, except in the case of goods that exist in unlimited supply, decisions must be made about who has a right to how much of what. The flow of goods from their point of origin to the hands of their possessor is, of course, a physical problem. How does the producer get them there? Do men, boats, or donkeys transport them? Distribution is also a moral issue. To whom *should* the goods be delivered, and who *should* be able to use or consume them? Along with production, distribution is necessary; distribution is simply a part of production. In other words, some people will specialize in carrying goods around. Distribution also involves *allocation.* Allocation is a necessary moral process, a determining of whose claims on goods are to be considered superior to others' claims on those goods, considering that supplies of the particular good are not enough to satiate everyone.

Battle with Society and Need for Coordination

New kinds of resistance to human effort manifest themselves in the production process, and for this reason, new kinds of efforts or strategies are needed to overcome the resistance. In broad terms, what is needed is coordination. That is, there must be a process by which a large number of very different actions go together to produce a single desired or useful effect. A preferred state of affairs is brought about. This process may be administered by a person who intends to bring about the effect. Or it may take the form of mechanisms, such as the economic *market,* which produce the result on their own rather than through action intended to do so. But regardless how it is brought about, coordination takes place. In one way or another, tasks are farmed out to various people. A proper balance exists between each person and his specific job and the jobs performed by all others so that there are not too many people providing certain goods and services while others are missing or in short supply. If an administrative order develops, directed by either person or process a transfer of people from one task to another will take place. Some will move from where there are too many to where there are too few, with the result that there will be the right number in all places. Physical distribution of capital goods (tools in a general sense) and consumer goods is, of course, part of such a transfer.

Similarly, there must be a moral order. There has to be a set of rules defining who may have how much of whatever there is not enough of for everyone to have all that he wants. Whether arising spontaneously or generated by individuals or committees, such rules must exist. Likewise, mechanisms whereby people develop a sense of obligation or are otherwise motivated to obey the rules must also exist. Someone or something maintains order within the system. There may be a cadre of police who attend to the matter. Or, alternatively, religious beliefs may play a role in maintaining order. For example, some religious group may believe that spirits hovering over the camp will do nasty things to whoever violates the rules or that violators will spend eternity in hell after they die. Or perhaps, customary ways may be used to shame violators, a fate that in some societies is very much like death. All of these mechanisms comprise *social control*.

Where the rules are unclear, or motivation to follow them is weak or distorted, there must be a way of settling disputes between one person or family and another. In the eighteenth chapter of the Book of Exodus in the Bible, Moses accomplished the task himself. He sat all day every day settling disputes among his people, until his father-in-law, Jethro, counseled him concerning matters of administrative science. Jethro suggested that Moses appoint leaders of tens, fifties, hundreds, and thousands to consider small cases, with only the major cases being presented to Moses. Moses himself should act, in effect, as the Supreme Court. This may not have been the first time such a judicial system was developed (Where did Jethro get the idea?), but it certainly indicates the early appearance of some type of judicial system. Stated briefly, there must be a system for the distribution of tasks and goods. Concentration of goods in the wrong locations is a new resistance from the world that requires new kinds of coping. Human effort has to contend with the absence of coordination and by dint of force, intelligence, and good will bring it into being. The resistance is different from the kind manifested in nature; therefore, the ways of doing battle with it have to be different. People wage war against this enemy by organizing to allocate, distribute and trade what they produce rather than by trying to produce more.

Strangely, when Americans talk about problems today, they often use phraseology suggestive of the battle with nature. They say that the poor are poor because they do not work or do not work hard enough or well enough. They speak of improving productivity so that more can be brought forth in an hour's labor. In awed tones, they talk about what computers and other technologies will enable society to produce in the future. In all of this discussion, they fail to recognize that for a long time now the American problem has been that we produce too much. We cannot make our lives better by producing more. Our warfare is with society, not with nature, and we will emerge successful only if our armaments are designed for this kind of strife.

Nature and society are different kinds of adversaries, and the ways of doing battle with them are likewise different. When nature is the adversary, the farmer must take care how he sows his seed. If he sows it in the wrong way, he has no crop. Similarly, the husbander of sheep and cattle stands to lose from an inability to fend off attacks on the herds by wild animals. There are times when nature is reluctant to do its part. Crops will not grow because the land is hard (unplowed) or rainfall is inadequate. At other times, nature goes on the attack, as when hail or swarms of locusts spoil the crops. To overcome the former and prevent the latter, we human beings do not as a rule have to improvise the required kinds of work. Traditions of how to farm, fish, build houses, and perform other tasks are inherited from the past and are tailored to the conditions nature imposes on those who treasure its concessions of food and other goods. The traditions are *knowledge*. If knowledge or efforts to make use of nature are inadequate, crops fail and people are deprived. People can sometimes get by with less, but sometimes they cannot, and they die. When the adversary is society, the techniques learned from the past are useless. Problems arising from people's linkages with each other cannot be solved by use of weapons crafted for an engagement with nature. As the enemy is different, so must be the form of battle. The effects of failure are the same; people are impoverished whether defeated by nature or by society. But the strategies for avoiding that defeat are *not* the same.

Economic Depression and Society

An economic *depression* is the most common form of such failures. The distribution of tasks and the allocation of goods are not effectively brought together. There are people who are willing and able to work, and there are people who want to consume and use the fruits of human labor. But the two are not effectively related to each other. The people who wish to labor are unable to *link up* with those who need their product in a relation of reciprocity, in a relation in which the worker gives what he makes to the consumer who reappears as a producer who gives things to the worker. There are no adequate arrangements for *trade*, for enabling people to exchange labor for goods and goods for labor. The result is that the worker is idle and produces little or nothing, and the consumer has nothing to consume. Since everyone is both worker and consumer, all people are unable to work and unable to consume. This situation is very much like a failure of communication. To see this, imagine two people who want something from each other and are willing to do things for each other. However, they speak different languages and cannot work out negotiations; thus neither gets nor receives anything from the other. A depression is similar, except what is lacking is not a shared language but *money*. In a depression, either people do not have money, or they do not circulate it sufficiently. Regardless of the reason for the shortage, people who want to sell goods cannot do so, since buyers lack cash. And because the seller gets no cash from buyers, he cannot buy what he needs from other sellers. An initial lack of money multiplies, as the normally successful sellers are unable to sell and therefore to buy. It is a vicious circle, all returning to a starting point. Economic activity--buying and selling--comes to a halt, and everyone is miserable. People are unhappy because they cannot work and sell and therefore lack dignity and even identity (an unemployed person feels like a "nobody."), and people are also miserable because they cannot purchase things to consume. Though everyone is willing to work and provide for others, and everyone wants to consume what others produce, no one is able to work out a solution. The culprit of the situation is money.

As illustration, imagine three men who have an excess of certain things while lacking others. Joe has more potatoes than he needs but suffers from a lack of corn. Pete has too much corn, but is in need of apples. Mike has excess apples while being in need of potatoes. Since Joe wants corn, he sets out to trade with Pete who can provide him with it. Pete, however, does not want Joe's potatoes and for this reason cannot trade directly with him. What he does want is apples, for which he must look to Mike. But Mike has no need for corn, which is what Pete has to offer in exchange for apples. What Mike does have a need of is potatoes, which Joe can provide, but we recall that Joe wants only corn. Nobody, it seems, can trade what he has in excess for what he needs.

A solution to the dilemma is, of course, readily at hand. Pete can give Joe the corn he so badly needs. Joe can as an exchange give potatoes, but to Mike instead of to Pete. Mike, then, will give apples to Pete, and everyone will be happy. All have given, and all have received. They have traded indirectly. Each has given something to a second person who gave another thing to a third who gave yet another thing to the first. Goods have flowed in a clockwise direction. For this to occur as an exchange--that is, as an action in which everyone acts solely in his own interest, communication would seem to be necessary. The three men must have a conference carried out in one way or another. In this conference, one of them will say "I have a great idea. Let's exchange in a circle; I will give what I have to one of you who will give something to the other of you who will give something to me." The other two will then nod their heads and say, "that is a good idea; let's do it." The conference is necessary because each is acting as he does in order to get something for himself and will, for that reason, not give anything away unless doing so results in his getting something that he wants for himself.

If such communication is impossible for any reason, there is another way in which the necessary coordination can be accomplished. This would be to provide each man with a certain fourth item that has value, something other than potatoes, corn, or apples. This fourth item must have value for all three of them; it must, however, have value only as an object to be exchanged for another object. It cannot have any utility or afford any pleasure on its own account. It must be something that people think can be exchanged for other things because--and only because--they think that others think so. There is a word for such an object. It is called "money." If Joe has some of it, he can give it to Pete for his corn. Pete can then turn it over to Mike in exchange for Mike's apples, and Mike can return it, in effect, to Joe as payment for the potatoes Joe gives him. Thus, what would in the most basic instance have been accomplished by communication is achieved instead by money. Money flows in a counter-clockwise direction while goods flow in a clockwise direction. Everyone gives, and everyone receives. The money in this case would seem to be a sort of ticket. Because the three men wanted to exchange indirectly, they created tickets as a device for carrying out that exchange.

In the beginning, all three have goods. Any excess of potatoes, corn, or apples possessed by one or the other of the men will eventually rot if the men do not transfer the excess produce to someone who wants it. If the produce spoils, it becomes a useless non-good. In this sense, the exchanges that take place augment the supply of goods; the process involves more than a simple exchange of items. If by "goods" we mean objects that satisfy desires and make life better for people, then it is logical to say that there are "more" goods because the exchanges took place. Thus exchange is like production. It means that there is "more" of what is produced because individuals obtain more of what they want. Since it is money that made the exchange circle possible, money has, in effect, generated goods. Money has done the same thing that a three-way telephone conversation does. Money becomes the means of communication.

Typically, the exchange does not take place among three people, but among a far larger number. In addition to Joe, Pete, and Mike there are Jim, Nancy, Margaret, and an additional few million. With more people trading, more steps enter into the clockwise flow of goods and the counterclockwise flow of money. The principle is the same, but it functions in a more complex way.

Further, there are both consumer goods and capital goods. Some of the people produce only the latter. These are objects that are of no value in themselves, but they are used to produce things which are of significance--consumer goods. Producers of capital goods have nothing if they do not trade. Unlike Joe, who at least has his potatoes and can eat the fruits of his labor, those who make capital goods cannot (by definition) consume their products.

As the diameter of the exchange circle increases, the number of steps increases; and as much productive prowess is devoted to bringing forth capital, rather than consumer goods, producing for one's own benefit fades into the background. The proportion of the typical producer's output which he consumes himself sinks to zero, and the part of it which he puts on the exchange-circle conveyer belt rises to 100 percent. Apart from an occasional garden featuring tomatoes in the back yard and possibly a pear or pecan tree, few people in American society work and make things with an intent to eat or use them themselves. Production for consumption disappears as a factor of economic life. The dairy farmer who buys his milk in the store like everyone else dramatizes this development.

Further, because tools and facilities are owned by certain people, many do not produce goods which they may then place in the exchange circle. What they bring forth belongs to their employer, and it is he who places them on the conveyer-belt, just as if he had made the goods himself. The people have only their labor to sell; it is their only product. They give the product to their employer, who gives them a wage (money) with which the laborers then buy things. Yet as far as the employer is concerned, the workers and what the workers produce are extensions of himself. Their labor is his labor, and the things which issue from their labor are his things. When communication breaks down, the labor becomes a stillborn good. Labor does not rot, like the potatoes; it simply never comes into existence when communication between employee and employer is severed. The potential worker gazes at the "no help wanted" sign and then goes home, assuming he has not yet been evicted from his home. At home he sits, either suffering because of his unemployment or happy to have an excuse to be lazy. His not working is a replica of the potato that is not consumed and therefore rots. Productive power goes unused, satisfies no need, and is lost forever. Again, failure in communication is failure of production.

Money functions similarly to communication. It enables the exchange circle to exist and to operate. Imagine what would happen if suddenly there were a money shortage. Consider the following scenario. Suppose everyone carries his cash in hole-ridden pockets, and approximately half of the money falls through the holes, onto the ground, and from there into oblivion. Now, much less money exists. Carefully note that money does not have an inherent "muchness" as do other entities. Money has quantity only in the sense that it can buy a certain quantity of goods. There is "less" money only when we assume that prices are constant, when the "amount" of money which is exchanged for various goods remains the same. Assume, then, that prices are constant; suddenly less money seems to exist. As a result, exchange does not occur. No one benefits from this halting of the conveyer belt, and all would do well to keep it going and ignore the absence of money. But all cannot act as an "all." Each participant acts on his own behalf, and conducting himself in this manner requires that each transaction be carried out *en toto*. In other words, each demands money before turning over whatever goods he has on

hand. Thus, the whole system grinds to a stop. The process could
have continued without money, but to do so would have required a
form of communication beyond money, and it was exactly the absence
of such communication that made the money system necessary to
begin with.

The above scenario is used here as an example of the tragic
tension between individual and group. In a community of total
goodwill, goods would have continued to flow. Each person's
tenderness for other persons would have replaced money as the
communicative oil that allows the economic machine to operate
smoothly. Yet when each individual takes responsibility for only
himself, the whole system collapses, and everyone suffers.

Dealing with Depression

Logically, two things could be done to get things moving. First,
more money could be put into people's hands. If we assume that the
rate at which money changes hands (number of transactions or
"velocity") is constant, giving people more dollars will result in more
of these dollars being circulated. People will be able to buy from
others who will in turn be able to buy from still others and so on and
on. Or, second, prices could be lowered. We could imagine that by
some miracle of communication, all prices were lowered
simultaneously; the money in circulation would be "more" than it was
before, and a similar increase in exchanges would take place.

For purposes of adding money to the pool, people could simply be
paid for being people; they could be given an allowance. Or,
unemployment compensation could be extended for longer periods of
time, perhaps indefinitely. Social security disability and retirement
allowances could be increased and the conditions for obtaining them
loosened. People could be put to work doing things that are useful to
the community such as building and repairing roads and parks, or they
could even be employed at labor that is of little use to the community
or to anyone in it. Usefulness is nice, but it is not necessary; what *is*
necessary is getting money in people's hands. Producing goods for
export, called trading, often functions as a means of providing people
with money. We give other people something so that they will give
us something in return. Yet, we often neither need nor want what the
people provide, so exporting goods is often "make work" just as is
producing arms for fighting imaginary enemies.

Lowering prices to get things going could be a purely "cyclical" occurrence. At the depth of a depression, it becomes possible to employ people for lower and lower wages, since so few jobs are available. With this change, employers begin to hire more workers, since they can get them at a better price. The workers may be merely settling for what they can get, but as prices of commodities go down, the quantity of goods which their wages can obtain moves upward. Workers may be able to buy as much as before, when their wages were higher, or at least they will be able to buy more with less money than they could have before. Their real wage goes down little or not at all, for the "muchness" of money has recovered its previous level. The number of dollars has gone down, but because the cost of goods and labor has gone down also, any given number of dollars is, relatively speaking, "more" money than it was before. This hypothetical scenario envisages a pure market economy, an idea analogous to that of a pure vacuum or a friction-free surface in physics. The lowering of prices and the recovery of money's quantitative value take place within this conceptual scheme. Yet to some degree, this theory materializes in the "real" world. Some aspects of the recovery from depression during the 1930s correspond to this pure market economic construct[3]. Yet things have been very different from this "pure" model since 1945. Though recessions in the United States have been many, they have not triggered any general lowering of prices. On the contrary, inflation has continued, even during recessions.

The increases in the relative quantity of money through lowering prices could in principle be administered by some regulatory body rather than by allowing market phenomena to control the process. For example, government could legislate price controls and set prices at a figure below their current level. Or, the leaders of industry could agree to simultaneously roll back prices and wages. Of course, this is not likely to happen. Putting money into people's hands by means of the available artifices seems simpler and involves fewer political dangers. In any case, it is important to note that money makes the exchange circle function, no matter how people get their hands on it.

Other Ills of Failed Battle with Society

Several things can go wrong with economic coordination. The system may simply fail to work, or even though the system works quite well, some of the people in society may be left out of it. An exchange circle exists; both labor and goods move in one direction, while money moves in the other. Yet some people are not part of the process. Neither as sellers of labor nor as producers of goods are these people needed; they could just as well disappear. However, they survive by numerous means: kinfolk and friends feed and support them; they eat the crumbs that fall from the plates of charitable organizations and government plans; they perform tasks that people consider unnecessary, but for which they will pay if the cost is low enough. Rarely do the excluded people simply die of starvation, though hunger in the United States is more common in this country than we are willing to admit.[4] We assume here that a surplus of people is not a tolerable state of affairs. Economies exist for people; people do not exist for economies. And just as it is bad if these economies do not work, it is also bad if they do not work for everyone. People may be surplus in the economic scene, but they are not unnecessary extras in truth or substance. After all, people are what economies are all about.

Similarly, an economy may work in the sense that everyone is involved, both as worker and as consumer. But there may be an insupportable flow of goods away from some and towards others in the exchange circle. While all may work, and all may produce, some gain control over and have use of much more of the product than do their neighbors. Certain members of the community have access to greater quantities of what issues from the processes of production. Their needs are taken care of, and they have vast supplies of overkill goods that are convenient to have but not true necessities. Some are able to enjoy a luxurious life style. We refer to such a bountiful way of life as "luxurious" partly because it is comfortable and pleasant, and partly because it envied and admired. Much of its affluence is redundant, as far as practical needs are concerned. And as Thorstein Veblen noted many decades ago, such prosperity has value for its possessors mainly in that it is "conspicuous."[5] In contrast, others in the community must make do with very little of everything. Their diets are monotonous, and their dwellings are humble. Their entertainments are home-grown and involve little glitter. Security is something they know little about, since even greater deprivation always lies in wait outside the door. Their comforts are few, and they have little or nothing that evokes envy or admiration. Without much, they hope only for a measure of dignity. They are *poor*.

Any ordinary member of American society who puts ideologies aside and takes a serious look at this economic situation must acknowledge its injustice. He may not know what to do about the situation, but he will label it unfair. The system's unfairness reveals yet another way in which the exchange circle performs badly. Although the economic machine (the "macro" factors) seems well oiled and many "indicators" may suggest a positive economic outlook, the machine is not operating well. The lubrication and signals pertain to the economy, but they do not pertain to people. And people are, after all, what is important. Stated simply, either an economy works well for people, or it does not work at all.

The Difficulty of Managing a Division of Labor

Coordination is an awesome undertaking. The desired state of affairs is one in which everyone works, each at a totally specialized task. We call this specialization total because the worker does not consume any of what he himself produces while on the job. Instead, he gives it away, while receiving all that he does consume from others. At the same time that everyone works, everyone also consumes. People lay claim to goods, either using them up or just using them; they eat goods, wear them, live in them, and drive them. All of this giving things to other people and receiving things from them requires coordination. It can take place if, and only if, the actions of each person coincide with those of every other person, forming what is a truly marvelous symphony of production and consumption.

Symphonies have advantages over economies. A composer envisages what cellos, flutes, trumpets, and other instruments will do, and he plans how each will perform so that all work together to create a harmonious whole. His final arrangement with its unity of diverse sounds is what the word "symphony" connotes. In addition to the composer's score, the orchestra also has a conductor. He directs the many performers, using the composer's score to bring forth a beautiful, concordant event.

In comparison and contrast, economies have neither composers nor conductors, yet people expect economic systems to work in orchestra-like coordination. Such expectations demand a lot, perhaps too much, from an economy. If misery is to be avoided and happiness wide spread, every productive activity must be coordinated with every other productive activity.   Production as a whole has to be mutually articulated with consumption.   Ludwig von Beethoven, where are you when we need you?

Many have spoken about the collapse of communism in recent years.   Critics often view its dismal performance as inevitable because they believe that as a "system" communism is flawed and destined to fail in every way.   Sometimes they attribute its failure more specifically to the ineptitude of Soviet Communist leaders.   However interpreted, many Americans view communism as the other fellow's problem and failure.   We assume that we will not suffer a similar fate because have never been Communist.   Americans would never allow a thing like that to happen in their territory! Actually, however, one might view the "failures" of Soviet Communism as an inability to perform   the   almost   impossible--to   coordinate   production   and consumption activities.

"But do we not do it better?" the American might ask.   Certainly it is true that consumer goods are more accessible in the United States than in what was the Soviet Union.   In a broader perspective, however, every horror story about long lines and empty shelves in Eastern Europe can be matched by stories just as grisly about the fates of people who live in capitalist societies.   The song "Sixteen Ton," lamenting the fate of the old-time American coal miner, is, after all, a protest against what happens under capitalism.   Instead of beginning with an accusation against either the communist or the capitalist order, perhaps   analysis   should   start   with   an   appreciation   for   the overwhelming difficulty of coordinating the things that people do. We may as well face facts: it is extremely difficult to set up or promote an economy that *works*.   It is also a tremendous task to set up an economy that is *fair*.   Arranging an economy which both works well and is fair becomes even more difficult.   It is not likely that simply adopting the right "system" will solve the problem.   It might be more a matter of how a "system" is managed rather than of which one is ideologically espoused when coordination is considered.   Any system may work if it is not taken too seriously as a system, that is, if modifications are allowed and if leaders are responsive to the will of the people as expressed through various institutional orders.

"Coordination" refers to any device by which divers activities are made to produce a single, desired effect.   Individuals most readily think of it as administration *by people*.   Somebody gives orders, and if others obey those orders, their activities will be coordinated.   It is certainly because of a composer's plan that a group of people making noises on musical instruments ends in a unified harmony, in a symphony. Similarly, if people would get busy and plan, and then would act on that plan, an economy could work well or at least function to an acceptable degree. Such an idea suggests "central planning," a conceptual thesis for which communism is famous (or infamous). Because the above discussion is basically abstract, this comparison will be set aside for the moment. The point remains that, in principle, it is possible for people to coordinate an economy efficiently.

Alternatively, coordination can be *by process*. The most obvious process type administration is the "market" in which people buy and sell and in which the individual's self-interested decisions coincide with what is required for the community as a whole. If too many people take up one line of production while others are neglected, the prices of the goods which suffer a shortage rise, while those items manufactured in abundance fall. In response to this development, producers shift from making what exists in excess to manufacturing what is not sufficiently available. An evening-out occurs; the process generates the right amount of everything which people want, offering them at the right prices. Also, producers striving to compete come forth with high-quality products and sell them at lower prices. They do so not because they sympathize with consumers who are hungry for low-priced quality, but because they wish to do well for themselves. Through these and other processes, administration would be achieved.

Again, the above is abstract postulation, and one would do well to shy away from comparing it with the specific market enthusiasm of the late 1980s and early 1990s. The interest here is in coordination of activities through processes rather than by people. Neither administration carried out by people or administration by process taps into the metaphysical center or core of reality from which everything that "works" arises. Instead, both types of administration deal with occurrences that are empirical or visible, with realities that are by their nature limited and finite; these realities are what they are, and nothing else. They simply function in the way, and to the extent, that they do. There is no guarantee that because one is the "right" way, it will work. Regardless of how administration is approached, either by people or by process, the obstacles to its success are formidable. If it is administration by people, those people are expected to orchestrate an economy and create sweet music. To do this, they must make good plans and obtain wonderful cooperation from those below them in the hierarchical order. To ask for such an ideal situation is probably to ask too much. Likewise, expecting any process to do something that will work for each individual and for the community as a whole places tremendous demands on the process. Communism, people are now convinced, has not worked, and for this reason they reject the idea of a centrally managed economy. An examination of Capitalism during the 1930s and in the period following World War II, however, would also raise doubts about process. Adam Smith's "unseen hand' becomes clumsy time and time again. In truth, it is extremely difficult to coordinate everything that has to be coordinated in order for any economic system to work both effectively and fairly. As soon as people think they have it figured out, something "blows" in the economy, and people realize that their concerted achievements have to be reorchestrated if they wish to have harmony. To understand this is perhaps the beginning of wisdom. Taking an honest look at the awesomeness of the task might make people hesitant to blame someone else for using the wrong approach and less likely to claim that they have the right one. Once the blaming and claiming halt, people will be ready to start thinking about problems--to engage in basic thinking.

Chapter 2

Money

Money is an interesting concept. People in modern societies are well aware of what money is. They can talk with one another about it with ease. They know what purpose it serves and what they can do with it. They also know a great deal about the world "out there" which is formed and shaped by money and all that pertains to it. Yet if a visitor from outer space--or possibly someone brought up in an isolated commune--were to ask them what it is, they would be hard pressed to give an answer. Perhaps they would explain that having money is desirable and that money enables people to acquire the things that they want. But clearly defining what money is would be difficult or impossible Yet such as they are, explanations reveal that money plays a leading role in individual lives and in modern society as a whole.

The previous chapter shows that money makes the exchange circle's functioning possible. Because money exists, people give things to others, though they do so to only take care of themselves. That is, when one person gives things to another, he does not do so out of compassion or to fulfill purely personal obligations. Instead, he gives as a participant in the economic community where people are busy at both giving and receiving. When he throws what he produces at the community, he expects it to bounce back in the form of a market-basket of goods which will serve his needs. His exchanging is circular.

This circular exchange pattern necessitates efficient administration. If people give and take, and take and give randomly, with no guarantee that they will be able to rid themselves of their excess and receive back the things they need, pandemonium results. Only when order emerges out of the chaos of producing and exchanging can people feel assured of systematic trade. Thus, administrators (people or processes, most notably market processes) become essential in imposing order. The phrase "exchange circle" itself suggests that there is circular form and that whatever leaves from a certain point will eventually return to that point.

All goods, by definition, have value and are part of the economic exchange circle where money communicates. The value of most goods varies according to the individual and the situation. Some goods have value to people not simply because the goods exist but because of what they do; tools and equipment fall into this category. On the other hand, consumer goods have inherent value; they have worth residing in them because they afford pleasure or fill needs. The value people place on goods relates not only to practical, physical desires but also to psychological or emotional needs; people may want things because they believe certain items will endow them with dignity and prestige, or evoke others' envy. Whatever the reasons, people do allocate certain value to goods.

Despite the diverse valuations people place upon goods, they can also abstract from the objects a generalized value. Exchange processes force people to do this. If one of one kind of thing is exchanged for two of another, the first object has half the value of the second, or the latter has double the value of the former. In the exchange, a certain number or amount of one thing has to have a value equivalent to a certain number of another thing. The two objects may have little in common except that they both have "wantability" in degrees measured by the numbers of each that make it equal to another. For example, having one's hair styled could be the same in value as ten hamburgers, half of a music lesson, a fourth of a session with a prostitute, or a twentieth of a lawn mower. And of course, if the hairstyling is equivalent to a specific measure of each of these, each of them also matches the worth of each of the others. *Value* rises like a mist from the ground and makes all things comparable.

However, as the saying "you can't buy love" suggests, some things are beyond monetary valuation and therefore have no comparable equivalents. The realm of personal relations displays no price tags. People and relationships with people have great value, but their worth cannot be compared to those things that are merely useful or which satisfy physical appetites. There is no quantifiable amount by which love affairs, family relationships, and friendships can compare to automobiles, pianos, and television sets. Indeed, any attempt to compare the personal to the non-personal seems odious; it appears to deny the personal its proper dignity and value. People often denounce those who attempt to "buy" personal relationships, as in the case of parents who shower their children with "goodies" in the hope of winning their affection, or the suitor who attempts to elicit romantic interest in his (or her!) beloved by bringing expensive gifts. This attitude explains why people condemn prostitution as being the monetary purchase of what properly belongs in the realm of personal relations. People often use the term "prostitution" to refer to any exchange in which money is offered for something that is personal and therefore not legitimately in the monetary realm. Presumably, a person can obtain love only by being lovable or by loving and can win honor only by being honorable in spirit and action. Even when people do give money for service, they may feel that there is an element of the personal in what is done for them. They therefore say "thank you"--perhaps to their cab driver or waiter--on the assumption that an expression of gratitude compensates where money leaves off. Thus, money facilitates or establishes comparisons only among things that are outside the personal realm--those things that are just collections of physical and visible attributes and which serve as the furniture of the personal life without being that life.

Money has no value in itself. The coins or pieces of paper which commonly represent it have no worth of their own. They serve merely as a practical means of exchange. People want money because others want it, while these others in turn want it because still others want it. Value is imputed to money by a shared perception of it within a group of people. It can have value only as long as each person believes that each other person considers it of value. This explains why gold is rarely called money. Even when people use gold for exchange, they do not refer to it as money. Instead, they call it "gold" because they see it as having value in itself, even though it really does not. It may glitter, but so do many other things for which no one would rush to California. That people view it as intrinsically valuable throws it into clear contrast with money which, by its nature, has no value of its own. Money's absence of value-of-its-own enables it to serve as the representative of abstract value, making it useful for exchange.

In *The philosophy of Money*, Georg Simmel noted a basic way in which money is different from all other things. Everything else, he said, has both quality and quantity. A supply of bread, for example, is a certain object, one called "bread." It has the texture and nature of bread. But of necessity, the supply of it is also specific in amount. A certain quantity, measured by weight, volume or number of pieces is at hand. So bread is present both in its nature and in a quantity. Money, however, has no quality. It has *only* quantity. There is no "thing" that is present in a certain amount. The quantity swallows up the quality.[6] Or, it could be said that it has no quality because it is every "thing" rather than a specific thing. It "is" whatever one can buy with it and so, unlike bread, is not one thing rather than another. But since it is an amount of any-thing, its quantity is its entire reality.

Simmel also argued that because of its peculiarly quantitative nature, money is able to effect a radical change in human society. All human relations and human activities in traditional society have a more personal character and express sentiments and loyalties more than is the case in modern civilization. With money absent or present with only some of its nature, it has to be so in a human community. But when money takes on its full nature as abstract value, society undergoes a metamorphosis. It appears as a set of social relations organized around the single theme of "value." These relations are of necessity more of the "business" and less of the personal kind.[7]

Money and Property

Lying behind the concept of money is the institution of property. It, like money, is something Americans take for granted and seem to understand and discuss easily. So much do they simply assume the concept of the ownership of property, that they can scarcely imagine social life without it or even think of community life in which property takes very different forms. As children, we were immersed in a world in which the objects in the world around us were continually assigned owners. A certain thing was said to be "mine," "yours," "his," "hers," "ours," or "theirs." In time, the meaning of these assertions seemed obvious to us and posed no problem. We might not have liked it that something we wanted was "Margaret's" rather than "ours," and we might, on occasion, have even challenged the validity of the statement that it belonged to her. But we had no problem about what the statement *meant*.

Actually, there is quite a bit of a problem about what assertions concerning ownership mean. Property exists in people's minds; it is a subjective reality. But if it is an idea, it is a shared idea. My belief

that something is "mine" or "John's" is not just my idea. It is an idea
that I and many others have. It exists in the space where minds meet,
or, better yet, in the communication that takes place between minds.
It is "our" idea or belief, and its being so belongs to its essence.
Unless a belief about ownership is shared within a group, the
ownership does not exist at all. It is not, like matters of opinion and
taste, an affair of the individual. It has to be shared by many to be
what it is. Another way of saying this is that property exists within
a moral order. A set of sentiments and feelings of obligation which
bind people together in a community comprises the essence of
property.

More exactly, property is a shared belief that certain people have
specific rights and obligations. If an automobile is "mine," I have
rights relative to the vehicle, and others have obligations to refrain
from interfering with my rights. There are three such rights, those of
use, control and disposal. I have a right to use that automobile,
typically for transportation, but I may also use it for any purpose that
does not violate an obligation laid upon me. I may, for example,
press it into service as an office or bedroom. I also have the right to
control the object. I can allow others to use the car, either because
it pleases me to do so or as an exchange for something else. And I
may dispose of it. I can transfer ownership of it, with all of the rights
involved, to someone else, again either as gift or in exchange for
goods or money.

Such rights are never absolute. In various ways, the community
limits a person's rights to use his property. Zoning regulations are an
example of such a limitation. Presumably one person's use of his
property may interfere with someone else's rights to an environment
which has pleasant sights, sounds, and smells and which is healthy.
And in deference to these rights, an owner of land is required to use
his property in only certain ways. Eminent domain provides another
illustration. Throughout the history of our society, it has been
believed that the community as a whole--that is, a very large number
of people-- has certain interests that require abridgement of the rights
of property owners. The community has a right, for example, to a
road that does not contain too many curves. Accordingly, specific
properties may be confiscated. The rights of owners continue to be
respected in the sense that *value* is not to be taken from them, only
a specific property. They are, that is, to be paid enough to buy an
equivalent property elsewhere. Even so, these limitations illustrate

that when we speak of property, we talk about rights that are specific and therefore limited.

In speaking of property, we often say that a person "has" one thing or another. This word suggests physical possession, as when a person holds an object in his hand or has it hidden somewhere. Actually, "having" occurs entirely and only in the moral order. To say someone "has" a thing is to say that people think he has such a right and are likely to respect it in what they do. Thus even if a thief steals my car, I still "have" a car. It just is not in my physical possession at the moment. Presumably it will be in due course. And if the thief parks my car in front of his house and then goes in and retires for the night, I could come and remove it without committing a wrong deed, for it is "my" car. Yet all of this is what people think, and is nothing other than what they think.

Further, that car can cease to be mine and become someone else's car only by an act of my will. Of course, no one can see my will, nor can I see that of another person. But signs of it are visible, as when I sign certain papers. I can "sign away" my ownership of an automobile or other object. However, the signature is only a sign. If someone held a gun to my head or threatened me with a whip to make me sign, my signature could be invalidated on the grounds that I did not surrender ownership of an object by an act of my will. The same would be true if I were drunk or emotionally unstable. Transfers of property are, then, acts of will. Just as property exists in a moral order, so do changes in property relations. In other societies, different gestures have served as a sign of consent. The Bible speaks of a man conveying consent to a transfer by removing his sandal and giving it to the other in front of town elders and other witnesses. This was "the custom in former times in Israel concerning redeeming and exchanging" (Ruth 4:7-8).

If property exists in a moral order, its forms and limitations will be determined by that order. It is not, that is, something that is absolute or cast in stone. It consists of a set of rights, and these rights must take their place among all of the other rights and obligations which are granted to or imposed upon the people within a community. Just what the rights are and are not will depend upon the total pattern of privilege and demand which affects all of the people within the group.

Money as a Claim on Goods

The previous discussions on money and the exchange circle, on money as abstract value, and on property and the moral order prepare the way for understanding how basic thinking perceives money. While this thinking acknowledges that money is a medium of exchange, it also recognizes something far more fundamental regarding its basic nature. Basic thinking realizes that money is a *claim on the existing pool of goods and services*. The person who has cash can stake out a claim on "things," and others will honor his claim. He will, that is, be able to appropriate for his own use or bring under his own control a share of whatever is available.

In other words, what people do with money is to appropriate objects that are scarce, valuable, and viewed as necessarily "belonging" to one person (legal entity) or another. They "buy" these things, as we say. Through purchase, they gain control over things and can command that the things be used for purposes of which they approve. Many of these uses are selfish, while in other cases owners devote goods and services to the promoting of the arts and sciences, or to the bettering of other people's lives. Whether selfish or unselfish, a person determines by an act of will what purposes his claim to certain goods and services will serve. Despite the seeming obviousness that people use money to lay claim to things, the point needs to be stated, for it can change one's view of money significantly. If we took all the sentences in which "money" or any synonym appeared, pulled that crucial word out, and replaced it with "claim on the existing pool of goods and services," our thinking would automatically become clearer and more enlightening. What we say would be forced into the basic mode. Exchanging the longer phrase for the word "money" would push us into the basic mode for two main reasons. First, it clarifies that money is what money does. It has no existence or value of its own; it is a claim and only a claim. Thus, if I have money, I can control what others do. I can induce them to give me things and to perform desirable services for me. However, my control of what others do is not "moral." Others are not under an obligation to accede to my wishes. They are free to post a "not for sale" sign by the goods that I want, or they can say that they "do not do" what I want them to do. But, usually, they--or someone-- will do as I wish. Someone will do so because my claim on goods will then transfer to him. And he, then, can go forth and stake his own claim on goods, his ability to do so having been generated by his granting me my wishes. I am able to use other people's selfishness to gratify my own. Since my giving things is an act of consent, money may be said to deal with an exercise of the will. It enables me to manipulate people, but I do so by engineering their consent. I make them will what I want them to will. Thus, the relationship is one of the manipulator and the manipulated, and money has its reality only in this relation. It has none of its own, but rather exists in the space between person and person. Existing there, it gives me a command over things and an ability to assign those things to uses which give me pleasure, fill my needs or serve causes of which I approve.

The second reason why calling money a "claim" forces people into the basic mode of thinking is associated with the pool of available goods and services. It clarifies that money has meaning *only* in relation to this collection of goods. Without the pool, money would have neither meaning nor value. If the goods disappeared entirely (which could happen because of natural disaster or war), money would be worthless. A man who had a loaf of bread in hand would not voluntarily surrender it for any amount of money. His loaf of bread would be worth more than money in any quantity. And he would recognize that others share his dim view of money and for that reason would not give him things for it. There would be no point then to acquiring money, because once the person has it in hand, there is nothing he can do with it. Since money has value only because *people think that people think* it has value, it would have then become, properly speaking, valueless. The circle would be broken, and money would no longer be--money. If, instead of disappearing altogether, the pool of goods merely shrunk in size, money would become less valuable than it had been previously. Either it would take more money to buy any given quantity of goods, or it would take the same amount of money plus something else. If goods were distributed on a first come, first serve basis, one would need to get to the stores early to get things. If rationing were the means being used to cope with shortages, it would take ration cards as well as cash to stock one's shelves. On the other hand, if the pool of goods grew, money would buy more goods than before; prices would go down. If shifts occurred in which some goods became more abundant and others less, there would be correlative shifts on the claims money would enable one to make.

Similarly, if a person's fortunes wax and his cash in hand increases, he will be able to claim a larger portion of goods available. As he sees it, he can claim more goods. But in basic terms, what he claims is a greater *proportion* of what is in the pool, since the pool is what gives money its meaning. When a person is very wealthy, he can claim a proportion of goods greater than could possibly serve him and greater than people would consider to be fair. Perhaps no one begrudges him the money; after all, society has its billionaires. But if he seeks to use his wealth to commandeer goods that exist in limited supply thus creating shortages for the rest of the people, he is being unfair. He might have wrested (earned) a billion dollars from the operation of the market, but does he have a right to possess what that money can buy for him? It is not clear that he does. The fact that rationing was in effect during the Second World War indicates than when all is said and done, the community (that is, people) does not think it fair for people who have large sums of money to be able to claim a correspondingly large proportion of life's necessities when those necessities are in short supply.

Conversely, if a person's fortunes wane, and the money he has in hand or in bank accounts diminishes, he can claim only a reduced portion of the goods available. Here too, one must question the fairness of his situation: is it right that he would be able to claim little or nothing? Would a fire, a serious illness in his family, or "bad luck" in business or the stock market properly put him in a position where he has no right to food, clothing and shelter? Is he properly obligated to either die or to survive only by the charity of others? Most people would not be inclined to think so. These questions become especially acute when sudden rises or falls in a person's fortunes bear no relation to what a person puts *into* the pool of goods. Since stocks and bonds, for example, have nothing to do with a person's productive activity, why should their rise and fall affect his claims? More generally, why should luck make such a difference?

Here, the contrast between usual and basic thinking clearly reveals itself. In usual thinking, people assume that a person who becomes wealthy by legitimate means has by definition increased his contribution to the pool of goods available. If he bought and sold companies or real estate, the belief is that he performed a buying and selling service--that in some real if not immediately apparent way, he added to the store of goods in a measure equal to that in which his wealth increased. Perhaps he engaged in organizational structuring or

did something that left producers better poised to actually produce.
The very fact that he got money *must* mean that he performed a
service which was of value to people. True, there is the concept of
"speculation," a term used to refer to acts of buying and selling that
serve no purpose other than to enrich the persons engaged in them.
They have no benefit for others and may even work mischief in the
market.   But people think that "speculation" is by its nature
exceptional and marginal.   It does not have a significant place in
economic life in which giving and getting are by their nature bound
up together.

In basic thinking, matters are different. Here there is no necessary
link between acquiring wealth and contributing to the pool of goods.
Certainly in a relation between two people there is such a link. I am
not going to give a thing of value to someone unless he gives me
something or does something for me. If, therefore, we assume that
neither of us engages in force or fraud, getting has to occur as a result
of giving. But matters are different when there is large society with
a complex exchange circle. Events take place within that circle that
obscure the relationship between contribution and acquisition. A man,
for example, buys a field. Some time after he makes this purchase,
business operations are undertaken nearby.   As a result of these
operations the value of the land increases several times over.   The
man can therefore sell the land at a large profit. The events that made
this "windfall" possible were unrelated to anything the man did. He
performed no service that benefitted anyone, yet he received a great
deal of money and, with it, an ability to commandeer the goods and
services which others provide. In basic terms, he is a leech; he is
living "off of" others no matter how much he may appear to have "his
own" money and to not require charity. In some cases, he lives very
well--off of others. He is different from the usual thief only in the
greater magnitude of what he gathers for himself from the stores that
others have labored to bring forth.

The goods in the pool are profane and anonymous.   Emile
Durkheim used the term "profane" to indicate that objects are what
they are; they are nothing other than what their observable
characteristics make them.   There is no special or added character
such as there is with, for example, a nation's flag.[8] The term is used
here with the same meaning. Objects are profane when they are only
what we see when we look at them, when they have no charisma
which affects their worth. If they have value, it is because they are

useful or because they are beautiful or otherwise give pleasure and comfort, and what people will give in exchange for them is determined by their value together with the extent to which they are readily available or scarce.

Certainly, humans value some objects because of what they mean. These objects--such as the American flag and religious pictures, books, figurines, and statues--carry important symbolic value for many people. These, however, remain in the realm of the profane where their value is determined in the same way as any other profane object. For example, the cost of producing and marketing a picture of the Last Supper, as well as the demand for it, determine its price. The mass-produced picture would not have the esteemed value Leonardo de Vinci's original clearly has because the value of the art work depends upon its status as the great master's original. Words such as "copy" and "reproduction" imply the insipid or profane character of the other pictures. The words suggest that what one sees when he looks at them is a "copy" or "reproduction," while "original" has a much greater value and may even be priceless because of an idea others have about it, namely that it is an original. Objects, such as original paintings, have a distinctive value because they are not part of the pool of goods and services.

As a rule only wealthy people, those who have a claim on goods and services far beyond what a person is able to use and enjoy, purchase originals. These people feel that buying these objects has caused them to rise above the market place. They can display objects whose value does not derive from characteristics but from the idea (belief) that they are of special worth, that they are the actual workmanship of someone well known. Perhaps the wealthy's buying is a good thing for them to do, for it enables them to do something with their excess claim on goods without subtracting from the goods available to others and without diverting productive forces, that is, labor and apparatus, from producing essential items (such as food, clothes, and housing) for people who cannot dabble in art. It is as though a person who has a great deal of money arbitrarily decides that a certain decoration is "more" than what it is, and he therefore is willing to surrender more money for it. His purchase of that decoration eats up his excess claim without diverting resources from other people, as would his building a very large home or importing caviar from abroad. For this reason making such a purchase is a good thing for people with excess claims (money) to do with those claims.

Both the objects in the pool and the claims upon them are *anonymous*. They are not attached to particular persons and are available to everyone. Therefore, when either claims or goods are available in quantity, anyone who has a claim (money) can obtain goods, and anyone possessing goods can sell them. For instance, if my car is broken and I have money, I can get it repaired. I may not be able to induce a particular mechanic to do the repairing; perhaps the mechanic will refuse because he does not like me or because he has planned to devote the day to his daughter since it is her birthday. Whatever his reasons for not wanting my money and thus not doing my bidding, I can find another mechanic who will. An anonymous "someone" out there who knows how to fix cars will do it. Expressions in the passive voice such as "I had it done" suggest that the identity of the agent or performer of an action is less important than his capability to perform.

Likewise, the person who knows how to fix cars and wishes to do so--wishes money and will do work in exchange for it--will be able to find customers. Even if I do not wish to go to him for some reason (perhaps because he hurt my feelings, or I do not like his politics, or his accent annoys me), someone else will choose him. Here, the customer's identity is insignificant; only his ability to pay matters. *Someone* out there will have an ailing automobile and will desire the mechanic's services.

All of this availability depends upon the relative equilibrium of supply and demand. If mechanics are scarce in the relation to the number of people who have money and troublesome vehicles, matters will be different. Prices may go way up and mechanics may become wealthy, or mechanics may bestow their services only on people who please them. If the reverse occurs, prices may go way down, and customers may patronize only the particular mechanics whom they choose. But as long as supply and demand are more or less balanced, the pool of goods will be anonymous as well as profane.

Money and Diminishing Returns

Once upon a time, a country boy and a city boy were having a chat. As they talked, the country boy mentioned that as he was growing up, his family always had an outhouse instead of a bathroom. "Gee," said the city boy, "with that, how do you go to the bathroom when it is ten degrees below zero outside?" The country boy answered, "quickly." This little story indicates that when technology and industry are available, money can do things for the person who has it. He can buy a modern, indoor bathroom with a pleasant ambiance. Such a bathroom--with appealing scenery, a pleasant smell, and a comfortable temperature--cannot make a miserable person happy, nor can the lack of it make a happy person miserable. Nevertheless, such a modern facility is very nice to have. With it, life is more pleasant and comfortable that it would be without it. Given a choice, people would rather have it than not. An indoor bathroom is just one of many modern comforts which money can obtain for individuals. In addition, people with money can get fresh fruits and vegetables perennially, buy televisions, travel by airplane, and the list continues. If not happy, life is at least more comfortable because of these things.

Characteristic of this repertoire of things, however, is that the items undergo diminishing returns. Each thing added to what we have does less to make life pleasant than did the previous one. If a person who has been living in the streets is given a one-room dwelling, his life is greatly improved. Add a second room, and his life improves even more, but this time the enhancement is less than was the first one. The difference between living in a large, multi-room dwelling and living in a single room is less than is the difference between having the one room and spending the night beneath the 10th Avenue Underpass. The same principle holds for food. Having some is a great improvement over having none. But as the diet improves, each improvement is worth less to the individual than the previous one. Having good food is certainly better than having food that is not good, but the contrast is less than is the gap between having food that is not good (not "delicious") and having none at all. And so it goes among all the things humans want. The first unit given an individual benefits him most; each successive unit benefits him less than did the previous one. Desires are satiable. Once people are satisfied, they can experience only marginal increases in enjoyment, as when a householder finds it merely nice to have an extra room.

While the desire for goods and services is satiable, such does not appear to be the case with money. The reason for this is that money is an intellectual construct. It is an idea conceived and elaborated on in the minds of people. As an idea, it is not restrained, as is the material of which the empirical or factual order is composed. It can soar to the skies and beyond. It is modeled on the system of numbers, and can do whatever numbers can do. And what numbers do is to go up indefinitely. We may not, practically speaking, be able to count past a certain point, but the numbers themselves know no such boundaries. They go up literally forever. No matter what a certain number may be--no matter how large it may be, it is always possible to add a certain other number to it or to increase it by a proportion of itself. Any person's income, to take an example, could have 10,000 dollars added to it or be increased by ten percent. And when either the amount or the proportion is added, the original figure is increased accordingly. We will refer to this feature of numbers which is also a feature of money as *upward linearity*.

While money exhibits upward linearity, its contribution to human happiness, effected by the purchase of things, does not. The first pile of money cast into a person's lap makes life better for him than when he had nothing. Now he can buy food, clothing, and shelter. The second allotment of money also helps. It enables him to buy more of life's necessities. But the second is less significant than the first. Each addition will benefit him less than did the previous one. While the first made it possible for him to survive, the second did no more than make life more pleasant, and a third would simply be convenient to have. As an analogy, we may cite the mathematical expression "X equals the square root of Y." As Y gets greater, so does X, but it does so less than does Y. If Y is doubled, X increases by only forty percent; if Y is multiplied by four, X only doubles. Additions to one variable translate into lesser additions to a second variable. As money increases so do happiness and well-being, but the increase in the latter is less than the increase in the former. Before long, additions to money add only to prestige and power and no longer to comfort and ease. On a graph, as the line representing money acquired and money possessed angles upward, the line representing happiness falls under it. After a while, the happiness factor levels off, indicating that at a certain point, additions in money cannot contribute to happiness. Often, people possessed of such funds find that they can do nothing with them other than invest in order to make still more. They use excess funds, that is, to get more of what they already have too much of!

Money and being "Well-Off"

As obvious as this may seem, most people do not see matters in such a light. Their views of things are not determined by things themselves but by the conversations they have about these things. As individuals talk to one another, they construct reality. And in this constructed reality, there exists a quality or variable which people call "being well off." As this view sees matters, each of us or all of us together are *well off* or *worse off* in one degree or another. Today we may be better off or worse off than we were five years ago. If something happens, we might be better off or not as well off as we would have been if it had not happened. Of course, we could be neither better nor worse off than we would have been--we could be merely at the same level as before or as we would have been if something had not happened.

The condition of being well off is, in people's minds, vaguely associated with having goods and services available to them or having a claim on goods (money) which they may use when they choose to do so. The association is vague in part because it includes an element of security as well as present possession. I may consider myself well off because I have money with which I may obtain help in case of emergency, such as an illness, or in case I have a sudden yearning to travel. But more significantly, the association between money and the state of being well off is vague because it is a phantom-like construct generated by conversation. It is what people and I talk to each other about and whose existence and nature we feel certain of, as our nodding of heads indicates when we carry on the conversation.

As a variable, being well-off is perceived as exhibiting the same upward linearity as does money. Whatever amount of money I have, I could be given more. My employer could give me a ten thousand dollar raise or a twenty percent increase in my salary, and I would thus feel myself to be better off. I might not want anything more than what I have already, or I may have reached a level of wealth where there really is no such thing as "more." Yet I will still perceive myself as being better off.

In his classic work *Suicide*, Emile Durkheim remarks that human desires are by their nature insatiable.[9] No matter what people have, they want more. And since the extent to which they are happy is determined by how what they have relates to what they want, they are condemned to misery. The only way they can achieve happiness is to impose a moral limit on their desires. A person may feel certain that his lot in life is limited, that there is no way he can become richer or achieve greater eminence. But he may also feel that the limit is morally right, that with that upper boundary his life is as it ought to be. Such a limit may then make it possible for a person to have that to which he aspires (though not what he potentially wants), and so to be happy. Durkheim notes that suicide rates go *up* when economic conditions suddenly improve in a territory. He explains this unexpected finding by referring to the concept of limit. He asserts that when people find themselves doing better economically than they are accustomed to doing, they lose their sense of limit. Their aspirations go up even more than do their actual conditions; thus they are more unhappy than before, even though they have more than before.

Human desires are satiable. Yet Durkheim's assertion about their unlimitedness is also correct. The upward linearity of money generates a double of itself in the condition of being well off. This condition can then improve in tandem with the increase of funds, and it can do so indefinitely. Funds, in turn, are based on a numerical system. So numbers take over; we see ourselves as in better or worse condition on the basis of a number of dollars that we have in hand or in bank accounts.

Imprinting of Money on Things

To accomplish this, money is *imprinted* on things. Humans view the things that money buys as blank pieces of paper rather than as things that may serve us in specific and therefore limited ways. We stamp a money value on them; we perceive them as having value in the same measure as the money whose image appears on them. Some things readily lend themselves to doing this. Jewels are probably the best example. Indeed, the word "jewel" means a stone that has value far exceeding that to which either its practical uses or its beauty entitles it. This is revealed in the great concern people often have about whether certain stones are "genuine" or "counterfeit." Those that are counterfeit are like true jewels in almost every respect. Only an expert, and one properly equipped, can distinguish them from real jewels. From the standpoint of the value things have for people in general, a difference that can be discerned by only an expert is really no difference at all. Differences are contrasts between objects that matter in some way; when objects exist to be put on display, differences can matter only if people in general can recognize them. Jewels in this sense are properly worth no more than counterfeit versions of themselves but are forced into being worth more by the process of imprinting. Much the same is true of wine. The differences in taste between kinds of wine are sometimes so small that it takes a connoisseur to discern them. The ordinary drinker, for this reason, does not know whether he is getting special enjoyment from a glass of wine until this expert tells him. One might think that if a person has to be told how much he is enjoying his wine there is something wrong. The wine is not really different. Yet people think it is different because of the judgment of the connoisseur--the person who "knows." Marginal differences in taste are enlarged many times over by the fact that people have ideas about the small ways in which one wine may be different from another.

Brand names and designer labels are yet more examples of the artifices used to imprint money on things. An item of clothing has a special value, not because of what it is--because of its characteristics-- but because of who designed it. The designer's fame or notoriety come to rest on the item and give it an essence it would otherwise lack. People often give marginal improvements in comfort, utility, or beauty a value larger than that to which the magnitude of the improvement would entitle them. This is the surest sign that people imprint money on things. A car motor purrs a little more softly; the vehicle rides a little more smoothly; it has cruise control; the electronically-powered windows save the driver from the onerous task of making his hand go around in a circle. Household appliances and other exemplars of technological and industrial blessedness boast similar advantages. When people magnify differences beyond practical and aesthetic value, money and not goods is clearly the focus of attention. People begin to determine value in a backwards manner. Whereas we expect things to cost money because they have value, it is now the other way around. Things become valuable because they cost money.

One more item belongs in the mix of how people think about and perceive economic realities. It is what Americans call "success," a term that needs quotation marks because it has special meaning to Americans. The background for this meaning in human societies in general is that certain activities or tasks are given greater honor than others. If one person does one kind of work while a second does another, inevitably one of the two will be regarded as more exalted than the other. His work is deemed by the community to be more worthy, either because of what it does for the community or for reasons not readily spelled out. In industrial societies, it seems inevitable that white collar workers, those whose function it is to manipulate symbols, enjoy higher rank than do blue collar laborers who work with things manually. In America, differences in occupation carry great import.

The special connotations of the word "success" are important. For Americans the good life is one in which they get ahead and become "successes." Doing so may mean doing well in a small, private business, perhaps one that becomes large. Or it may mean climbing the managerial hierarchy of a large firm. It may also mean being a doctor whose examination rooms are full, a lawyer who pleads cases before high courts, or a scientist who makes a breakthrough. Emphasis on "success" as a life-goal for the general populace is a characteristic mark of American society.

While people in highly honored positions are usually paid better than others, honor and pay are two different things, and the correlation between them is far from perfect. It is not difficult to find examples in which the two diverge. Truck drivers and plumbers often have good incomes, but they rank low on the social totem-pole. People whose occupations are illegal or viewed as immoral rank extremely low. In contrast, there are occupations that Americans honor highly but which pay relatively little; teachers and clergymen are good examples. When people cheat in order to enhance their reputations or achieve fame, economic rewards are not always their foremost motivator. For example, some unprincipled scientists have falsified research findings in order to make a name for themselves, with little thought of getting rich in the process.

Yet for the most part, the correlation of honor and pay holds true, even if imperfectly. One is imprinted on the other. Occupations which people regard highly are usually also well-paying. And the money reward serves to validate the occupation's prestige. A job has a certain glory associated with it, but there are dollar signs on the glory that firm it up and protect it from any threat. The reverse is also true. "Success" in the hierarchy of occupations is imprinted on the money that people receive. It is real or legitimate money because it came from that occupation. The worker earned it in a morally upright way. The opposite is money that is "tainted" because the person gained it in a reprehensible manner; the evil character of an activity stains the money derived from it.

Four features ascend the economic graph: money, which measures numerically from zero to infinity; being "well off," which by societal consensus is parallel with the ascending line of money; occupational prestige, which substantially, though not perfectly, correlates with money (and therefore with being "successful" and "well off"); and access to goods and services, which is associated with the other features but in a diminishing returns sense. Each increment of money contributes less to usefulness and comfort than it did the one before it. In this sense, the value of money to an individual does not rise in tandem with the rise of money itself but veers downward from it. If, however, money is imprinted on goods, their value may be forced into a line parallel with that of money and thus also to the related conditions--being well off and successful rises infinitely just as do numbers.

Basic Thinking and Money

Having considered what money is as a fact of social life, we can now see how basic thinking deals with money. To start, note that what people want in this world is a set of goods and services because these objects help people find the good life. The objects themselves do not make life fulfilling; it is mainly in the realm of personal relations that fulfillment either takes place or fails to take place, yet people certainly do better with a supply of goods and services than without it.

In the effort to acquire goods and gain access to services, people are inevitably involved with money. So quickly and intimately do they become involved with it that money becomes, in effect, a surrogate for goods in general. The person who has an ample supply of it already has an anticipation of possessing a galaxy of goods. To move from anticipation to actual holding of the goods, he needs only to "shop." All he must do is to select what he wants from the vast stores of desirable things and then hand over some bills, write a check, or offer his credit card. If anticipation can be viewed as a kind of possession, we could say that having money *is* having all of those wonderful things. This close resemblance of money to an array of goods exists, however, only in the relationship between an individual and society. To acquire goods is to obtain them from people--from many people, indeed from a large army of anonymous people. But since people turn over what they have in hand only for money, money is, we might say, the bridge over which goods and services travel. If I deliver goods to others, those goods travel across money to get to the others. If I receive goods from them, the same conduit is used; the goods float on money to get from the others to me. Money is the bridge that rises above the reciprocal selfishness that divides one person from another and enables them to share what they have as though they were *un*selfish. This is what money is. This is exactly what it is, and this is *all* that it is.

Once people see money this way, certain features of the world appear in a light different from that in which people customarily see them. Three of the features are worthy of consideration. First is the arbitrariness of using dollar figures to quantify collections of consumer and capital goods. Second is the erroneous association of economic "growth" with the welfare of people. And third is the unfortunate reign of money over people's framing of their life aspirations.

Arbitrariness of Using Dollar Figures

In many ways, people use dollar figures to ascribe "muchness" to piles of goods and services. To take one case, suppose economists and others discuss trade balances or imbalances between two nations. Each of the countries has exported goods to the other, but one of the two has shipped off "more" than has the other. The designation that one collection of goods is of greater quantity than the other is quite arbitrary since the goods involved are heterogeneous. Perhaps one country shipped off bananas, coffee, cotton, and sugar to the second, while the latter nation sent vehicles and machines to the first. (Such an exchange was typical between industrial nations and agricultural societies before the industrial countries saw those societies as sources of cheap industrial labor.) On one side of the aisle is a large pile of agricultural produce, and on the other is a collection of machines. How can it be that one is "more" than the other? The answer is because somebody assigned dollar values to each item on both sides of the aisle, added them up, and designated that as the value of the entire collection. Thus, one pile of goods may be greater than the other; and the country which receives more than it gives has a "debt" to the other country.

Involved in this process is the assumption that every object has a price, a designation assumed to have an objective reality. This reality is expressed as a certain number of dollars, which is then taken to be what the object is "worth"--in truth and not just to this or that person. It is not simply a matter of what I am willing to pay for something but of what its true and proper price is. If that price is greater than I am willing to pay, I do not buy, and that is that. If the price is less, I get the object partly for free because the object's price is less than I would be willing to pay. I am not having to pay what the object is worth to me.

Behind this seeming objectivity of prices is the market, which people view as a reality *sui generis*. It is thought to possess a substance of its own, apart from the individuals who are involved in it. The market consists of exchanges that take place between persons (or organizations). In this sense, exchange is at the center of it. But there is a very large number of these exchanges, and all of them together comprise what we mean by "the market." There are several effects of the simultaneous and continuous occurrence of the exchanges. Among them are the allocation of people and resources and the determination of prices. From the standpoint of any person, these effects are objective. They are events that take place "out there" and are in no way subject to his influence. He must deal with them as "facts of life" that decree what is required of him if he is to make his way in the world. The wealthy nations think of themselves as being like that individual. They determine prices, yet when they have done so, they treat these prices as *data*; they view them as "givens" which indicate how much of one thing is be traded for how much of something else. They thus make it possible for one nation's offering to be considered to be "less" than what it receives from another, so that it is "in debt" to the other. This objectivity is spurious. There is no world "market" that shapes economic life through a balancing of efforts on one side with wishes or demand on the other. The world's people do not have enough options to make such a market possible. In the world as it is, the prices of objects are nothing other than what someone has to pay in order to obtain the objects. If a person wants coffee but wants it for less than what a seller demands for it, he will have to do without his morning cup. If a seller wants money, but does not want--need--it enough to surrender his coffee for less than a certain amount, he will have to make do without receiving that money from that source.

If, as is likely, one party to the negotiation has less need than the other, commonly because he has more trading partners available to him, he will have more power. For this reason he will be able to get what he wants on "favorable terms." The buyer will be able to buy at a low price, or the seller will be able to deliver goods for a high price, however "high" and "low" are determined in the specific situation. There is no objectively-determined correct price, and there is nothing dignified, moral, or fair about trading on the basis of prices as they are.

Today, wealthy nations trade with poor nations and then assert that the latter have received more than they gave and therefore have a debt. Because of this, the wealthy nations make demands that the poor nations pay off their debt or that a program be set up according to which the debtor country will make payments on the debt. These debts accrue interest, and so grow as time passes. Indeed, they often grow even when the debtors are making payments. These debts become so large and grow so rapidly that there is no possibility that the debt can ever be paid. After all, to pay them, the poor nations must ship off the products of their farms and mines, and there are limits to just how much of these the wealthier nations want. Once that limit is reached, there is no other way the debtor country can pay. And further, if these tropical countries do come up with more bananas and coffee, the prices of these commodities would go down--the greater number of bananas would no longer be a greater value. In effect, to obtain bananas and coffee, the wealthy nations pay the poor countries an amount which the wealthy nations determine themselves. The poor countries have no real control.

The above situation typifies power's influence. The more powerful take from the less. The strong take what they can and give what they must--in order to keep taking. Yet to talk about what they do, the powerful groups use euphemisms for words and concepts that give the process an air of dignity and propriety. They speak of having sent "more" than they received, of there being a debt, and of what should be done to enable the poor countries to pay the debt. Their rhetoric becomes conventional wisdom. Thus, the public accepts their lingo as credible, as definitive reality. Yet what lies underneath is simply the powerful exercising their might over the weaker nations. This subject will be taken up in greater detail in Chapter Eleven.

Economic "Growth" and Welfare of People

The Gross National Product and other measurements dealing with an economy's growth are merely dollar figures that quantify goods. The widely used GNP (or GDP) figure refers only to those goods that, having been produced, are exchanged in the national market; it does not include the goods that people both produce and consume without exchanging them in the system. Being abstract, the GNP distills value from a heterogeneous collection of goods and services. Using GNP standards, goods, no matter how different in character, command comparable prices and are not otherwise distinguished from each other. Nothing in principle is wrong with using such abstractions. After all, we abstract every time we talk. But the usefulness of abstractions depends upon leaving out the less important features of the situation while retaining the important ones.

When what is left out in the process of abstracting is important, the numbers used in abstracting lose much of their meaning. If we have a pile of goods, and a price affixed to them, we can compare their monetary values. But if they are very different and are of value in very different ways, figures calculated from their prices are not very meaningful and comparisons of these figures are even less so. Thus the GNP is really a numbers game that has value only in certain and very limited ways.

Even less instructive are comments about the "growth" of economies. Frequently, people use percentage rates to discuss economic growth, comparing the past with the present and one country to another. Numbers assume a pseudo-reality. They are, in effect, forced to stand in for aspects of life that cannot properly be quantified. As a result, realities that do not, in fact, fit tightly within a scheme are treated as though they did and so assume a false precision. Exact figures which are used to represent what are really fuzzy realities are not truly exact figures. Statements about the growth of an economy can be made, but they are gross and not exact statements and should not be made with numbers. One could say that a certain society has added "a great deal" to its store of apparatus and tools and to its "infrastructure"--roads, railroads, and the like--and so is able to produce more of what people want than it did before. This is as much precision as can legitimately be made. The economy has grown "some"; that is all.

Both the GNP figures themselves and those representing its growth suggest a reality which people have conjured up simply by talking about it. This genie which people have called forth from an intellectual Aladdin's lamp is *the economy*. They have ushered this reality into existence, and they treat it as important. The economy has become humanity's prime concern. People treat it as a surrogate for what is really important--how people are faring. Most use it much as they use the concept of average (mean or median), as a shorthand for speaking about people. When someone says that the economy is growing, others assume that all people are doing better or that they will soon be doing better.

However, the economy is not an average. It is instead a constructed reality, a thing that exists because everyone says it does and because people act on the basis of its being real. Its relation to people is extremely vague, for an economy can grow while people fare no better than before, or it can shrink while the lot of most citizens improves. If what we want is to talk about how things are *with people*, we would do better to speak less of the economy and to direct our attention to people themselves.

Centering discussion on human conditions requires that we engage in statistical talk. This is a manner of speaking in which we use numbers in order to make single statements which report on a very large number of observations. Statistics, in this sense, are like blotters: they soak up a great deal. If someone says, for example, that forty-three percent of voters voted for Bill Clinton for president in the 1992 election, he makes a single statement. But that statement gathers into itself an observation of what each of the many voters in the election did when he/she voted. Even though the figure would be the same even if a certain person had voted differently, that is only because it is not carried to enough decimal places. In principle, carried far enough, any given Tom, Dick, Harry, or Margaret's vote would affect the figure. This is what statistics does, and it is statistics's virtue. If we want to know how it goes *with people* and not just about a phantom such as "the economy," we need to speak statistically. The people are, we may note, many, and yet what we want to know and say has to do with all of them.

It is true that statistics deceive as well as reveal. They do so most notably because they "hide" information. If each observation is to be included in the one statement, it has to be drastically simplified. It has to take the form of an "either-or" or a number. If we want figures on poverty in the United States, for example, we have to determine that each person--or each family--either is or is not "poor." And we must so define "poor" that any observer would make the same judgment about each person as would any other observer. So we have to define poverty in specific ways. Our doing so will inevitably obscure important differences both among the poor and among the non-poor. A few cases would even seem to be wrongly classified. Some called "poor" would be living rather well and some denied that title would be truly deprived. Such is the danger of statistics. The advantage, however, is also notable. This advantage is that it becomes possible to say something about a very large number of individual people. And this is what we need to do if we want to know how "things are" with Americans or with any particular group of Americans.

Money and Life Aspiration

Another way in which basic thinking can make us see our world differently has to do with an individual's life aspirations. Americans as a group do not appear to be obsessed with money. They seem, rather, to regard it in a very practical way. This is true of many, perhaps most, for a simple reason: they have little choice. They have to do all they can to maximize their incomes in order to live a certain way. The voracious wolf is at their doors; any sudden drop in income or any unexpected and large expenditure (such as an illness) could cause them serious damage. Therefore, it is not surprising that they work as much as possible, have dual family incomes whenever they can, and always opt for the highest paying job. To them, it is all very practical.

Even apart from this, Americans do not seem to make decisions entirely in the interest of maximizing income. In thinking about careers, young people commonly reflect on what they want to do and on what they find pleasant and fulfilling. They are encouraged to do so in many ways. People in general seem to believe in it and approve of it. If some careers hold less promise of wealth than others, people give approval to a person's determination to pursue one of them because it is what he wants to do.

Additionally, when young people contemplating careers consider the options open to them, they see these choices differently because of differences in their life experiences. Differences in what they know and in the events to which they have been exposed affect their view of matters. Even though they live in the same society, some of them will see their common reality from different angles. For instance, two young men who are similar in character, ability, and interest choose dissimilar occupations--one becomes a wealthy businessman, while the other becomes a police officer with a modest income. Analyzing the characteristics of each man does not answer why one became a businessman and the other cast his lot with the police force. Rather, each man's individual perception of the world at a certain time affected his decision. To the first, a business career seemed wide open and full of possibilities. To the second, a law enforcement career loomed as a realistic and available job opportunity. The difference between the two may be factual as well as perceptual. That is, each may have personal contacts, "qualifications" or knowledge which are different from those of the other. Once the two men had made their decisions, they acted upon them, and in so doing widened the gulf between them. Each now has a vested interest in the path he has chosen. In summary, both job preferences and angle of vision prevent people from making decisions based on strict economic rationality. In general, when people make career decisions and take career actions, they do so within concrete situations and by taking advantage of whatever is offered within those situations.

Lurking behind all of this, however, is a conceptual germ, an idea that is able to affect and infect what people do at various points. It is the correlation of money with the condition of being "well off." The amount of money a person possesses is believed to determine how well off he is. The more he has, the better off he considers himself to be. Money here is money *sui generis*, a thing-in-itself. It is not good because of the things one can buy with it; it is a special reality "constructed" by societal conversation. Actually, in modern society people do not spend money for things because they want them. Rather, they want them because it takes money to get them. Money, as already noted, is *imprinted* on things, and each person considers himself "well off" because he possesses these things. He does not discover himself to be better off because he owns a Mercedes; he simply assumes that he is as an article of faith.

Improving one's estate is of great importance to most people. They work in various occupational fields, striving to increase their incomes as much as possible so that they can become better off. For example, in contrast to teachers, who very seldom have any power in determining their salaries, physicians can control their incomes. Because of the importance of their services, the smaller number of people in that line of work, and their ability to set fees and change rates as they please--especially if they have a private practice, physicians can manage their own salaries. In Chicago, a group of doctors in a group practice raised their office visit fees from thirty-five to forty-five dollars. One in the group refused to do so. He argued that their patients could not pay what they had been charging and so certainly could not pay more. This altruist was promptly dismissed from the group. While not all physicians are so greedy, similar stories could be told many times. A large number of people believe that if there is a way to get incomes up, then up they must go. Most feel that it is fair for them to get whatever they are able to get; they feel no need to justify their actions. By their ingenuity they master the task of explaining away their desire to be "better off."

The essence of basic thinking here is that income is strictly a means to an end. It is a means to the end of acquiring the things which a person needs to live comfortably and enjoy life. These things comprise the furniture of the good life, so to speak; they make it possible for people to carry out the personal dramas and projects that make life fulfilling. To enjoy life, it is necessary to have some of these things, and it is helpful to have others of them. But there are limits. Beyond a certain point, only improved personal relations can make life better; adding to the furniture cannot. Once a person has become comfortable, he cannot become more so by having more fine chairs in which to sit. He has all he can use. Also, acquiring more is not always acquiring "more." That is, objects viewed as better and therefore more expensive are often better only because they cost more. They have money imprinted on them, but they do not actually contribute significantly to comfort, ease, pleasure, or safety. To see one's self as "better off" because of possessing them is to hold a superstition.

To push the matter a little further, we may imagine a person whose services are in demand and who controls his own income. This individual considers the pool of goods out there and what kind of claim he should have upon it. To him, it seems fair that his share is larger than that of others. After all, he went to school to learn how to do his job while others were already earning wages. He made sacrifices, exerted effort, and acquired skill as others did not. But even granting this, he might think that there is a limit to what his greater share of goods should be. Even if he does deserve to be well rewarded, his view is that this reward should be a certain amount and no more.

The principle behind this thinking is that one person's share should not reach the skies or consume half the pie while many others are groveling for leftovers or dividing the remaining half of the pie into several tiny pieces. Instead, the person with the enormous share ought to act like the football coach who does not wish to win by a large margin. When his team is three touchdowns ahead, he throws his second string players into the game. In doing this, he gives the second string practice, spares the losing team excess humiliation, and most importantly, keeps the game interesting so that fans will continue buying tickets. Similarly, the professional might see practical and moral dangers in too vigorous an effort to maximize income. Even if the Lord does not call upon him to account for his actions, he could fear that gaining too much could have consequences in society that may, in the end, deprive him of what he has.

Detached from claim on the existing pool of goods, money goes awry. It is like a helium balloon that is cut away from other objects and so rises by itself. The more a person has, the better off he thinks he is. And since this upward linearity can go on forever, he always wants more. What is necessary here is to *reattach* the processes of "putting in" and "taking out." We need to see the rewards which we claim from society in relation to the contributions we make to it. These contributions may be great, but they are also limited, and so should be what we claim from society. The limits, then, are of two kinds. There are limits to what we need, indeed to what we can use, and there are limits to what we deserve.

When the Corporation Exceeds Limits

When it is a corporation whose helium balloon rises, matters are more complicated. There could be for instance, a corporation that manufactures and markets toothpaste. Most agree that the community benefits from this organization's activity. Toothpaste may not be essential to the good life, but it certainly is nice to have. As with many other things, people could live without toothpaste, but they would rather live with it; for toothpaste tastes good, makes breath sweeter and life more pleasant, and it might even have hygienic value! In any case, by producing and selling toothpaste, the corporation participates creditably in community life.

The company takes its place as a valued unit within the society. The corporation's employees, managers, and stockholders participate in community life as receivers as well as givers. They produce only toothpaste, but like everyone else who produces any thing, they have a right to see that thing burst into pieces and return to them as food, clothing, shelter, and TERM. They have a right to the profit that divides into wages, salaries, and dividends. This profit, however, should not be maximized to its fullest potential, nor should it be gauged to maximize the organization's corporate empire. The profit should be enough, and that is it.

When managers do set maximization of profit or empire as the goal, a host of evils follows. Indeed, much of the world's misery has its roots in this pursuit of profit. Once the corporation sets out to make the greatest profit possible, it sets in motion processes which no one controls. Its course is set; it has to do whatever holds the promise of reaching the goal, including such things as relocating operations in areas where cheap labor is available and shortchanging the safety not only of workers but also of the products which consumers will be using. The exigencies of profit-making shape managerial decisions.

When one corporation engages in such practices, others find it difficult not to follow suit. Since the one corporation is utilizing cheap labor, competing corporations must do the same to hold down their own prices. Consumers show little sympathy for the firm that charges higher prices because it insists on treating its workers well or being concerned about the environment. Cutthroat practices are no longer just a matter of maximizing profit; they are a necessity for survival. Companies have to meet the competition to stay afloat, and when certain organizations use devices to acquire the greatest amount of money, others have to resort to the same methods just to stay in business. As a result, corporations' maximization projects determine the shape of the world economy.

Conclusions

In the field of theology, Rudolph Bultmann undertook a project he called *demythologization*. By this august term he was referring to a restatement of a theological content, one in which terms which refer to something outside of the dramas of human life are replaced by those that are within it. Time-space terms taken to refer to supernatural realities would give way to expressions pertaining to either the empirical order or to an "existential" analysis of human existence. Things are to be treated more as what they actually *are*.[10]

This is what we need to do with money. It too needs to be demythologized or demystified. It too should be seen as what it is and as nothing other than what it is. The project of seeing it this way will not be easy. The mythologizing tendency is very strong. Money very quickly takes on for us a "more" that obscures its true and proper nature. The upward linearity people assign to it is just as false and alien to truth as are the gods of folklore and religious belief. What is called for is coming back down to earth, seeing money for what it is and seeing life and the furniture of life for what they are.

Behind the mythologizing of money is the desire for *prestige*, the wish to be "big and important" in one's community. This is a strange desire. It exists in a no-man's land between selfishness and unselfishness. If we were altogether unselfish, we would have no wish for prestige. We would want only to live in full community with others. If we were fully selfish, prestige would not interest us; only gratification of physical desires would do so. The person who wants to be "eminent" reaches out to others and sees himself as he thinks those others see him. In this sense he goes outside himself and is not simply selfish. But he does not go far enough to be *un*selfish. He imagines the world as seen by others only in order to build himself up within that larger world.

To tame money and bring it down to size, therefore, is an act of discipline. A person needs to see his wish for prestige in its true dimensions so that he can decide if and how he wishes to act on it. If he understands it rightly, he will at some points reject its siren call and decide to come back down to an earth in which he strives simply to enjoy life and be happy. He will in a way be less selfish, since he is grasping less for himself and sharing more with others. But in another way, he is more selfish. He is noting where a rock-bottom enjoyable life is to be found, and he is going after it. Just as he engages in basic thinking, so he seeks a basic life.

Chapter 3

Community

Human beings live a seeming contradiction. Each is a lone person, complete in himself/herself, yet each is also a member of a society and is formed and shaped by it. Both aspects, individual and communal, are significant in assessing what human beings are. On the one hand, everyone is a unique individual. Each person is a center of desire and decision; each can act independently; each is moved to act by what he finds in himself, which may be a desire, a sentiment or conviction, together with what he sees as being outside of himself, by his own special view of nature and society. On the other hand, humans are members of communities; they move in concert with others. Custom pushes them to behave in certain ways, and fashion constrains them to do one thing rather than another. These two features of human existence play tug-of-war with each other. At one moment, the individual claims, "I am my own person"; but at another, he professes loyalty to family, community, and nation. What humanity really is exists in the tension between these two opposites.

America places emphasis on individualism. We Americans stress the freedom of the individual and believe that people's faring well in life is a matter of how hard a person works to promote his own interests. The expression, "I will look out for me, you will look out for you, and the other fellow will look out for himself/herself," reflects the common mode of thinking and acting. The rule is each person for himself. No one waits for handouts, either from his neighbors or his government. People who want things must either produce those things or produce things that can be exchanged for them. The general rule is to work hard so that a person can take care of himself. One of the most insulting things that an American can

comment about another is that the individual thinks the world owes
him a living.

Americans' notion of rugged individualism and of a demanding
work ethic reflects their idea of what people and society *are*. It also
represents what they think people and society *should be*. The person
who struggles hard to reach his own individual pot of gold at the end
of the rainbow is, according to this way of thinking,   living in
freedom, which is America's highest value.   Assuming that the
individual pursues his goals in purely economic ways by trading and
by manufacturing and selling (not by stealing or defrauding),
Americans consider him a proper human being and approve of his
acting in his own, that is his selfish, interest.   Rationalizing the
matter, we Americans believe that he is doing what is natural for him,
while simultaneously acting in the best interest of the community as
a whole; for according to the laws of the market-place, his selfish
actions will combine with those of innumerable others to comprise the
"greatest good for the greatest number."   All people will benefit
because each person sets out to do what is best for himself.   This is
not something that just tends to happen; it occurs because it is in
harmony with the basic laws of reality.   In adopting this kind of
lifestyle, the individual taps into nature itself and acts in accordance
with its unchangeable laws.   His actions are healthy both for himself
and for the community to which he belongs.   Americans consider
selfish actions, as long as they pertain to economics, as serving the
interest of all people.   Purely unselfish actions are acceptable as long
as they are peripheral to the main line of activity. Thus, Americans
approve of donating money and time to worthy causes, as long as
such charitable giving is an activity carried out on the side. According
to this way of thinking, most of what people do should be selfish;
thus, the greatest honor goes to those who do well for themselves.

Human Beings are Communal

Such an outlook is fundamentally in error. Like it or not, humans
are social and communal beings.   Our lives are tied up with those
around us.   In the deepest and broadest sense, how we fare--whether
our lives are truly good--depends upon those others as well as upon
ourselves.   It depends, moreover, on how what we do affects others.
A person's contribution to those around him is not properly just a by-
product of the activity in which he promotes his own interests.   It is,

instead, part and parcel of what makes his own life good. My life is good because others benefit from my decisions and activities. Fulfillment for me depends on how others benefit from me. This is the human condition, for we are social creatures.

Further, humans do not tap into a law of nature by buying and selling in order to advance their individual interests. The laws of the market, like all laws of natural phenomena, are merely tendencies. Under certain circumstances, to certain degrees, and in certain ways, a large number of selfish actions can add up to the good of all. But nothing guarantees that this will always or even usually happen. To determine if autonomous actions will help all, examination of each particular case is necessary. If market mechanisms appear to operate for the common welfare, well and good; but if they do not, we should be wary. It is strictly a case-by-case matter because, in truth, there are no laws of nature underlying economic events. What happens is what happens, nothing more and nothing less. People should be extremely hesitant to use notions that associate economic matters with natural law. The free entrepreneur so celebrated in America's folk and *belle lettre* traditions is not as much of an individual as he is portrayed as being. A true individual would decide on his own what is important and for what objects and values he wishes to strive. The people surrounding this self-focused person, full as they are of tradition and fashion, fade into the background as he determines both what he wants and how he is going to get it. He often appears strange or even insane because he serves values which he freely espouses but which are not part of what "everybody" takes for granted. Portrayals of the free entrepreneur in American tradition bear no resemblance to this individual. What the American entrepreneur wants, rather, is what people in general want. It is everybody's dream or pot of gold, and it is what every person thinks every other person wishes to have. It begins, of course, with money, but it branches out from there. With money, one buys things, but the things one chooses to buy are commonly very much like what other people choose to buy. Once wealthy, the free entrepreneur buys what "people" search for and purchase, and he becomes a highly standardized product himself. He is so similar to those self-made people around him that it would take an expert to distinguish him from the others.

Calling such individuals "free" entrepreneurs is a misnomer, for they are not free. To be free is to have some idiosyncrasies; it is to have projects or tastes that are peculiarly one's own; and it is to make decisions that are different from those that other people would make in identical circumstances. The entrepreneur is not free in these ways. His decision to be an entrepreneur and to take up a particular line of industry involves predicting which of the limited options open to him is likely to yield him a good profit. He may produce and sell paper bags, cold medicines, or golf clubs; but few purely individual considerations enter into his decisions. Computer-like, he assesses opportunities and obstacles, and then makes an educated guess. Once in a line of industry, his mental operations become calculations rather than thinking.   Why he makes certain decisions involves his circumstances, not his individual preferences. He determines what course will make him prosperous. His concern is not with whether he wants to prosper, but with how to achieve that goal. His decision is not unique, for any other intelligent person in his situation would choose similarly. Nothing truly individual enters the process. For example, none of his personal tastes or values affect his advertising choices; he relies only on his ability to discern what would induce people to buy what he has to sell.   This *un*freedom of the businessman explains why the field of economics can be a science. One needs only to know the circumstances in which people find themselves, and he can predict how they will act, since they always act "rationally," and if this knowledge of circumstances applies to many people, he can foretell what will happen in "the economy."

The ideology of the free individual commonly presents the individual as both real and ideal. It asserts that when a person is liberated from primitive superstition and the constraints of government regulation, he can act as the free individual. He can calculate where his economic interests lie and then act on the basis of that calculation. The American ideology holds that to see each human in this way is to be realistic about the kind of creature human beings are. Yet the American tradition also considers such a person the ideal; each individual *should* be that kind of person and *should* act in this way. The free entrepreneur's behavior reflects not just his innate nature but also his level of integrity and virtue. Such a person brings to fruition a goodness which lies dormant in his bosom and which springs forth in economic decision-making. Actions based on the calculations of one's economic self-interest are blessed actions. A covering of rightness falls upon them and renders them sacred.

The connotations engendered in calling America's economic system "free" reflect this idealization of economic calculation. Few items in the American vocabulary are as sacrosanct as the word "free." America is, after all, the land of the brave and free; and in the Pledge of Allegiance, Americans declare liberty and justice for all. But freedom is abstract, and being so, lends itself to premature identification with some concrete item taken to be expressive of it. The concept of the free entrepreneur becomes a magnet that attracts all the pieces into which freedom is fragmented. Instead of being seen as an expression of freedom, the free entrepreneur becomes identical with it--freedom simply equals becoming an economic calculator. And because to be free is to possess America's most cherished ideal, economic calculation is par excellence the behavior which is moral and good. Such a belief system is monumentally erroneous. We human beings are unavoidably and by nature social. We live and breathe, suffer and rejoice, experience frustration and fulfillment in community with one another. There is no possible way to evade it, nor is there reason to do so.

The individualist gospel itself recognizes humanity's communal nature, for it sees the welfare of the community as a whole as the *ultimate* payoff for (and therefore the ultimate justification of) selfish economic calculation. This gospel begins with the assertion that it is right for an individual to pursue wealth for himself because it is in his nature to do so, and it is the substance of his "freedom." Eventually, however, the American gospel reaches a point in its assertions where it argues that pursuing wealth combines with similarly selfish actions of many others to promote the welfare of all. Thus, despite the moral preoccupation with the individual, *ultimate* justification for the economic actor is the belief that in the long run, he serves the community as a whole! Saying this assumes that the interests of the community as a whole are, essentially, the basis for determining right and wrong.

Indeed, even to speak of right and wrong (good and evil), is to become implicated in a logical universe alien to radical individualism. The whole point about the philosophy of the economic actor is that there is no right and wrong. What does or does not promote his own economic interests is not a moral matter. He is free precisely in the sense that his interests alone determine what he will do. He is no more burdened by obligation (other than to play the economic game by the rules) than he is by government. It is one thing to say that economic actors *do* behave this way, but to assert that they *should* behave this way--as the individualist ideologues do--changes the whole playing field. "Ought" and "should" become part of the game, inevitably linking the economic players with society. The obligatory "should" is society's way of drawing everyone into its orbit. It will not let the individual simply calculate his interests. It insists that decisions take account of and adapt themselves to society's overall corporate interest. Society speaks to each person and commands that at certain points he set aside selfish interests and address the needs of fellow human beings, as individuals and as a community.

If someone suggests that people *should* act solely in their own economic self-interest, he utters a simple contradiction, just as he does if he professes that it is good to be immoral. Otherwise, his words imply that acting in one's selfish interest is really acting in the interest of the community. If this is what the words mean, the person admits that acting selfishly may be good--but only some of the time and under certain circumstances. Economic actions are good because, and therefore only when, and to the extent, that they serve the community. Economic self-interest is, in this sense, made relative. It is good "maybe" and "sometimes" and "if," rather than "always" or "in the nature of the case." People consider the interest of the community as a whole as the final criterion by which to judge actions. To act in one's interest is sometimes good, sometimes bad, depending upon whether doing so serves the community.

If the welfare of the community as a whole is the criterion in the final analysis, why not accept it as being so from the start? Why not simply acknowledge that good lies in service to the community and that humans are social? After doing so, everyone can admit that *sometimes* people simultaneously serve the community and advance their own economic self-interest, just as people *sometimes* (even often) serve the community and realize that helping it has helped them and brought them an intrinsic sense of fulfillment. Whether one's motivation is enrichment of self or fulfillment in helping others, what results, service to the community, is what is good. Food, clothing, shelter, and apple pie are necessary for life to be worth living; the same is true of being decent, honest, and kind. The conscience, like it or not, is an undeniable part of a person, and no one can enjoy life when ignoring or doing battle with it. Fully accepting that humans are social enables one to make peace with the conscience and move forward. We may as well admit that we are communal.

The Nature of Human Action

Before advancing, let us take a closer look at what is involved. Imagine that someone driving in heavy traffic is waiting to turn left at an intersection with a traffic light. At first, there are ten to twenty cars in front of him also waiting to make the same left turn. After two or three changes of the light, he finds himself close enough to the turn at the next change. Many cars are now behind him, with impatient drivers wishing that they had never gotten on the road or that they had taken a different route. Because he is so close to the light, what he does will not only affect him but also the cars behind him. Whether they make it through the next light will depend on how fast he is in getting out of their way. Now, he may not have a great deal of enthusiasm for quickly clearing the intersection. When *he* was many cars back, he wanted those in front of him to rush; but now, no longer at the rear of the line, what those in front of him did a few minutes ago does not matter. He knows that *he* will get through the next light in any event. Whether the people behind him get to where they are going soon concerns them but not him. He may wish to refrain from going fast in order to avoid running the risk of having an accident or so that he does not have to concentrate so hard on what he is doing. In this sense, it is in his interest to go slowly; if the people behind him are late for appointments or become frustrated while waiting, it is their problem, not his. He might wish that other drivers would cooperate with him; but as far as his interests are concerned, he has no reason to do what he wishes others would do. When the light changes, he takes a few extra seconds to start up-- perhaps the equivalent of one or two cars going through the light--and stays far behind the car in front of him. He comfortably continues thinking or talking. In the meantime, the people behind him wish he would move more quickly, since it is in their interest for him to do so. But as with him, when they are in the front, quick movement will no longer be in their interest, and what matters to the people behind them will no longer be their concern. People are lined up, it would seem, to act selfishly.

Similarly, a driver will frequently be trying to turn right out of a driveway into a heavy line of traffic. If he waits for a break in the traffic, he may wait a very long time. The cars go by one after the other, all indifferent to his need to take his place among them. Sooner or later, however, an altruist may appear who stops and lets him in. That "nice guy" is clearly not acting in his own interest at that moment. At the least, he is delayed by having one more car in front of him. Yet if everyone showed this kind of consideration, no one would be the loser. Each person's sacrifice in letting someone in would be matched by the benefit of being let in when it is his turn to be the one trying to move into traffic. The trouble is that the benefit is not afforded "right now" to the person who shows consideration, and it will never be forthcoming if he is the only one that does it. The almighty "I" continues to do best by surging ahead and not letting that poor fellow get into the street.

More is involved here than just being considerate or inconsiderate. If I were to make my left turn quickly so that those behind me can make it, I would do so at a cost. I would have to be more alert, which involves effort and strain, and run the risk of possibly causing an accident. Similarly, if I were the courteous driver who stops to let other cars enter the lane of traffic, I would slightly delay myself and those behind me. If *all* drivers displayed such consideration, the cost to me would be nonexistent. What other drivers do for me, at cost to them, makes up for what I do for them, at cost to me. So if I *and others* do it, there would be no net expense for me. If the traffic moves more quickly through intersections, the cost becomes a payoff for everyone because all are getting places more quickly. There is more than simply trade-off benefit.

This scenario is a microcosm of a basic dilemma of social life. If all of us did certain things, everyone would benefit. But it does not help the individual when he alone does considerate things. If others do them too, I benefit; but I do not benefit from my own doing them. I might be glad if those drivers in front of me went through the intersection quickly, or if a driver stopped to let me turn into the road, but I feel no compunction to be so considerate myself. Their kindness benefits me, but mine does not benefit--me. No amount of calculation is going to give me a selfish reason to show consideration. In this sense, a community of selfish people is condemned to misery. All would benefit if all were considerate; but no single considerate person benefits when he alone is unselfish.

Someone could cry out, "Hey fellows, let's all do it, because if we are *all* considerate, we will *all* benefit." With everyone cooperating, no one is forced to be single-handedly unselfish. All are selfish and unselfish at the same time. This would certainly be a fortunate outcome, but there is little reason to expect it to take place. The required sense of community and ease of communication do not exist. There is no "hey fellows" followed by a nodding of heads and an agreement that all will act in certain ways. There is not enough of a "we." If others are being considerate, any individual could renege on his part of the bargain and benefit by so doing. If others are *in*considerate, he protects his own interests by acting selfishly himself. Regardless how others act, a lone individual fares best by watching out for "number one" while leaving others to do whatever they will. In the final analysis, then, a person acts unselfishly only for a *moral reason*. People may move a certain distance towards being cooperative when they pursue their own interests intelligently rather than stupidly (when they do so in an "enlightened" way), but without morality being on hand to push them through the remaining stretch of road, they will get stalled at one or another point. Deals in which people make their interests coincide can go a distance, but a gap which selfish interest cannot get over remains. If people do go the distance and act considerately, they do so for one of two reasons: either they think they should, or they sympathize with others' plights. Both of these motivations are what Emile Durkheim, many years ago, called *sentiments*.[11] They are part of morality. In one, the element of obligation is most prominent; each person's conscience prompts him to do what he "ought." In the other, compassion or fellow-feeling comes to the fore: the person suffers with the suffering of others and, as we say, "gives a damn"; he has a wish to promote others' happiness. Just as a person can travel a long way on foot but needs a boat to cross the river, so people can do much with enlightened self-interest, but without the help of morality, one cannot complete the last leg of the journey.

We human beings are communal. We are bound by ties of affection and loyalty to others and to the community as a whole. A variety of feelings and thoughts initiated in the conscience affect our decisions. From patriotic fervor to cold, hard principle and from a finicky love of order to outbursts of kindness--all fall under morality. As morality, they are really ties of affection and loyalty; to feel bound to a certain group is the same thing as feeling that one ought to behave a certain way. *Esprit de corps* and morality are correlative phenomena. Further, everyone benefits from being bonded to community and from being morally motivated. Innumerable rewards result from the cooperation and absence of conflict that group feeling and morality make possible. The cohesive "we" is the force that generates the good life. Without it, people's efforts to cooperate only in order to serve their respective selfish interests will not suffice. A person benefits from the cooperation of others, but his own effort at cooperation does nothing for him. In fact, he suffers because of his own cooperation. He sacrifices the benefits he could receive from selfish actions. Yet if he and all the others were selfish, all would suffer. Obviously, morality is necessary. The individual cooperates, not because he sees benefit for himself in doing so, but because he feels he *should*.

Once the community establishes cooperative responsibilities, other considerations come to the fore. Within the community, distribution and organization are important. Many jobs must be done. People need motivation to do them, and they have to distribute themselves among the various tasks that must be performed if the community is to survive and prosper. It would not do for everyone to perform one kind of work while others go undone. Similarly, the fruits of labor must be distributed. Food, clothing, shelter, and TERM (transportation, education, recreation and medical care) have to be handed out equitably so that each has enough to survive.

The two factors that make this discussion of community logistics distinctive need to be specifically mentioned: first, community is the central focus; and second, thinking should be basic. This kind of thinking is the way people do think when accretions and superfluities have been removed. In the ordinary state, thinking is bombarded with the concepts of money and jobs; these ideas fill the mind and dominate the process of thought. But when the accretions are removed and minds are allowed to sink back to the fundamental starting point, thinking becomes clearer and can properly be called basic. The intent here is to engage in basic thinking about the distribution of both tasks and goods.

A Hypothetical Community

As a way of entering the basic mode, consider the following hypothetical situation as a representation of a truly basic community: it is a community about which one can think in basic terms. It is small and simple, and has no accretions--such as money or a job market--because it started from scratch to organize itself. By examining it, one might see in a new way what it is to begin from the beginning in thinking about the problems and questions which beset humans. The society discussed will lack many features of the communities and nations we know. But the point is to make *simplifying assumptions* that enable us to see the kinds of judgment which we ourselves make when we deal with fundamental issues.

We may imagine that a great disaster has afflicted the entire world. As a result of this nearly apocalyptic change in the Earth, about one thousand people find themselves together in one place. Perhaps they are the only people left on Earth, or at least they are so separated from other groups that they think of themselves as being the only humans left alive on Earth. Finding themselves together and possessing no more than meager supplies of food, clothing, and other necessities, the group's prime concern is survival. They decide that there is one thing they must do; they must cooperate with one another and form themselves into a cohesive group. Only so, they see, will they have a chance to go on living, to "pull through." Organization thus becomes important to the community. Further, they realize that coordinating their efforts requires leadership; and to the end of having it, they decide that a few persons within the group should have authority to exercise dictatorial powers over the rest of them. They see themselves as being like a ship's crew in which all of the seamen see that their chances for survival depend upon their acting together, and that their doing so depends, in turn, upon total obedience to a "captain," a single leader.

To understand this *esprit de corps* within the group, imagine some additional problems within the setting--perhaps serious threats lurk behind the horizon. There may be storms, vicious animals, creatures from another planet, or another hostile human group. Having to cope with an enemy while obtaining life's necessities obviously requires close-knit organization, so the people readily assent. Whatever the reason, the community of one thousand souls grants all but total authority to a person or small committee. Inevitably, among the group are many who possess leadership abilities. The few who are exceptionally endowed emerge as leaders, while others with leadership potential and robust community spirit readily accept the primacy of the chosen few and take their place among the rank-and-file or settle for positions as lieutenants serving under the leaders. Indeed, far from competing with the top-echelon leaders, these people help to deflect such jealousies that sometimes appear within the group and so protect those leaders at the peak of the hierarchy.

Leadership attains a prominent role in the hypothetical community not because leadership itself is important but because coordination is, and leadership makes coordination possible. The people comprising our small community are able to act in total cooperation. What each does is predicated on what each other person does, and all the actions together form a single group action. Like soldiers carrying out a military strategy, they act in concert. Further, communication is so good that the thousand people are like a collection of workers who wear headphones and hear directives from a central source at the very instant the directives are issued. Thus, coordination among such a relatively small group is nearly perfect.

Acting on the orders of their leaders, the people get busy with their essential tasks. First, they assess what goods they have already so that they can divide them among the group. Food already in store is the top priority; to keep alive, all must eat as well as possible. The same applies to clothing and shelter, either in caves, in other natural sanctuaries, in remaining buildings, or in structures that can be improvised quickly.

Second, the people organize to produce food and other necessities. They identify plant products that are produced naturally and only need to be gathered, and they cultivate others. With only a thousand people in a large territory, gathering becomes a major part of the productive process. The same applies to using animals for food and clothing; the members hunt and kill some animals and domesticate and breed others. While food is the priority, clothing and shelter are also important; thus, manufacturing plays a role in the newly organized community. They use sailboats and other humanly-developed vehicles, as well as horses or other animals, for transportation. The community uses any extant technology to form a medical center. They also create means for children to get care and education. Once survival is assured, the organized community develops recreational activities. Also, a few people feel called to organize religion of a sort that is desired. Behind every productive activity, of course, are the sets of materials, tools, and apparatus used in the activity; at first many work as producers of the tools and equipment used in production rather than as producers of consumer goods. In time, some of these tools will be available in adequate amounts so that more of the total labor-power can work to produce goods for consumption.

Third, the community focuses on protecting itself from threats such as winds, floods, and other natural forces. For instance, if the area is subject to harsh winters, the community must take measures to survive the cold. Also, the group must develop means to counter such dangerous animals as may be prowling around and any hostile foreigners who may covet their goods or territory, or want to enslave their people. All protective measures require equipment of one or another sort, and this must be produced from whatever materials are at hand.

Once production is under way and goods are available, the people consider distribution. Since the community is small, the task of getting goods into people's hands is not difficult, except for a few jobs which require people to be in remote locations. Little, if any, of the work of the community is that of delivering goods. The question of who has a right to how much of what is, however, an important matter to the community. Clearly, they will have to make decisions about this. Unless the *esprit de corps* has blossomed into perfect brotherhood, they will need to allocate goods that are scarce to individuals within the group. Allocation must be just and fair, not only because being fair is intrinsically good but also because it is necessary to avoid resentment. It is important to keep ill feelings to a minimum. So the people develop a code of justice which determines, among other things, who has rights to things that are scarce--that do not exist in sufficient supply for everyone to have all he wants. In constructing the code, the people hope that everyone will be satisfied with it. That is, they hope that people will *feel* that the distribution is fair. Avoiding resentment is especially important here because rebellion is more possible in such a small group.

An existing order in this small society does not appear to be the work of an awesome "they," as is the case in large societies. It is not a daunting "the way things are" but is, instead, close at hand and open for discussion. For this reason, when we think of such a society, it is easier to clarify our own feelings about what is right and decent and good.

To start such thinking, we note that every member of the community should get--or has a right to--enough of whatever is scarce to survive. If the supply of food is only enough for each person to have the minimum required to stay alive, every individual has a right to this allotment. If beyond that minimum survival supply there is a some more that the people believe to be necessary for good health and general well-being, the rule of equal proportions for all still holds. The standard of justice is very simple: either every person gets an equal amount, or every person gets what he needs. People who are physically larger or whose work requires much exercise need more; a two-hundred-pound man who lifts and pushes heavy objects all day long certainly needs more than does a person who weighs half as much and who does not expend much energy. If there are to be differences in allotment, need alone serves as its basis. Neither a person's position within the community nor the services he performs render him as meriting more.

The basic moral judgment here is that the survival of all takes priority over reward to a few. The right of each person to survive, and perhaps at the minimum level of wholesomeness is fundamental. Certainly, people feel that all should be rewarded for what they do, and that people who perform more tasks or perform them better are entitled to more rewards than others. But this is secondary or marginal. The right to a minimum level of well-being comes before all other considerations, though it is not easy to specify just what that level is. Therefore, when supplies are gravely limited, an evenhanded distribution to each on the basis of need is the rule. This fits with, or perhaps we should say clarifies, our basic moral thoughts and feelings. In the beginning, this even distribution is the rule. The first break in the heavy armor of that regulation arises with malingering. There may be people in the community who choose to do no work or to do consistently less than their share. If there are such people, the remainder of the community will feel that it is necessary to do something about it. Some kind of move must be made against those who shirk their work responsibilities, just as something has to be done about any other behavior which is harmful to the group as a whole. An obvious disciplinary action is to slight the malingerers at distribution time, denying them food and other goods. This may not be the only way to punish them, but it is a way which is readily at hand; and it fits the biblical injunction, " . . . if they will not work, let them not eat . . ." (Thessalonians 3:10). Other possible punishments include ostracism, ritual humiliations, beatings, or imprisonment. In general, something can be done to or something can be taken away from those who dodge their duties.

However, if the community is to deprive the slothful of goods, they must acknowledge that doing so is just one of many possible actions. It is a move against someone on the grounds that the person has failed the group by an act of will. He had the power to fulfill his responsibility to the community, and he chose not to do so. It is not that he lacks a right to sustenance; it is rather, that he has made a decision opposed to the interests of the group, and thus the group takes an action against him. It is, therefore, crucial that the person's failure to work be voluntary. If he does not work because of disabilities that are beyond his control or because no work exists for him in the community, matters are altogether different. He retains the right to food, clothing, and shelter along with everyone else in the community. He does not rely on kind acts of charity from compassionate others; rather, he receives that which is his due just as does everyone else.

The thinking in this hypothetical community is different from that to which our American tradition is accustomed. The imaginary community does not say that the person who fails to work does not produce and therefore should not consume. That kind of statement assumes that people are individuals first and members of communities in only a secondary sense. By contrast, the assumption here is that people are *in essence* members of a group. As members, they have an obligation to work and a right to a share of the goods available. Yet there may be persons within the group who choose not to work or who do less work than the community has a right to expect from them. When this occurs, the group must make a decision. It can decide to condone the malingering with a shrug of the shoulders and a judgment that their work is not that essential anyway, while others are pushed by preference or by conscience to stay busy. Or, the group can also apply pressure to minimize or eliminate sloth. Making consumption conditional upon laboring is simply the most obvious kind of pressure. In time and after much work, goods may increase to the point where a surplus remains when basic needs have been met. When this happens, the community decides how to allocate the surplus. It, like the essential goods, could be distributed equally or on the basis of need or desire; or it could be differentially allocated in order to promote good behavior, especially good productive behavior. In a situation opposite to that of the malingerer, a certain worker puts in longer hours and does better quality work with greater efficiency than do others. The community decides that he will be given the greatest share of whatever is surplus among the goods produced. Perhaps they think it morally right to do so, or they consider it to be in the group's interest, since such a policy encourages people to work harder and better.

The community must be cautious with its rewarding. If it is to be in the group's interest to allow rewards for good workers, the reward has to be less than the increment of goods which results from the superior labors of those who work especially hard or well. Perhaps the group decides that if a certain person produces one hundred more of something than do other workers, his reward should be no more than fifty, with the remaining fifty being distributed among the rest of the group. Doing otherwise would defeat the purpose of rewarding him for his extra productivity, since only the worker himself would benefit from his excellent performance. There would be no moral "message" in the policy of rewarding good work unless the community itself gets some of the benefit of it.

Another reason for caution is that the increment of product that arises from superior work performance may be of the "shiny chrome" variety. It may appear to be an increase in the quantity or quality of goods available without in fact being so. Once a program of rewarding better-than-average work is in place, some people will work harder or better in order to achieve the reward. Either they want the goods themselves, or they want the prestige which such goods bring. Their excess zeal may not however lead them to produce a genuine increase of goods. It may, instead, result in only the appearance of such an increment. The chrome may shine more than it did before, while the product underneath is no better. People are always dealing with products, but in dealing with them, they deal with appearances. Some part of a product, often a minor part, presents itself, and everyone takes it as an announcement of what the remainder of the product is. To many people, the shine of a car's chrome signals its quality; its shininess--its exterior appearance--is visible to all, but much of the car remains hidden from view, especially from the view of those who are not mechanics. People base many of their decisions about products, notably decisions to buy and rent, on appearances because they cannot include in their calculations the features that are hidden and difficult to take into account. Anyone motivated to produce is therefore under constant temptation to maximize appearance rather than substance. The one who succumbs to the temptation chooses to shine the chrome rather than improve the engine. As long as people work because they feel this is what members of the community are supposed to do, they have minimum reason to concentrate on shiny chrome instead of the substance of a product. But when superior performance means glory, the Tempter emerges out of the shadows and shows the good worker shortcuts to wealth and honor. If the honest worker succumbs and begins producing goods with surface appeal rather than quality, the purpose of rewarding quality workmanship and performance has been defeated.

Differences in the importance of various production tasks should *not* lead to differences in rewards to workers. Some laborers use mind and muscle to bring forth life's necessities. Others work equally hard producing adornments, or amenities that are not necessary. The latter could disappear with only minor damage to the community; the former could not stop working without threatening life itself. It is inevitable that both types of labor will exist; and unless everyone does the same kind of work, some jobs will be more important than others. However, this does not mean that people who perform essential tasks should obtain a greater share of the product than those who perform tasks of lesser importance. After all, a division of labor exists. Within it, some people are busy bringing forth necessities while others apply themselves to producing adornments that add charm and beauty to the environment. It is not essential that everyone perform necessary work; the community *wants* some to create eye-appealing embellishments. And in view of this, there is no reason why one type of work should be rewarded more than others. It is important that work be done, so let everyone do a share. If a specific task is a part of the share, that is all that is important. The place of a task in an ordering of priorities is not.

Further, in many or most cases, a person who works does not produce a whole object. Instead, he works and combines his work with that of others to produce the object. Hence, no one's work is in an obvious way more important than anyone else's. Consider a football team. In a football game, one side wins because of a score made in the last minute of the game. One player carried the ball across the goal line, but he alone should not get the sole credit for the score. The man who threw it to him and the men who blocked opposing tacklers also deserve recognition. Clearly, everyone's contribution is equally important. Inquiring whose part required more effort or ability ends in the discovery that one task may demand more of someone than another, but both tasks are essential. Similarly, if two or more people in the community cooperate in a productive task, making shoes, for example, all of them make the product and no one has done "more" than the others. In viewing the survival of the group as a kind of product, clearly, all play a role in bringing it off the assembly line, but no one does more than play a role.

To summarize, when surplus goods exist, the community gives some of the extra to a few good workers as a way of encouraging good performance. However, if there is to be a real point in doing this, the community must make certain that the reward is less than the extra production, for only then can the whole community benefit from the reward system. It must also seek to avoid "shiny chrome" production, which can occur as a result of careless reward distribution. The community's concerns must also stress that doing work which is essential does not necessitate special rewards. Doing work well and efficiently, no matter what the task, is what deserves such rewards. And even here, the community must acknowledge and emphasize that, unless he works alone, no single person produces things by himself; instead, the worker merely plays a role in the production process.

While our hypothetical community of one thousand souls bears little resemblance to a modern industrial society, there is point to considering it. Doing so enables us to see what kinds of moral judgment we make when issues are sufficiently simplified. We make judgments in response to situations. When these situations are uncomplicated and clear in their essential features, we can be more aware of our own moral responses than is the case when there is a host of confounding factors.

Incentives and Work

Reward that encourages good performance is called *incentive*. The term has sacred character in the lexicon of free enterprise. Indeed, it has its place in free market thought that is roughly analogous to that of the *logos* in the first chapter of the Gospel of John. Just as the *logos* is the creative edge of the transcendent God-the-Father, so the *incentive* is the agency through which the free enterprise system is thought to achieve its wonders. Assuming, as neoclassical economics does, that people are calculators and maximizers and that the good or utility which they wish to maximize is fixed and consists of a limited array of items (houses and cars but not a tranquil conscience), then of course incentives are quite useful and important. The structure of the incentives determines people's behaviors.

In comparison to its place in free enterprise thought, however, the incentive is less awesome in the present analysis. It has no metaphysical character or theological substance. The incentive is one of the many factors that move people to work and to work well. Community spirit (as in the community of one thousand), conscience, pride in workmanship, sheer enjoyment, and hope for recognition are other factors not connected with rewards in the form of goods or market rewards. This discussion has attempted to bring the *incentive* back down to Earth and to view it as being what it is, just what it is, and nothing other than what it is.

Certainly, people often perform well at their jobs and in other ways behave as we might wish them to because of incentives, because, that is, they get what they want by so doing. We all benefit by having things or receiving services provided by people who are moved neither by conscience nor by affection to do so. They give us things or perform services for us because they will be paid. A great deal of the courtesy and friendliness which improve our days are extended for the same reason. Alternatively, when people have no reason to treat us well, they often do not, in fact, treat us well. The behavior of agents of the Internal Revenue Service which is often quite cold, in contrast to the warmth displayed by salesmen, illustrates this point. So much is the case that we often "trust" people only when they have selfish reason to be trustworthy. We think they will be kind to us if--and only if--there is "something in it for them" that moves them to be so.

This cannot, however, be asserted without qualification. Too much incentive often moves people to act against rather than for the interests of the community. The word "speculation" as used in connection with real estate dealings and other financial adventures conveys this idea. One advances his selfish interests by doing things that benefit no one other than himself and his associates. Also, in the area of medical service, we can well imagine that America might have a better corps of physicians if there were *less* reward for medical practice. People with high IQ's who are motivated primarily by a wish for money might stay away from the profession of medicine and leave it to others who really want to be doctors. And we might suggest that the really best "incentive" occurs when a worker partly advances his own interest and partly serves the community in what he does. This, rather than the advance of selfish interest by itself, might be the best motivator. And if it is, it would have the added benefit that it would move people to shape their activities to fit the needs of the community rather than just to maximize their own incomes.

Community vs Social Contract

The hypothetical community of one thousand souls is, in the view of its members, a community and not just an aggregate of individuals. In its ideal form, it would be a gathering of people who are in total solidarity with each other. Each person would care fully about each of the others and about the community as a whole. There would for that reason be no conflict between an individual's selfish interest and his commitment to the group. If an unpleasant or greedy person appeared here or there, he would be little more than an itch on the surface of the community's life.

This picture of perfect brotherhood has, however, been compromised in what has been said here. The discussion allowed space for recalcitrance in individuals, as in suggesting that food could be granted to or withheld from persons to induce them to work rather than to malinger. It was also suggested that surplus goods could be held or given away in an effort to reward people who work longer, harder, or better than others.

In addition to being communal, the hypothetical society is also administered by people. This administration can be either democratic or dictatorial. That is, there could be a person or small group who command while others obey, or there could be a "town meeting" governance in which everyone participates in the making of group decisions. Or people could all rule, but through representatives they elect. Whatever its form, administration is carried out by people. Human beings seek to direct their own destinies; they do not leave them to the tender mercies of processes that take place when each person or group acts on his own. The community is--communal. The opposing view of humans beings and community asserts that we are individuals who make a *social contract* with each other. We begin as individuals pursuing the abundant life for ourselves. But we discover in the course of that quest that we must cope with other persons. These others are both problems and resources. They are problems because they want what we want, and they may struggle to get it for themselves rather than letting us have it. Sometimes they try to reach the goal first, thus competing with us for whatever is not available in abundance. Other times, they wage a battle with us for it; they take positive steps to prevent us from getting what we want. We and they are in conflict. We naturally waste much energy in this competition and conflict. By making contracts with each other to cooperate, we avoid that waste. In effect, we save our energy for the battle with nature. On the other hand, other humans can also be resources. We humans are limited and small. There are many things no one of us can do alone, but which several of us acting cooperatively can do, even though we are fundamentally separated and can act together only by means of a "contract" which assures that each of us benefits in a selfish way from the cooperative action.

As a model of human life, this view of the human being as primarily an individual who acts in his own interest and who only secondarily joins in social contract with others is erroneous. It runs afoul of the basic facts of human social life, principally that it is never in an individual's interest to show consideration for others and that he will do so only if moved by sentiments and not just by calculation. Many years ago, sociologist Emile Durkheim sought to establish this point in his quarrel with "utilitarians." These were thinkers who said that all human behavior arises from calculations of one's own interest, and that people become "social" when and if they discern that it is in their interest to cooperate with others. Durkheim asserted that it is not, in fact, in an individual's interest to cooperate and that sentiments, rather than calculation, are the foundation of social life.[12] More recently, Amitai Etzioni has taken up the same banner in his *The Moral Dimension*.[13] He takes as his adversary the "neoclassical" school of economic thought which seeks to provide an "economic explanation" for all human behavior.

Gary Becker's *Treatise on the Family*[14] is good example of this neo-classical point of view. It is a singularly vulnerable point of view, threatened on one side by factual contradiction and on the other by reduction to tautology. That is, if we try to interpret all human behavior as implementation of calculations of one's selfish interest in the usual sense, we run into contradictions at every turn. People are obviously moved by conscience or compassion in much that they do. The human scene as we witness it is full of examples of acts of kindness and compassion that afford no material benefit for those who perform them. In innumerable instances, people deal honestly with others when it costs them dearly to do so. Also, there is the case of soldiers in combat. In fact, the soldier, much lauded by "conservative" thinking in our society, behaves in supremely *un*economic ways. There is no way to make "economic" (calculative) sense of a young man engaging in combat when he knows that there is a great risk that he will be killed in the action.

Becker and his colleagues seek to save their viewpoint by suggesting that an individual's "interest" may include many things others than material rewards of the usual sort. In addition, it embraces honor, affection, and the like. But arguing this way, they make their theory impregnable and therefore leave it empty of content. No matter what people do, they can explain it by positing another "desire" or "need." In so doing, this school of thought ceases to say anything. By explaining any and all possible facts, it fails to do what explanations or theories must do, which is to anticipate that certain things will be observed and others will not. It must, that is, be "falsifiable." It must be exposed to the possibility of being disproved if subsequent observation finds certain facts to be true. If, by contrast to this, it "explains" everything, it in fact explains nothing. What it does is to *name* behavior rather than explain it. It utters a tautology, a statement that is true by definition and which conveys no information. It is vacuous.

Clearly, then, a group of human beings living together cannot be viewed as a collection of free individuals who simply found it convenient to make a "contract" with each other. Rather, their being a community must be viewed as the primary fact. The community as such is what is real and solid. Individuals are members of the group more than they are anything else, and they are lone individuals in only a secondary and derivative sense.

A central feature of any such society is administration. To exist as a society, it is necessary for a community to see to it that the activities of its various members cohere. What one person does must combine with what others do to produce a single effect. And to achieve this, administration of some sort is necessary. There must, that is, be an organ that makes and implements decisions for the group as a whole. Since the society is not a "contract," this organ is an integral component of community life and not just a device for making contracts among individuals.

Inevitably, societies require some central control. At a minimum, this control has to create and administer a monetary system. Objects that are scarce and by consent of everyone viewed as precious, such as gold, may sometimes serve as money in some ways and to some degree even in the absence of an administration with coercive power.

Yet it seems clear that in society, the creation and management of money has to be administered; it cannot just happen. Also, people must attend to law and order. This too does not take place without actions designed to make it do so. What we see here is administration *by people.*

However, as noted in Chapter One there is another way of achieving the coordination which is essential when there is a division of labor. It was missing, or at least not discussed, in the hypothetical community of one thousand. It is *process.* Process is a series of events that take places automatically without being directed by human beings. These events, taken as a whole, are viewed as having effects of their own, effects that may be desirable. They may even achieve what administration by people undertakes to achieve. What happens is that people act, and their actions have aggregate effects. These effects occur as a consequence of what many people do even though it is not the intention of any one of them. People are busy pursuing their own personal objectives, but they do so within a "market" and so bring about a coordination of activities of the sort the society needs.

Each person within the group observes, among other things, what others produce and what others buy. On the basis of these observations, they plan and adjust their own production activities and their purchasing and consumption plans. It is not just a person who does this, but many people, and as a result of the constant adjusting by each unit within the mass, a necessary balancing of productive and consumption activities takes place.

For this to happen, there have to be *fixed channels* in which activity flows. As automobile drivers can choose which road to take but cannot drive across the field, people must select among some, but not all, of the things that they can possibly do. They must follow the rules. It is perfectly all right for them to seek what they want, even to seek it in great and superfluous quantity. However, they must seek it in a certain way and not in others, on pain of being perceived as bad and thus punished by a central authority. A man who aspires to attain wealth, sets up a business and, by competing, forces his competitor into bankruptcy would not be condemned as a criminal. But it would be unacceptable for him to blow up the competitor's facilities, for if he does he will not only be accused of ungentlemanly conduct, but more than likely will be punished for unlawful behavior.

These fixed channels are essential. They are what make the difference between chaos and process. Without them, there would be what Thomas Hobbes called the "war of all against all." It is a condition in which there is only violent pandemonium with no pattern or process; it is social chaos.[15] With patterns, process manifests itself. Each person confronts a collection of others whose actions are understandable and predictable, enabling him to carry out an agenda; he can plan his actions in a series of steps. While he is doing so, all others are doing likewise. His actions and those of others combine to form a discernible pattern, and a process can begin to unfold.

Notable about these fixed channels is that they are moral in nature. They are rules that many people--the community--think people should follow. The force that keeps people's actions within the channels is the force of obligation, or the "ought." Certainly there are political and economic ingredients in the channels. A person or an official of a company obeys rules because they are laws, and unhappy consequences await him who strays from the path. And in many ways, conducting business in an ethical manner is also carrying out the program which is most effective for achieving good profits. Honesty is, sometimes, "the best policy." These calculative or prudential reasons, however, do not comprise the whole or the essence of the channels. Laws would never be established or enforced if someone did not think that they express what is good and right. And there would be no community that rewards honest businessmen if moral sentiments were not a major part of it.

The process is one in which businesses wax and wane. If too many people take up a particular kind of production, the goods brought forth will exist in surplus, and sellers will have to compete by charging lower prices. As prices go below a certain point, some businesses fail or decide to look for greener pastures; consequently, the surplus will cease to exist. If in the meantime too few have put their efforts into another line of manufacturing, certain goods will be in short supply, and buyers will have to compete by offering more for them. These high prices will then attract other potential producers, and in due course supply will increase, and buyers will resort to reducing what they offer. As people seek to fare well in producing and exchanging, they pay heed to signals in the form of higher and lower prices and shift their efforts away from areas of excess towards areas of shortage. Nobody decides that there are too many shoes and not enough shirts and gives an order that less of the one and more of the other should be manufactured; nobody decides anything about what "should" be. What happens instead is that each person sees signals and shifts his activity to lines of production that bear promise. As a large number do so, the system achieves a balance of supply and demand. Processes take place to which people refer respectfully as *market mechanisms*. They are, in terms of the present analysis, an alternative form of administration. Market mechanisms are an alternative to administration by people who give directives designed to implement a plan. Instead of people doing the planning, an impersonal process does it.

Viewed this way, the market process is not inherently better or worse than administration by people. Both have advantages and disadvantages. The *dis*advantage of administration by people is that it requires a more ready compliance with directives than is forthcoming. Except for unusual circumstances, such as those of war or a ship crew, people do not decide what to do entirely on the basis of directives. Instead, they move in one direction or another in pursuit of goods, prestige, and pleasure; and they do so to a degree that is so great that operations do not flow as the directors plan. They do not work as well as they would if people did follow directives, assuming that the directives are good ones. The lack of cooperation may then induce top leaders to make efforts at improving it. They may use varying forms of persuasion and coercion, and in so doing generate a host of unpleasant processes. To take note of this is to see the truth whose importance will be overestimated or underestimated, depending on who is doing the estimating. Neither is process altogether innocent. Its flaws come readily into view. Process seems to have a certain *lethargy* that is damaging to participants. An entrepreneur who enters a crowded field may not know that he has too many competitors until it is too late. By the time he realizes that the shoes he is producing are redundant and therefore unmarketable, he has already spent his capital, his time, and his energy. It is well and good to say that he should shift to shirts, if that item is scarce (an unlikely state of affairs), but he has already lost too much in his shoe venture. Even if he can convert to shirts, by the time he has made the necessary changes in equipment and procedure, shirts too may be available in excessive quantity. After all, he and many others made the same decision at the same time; each was deciding for himself without any coordination. The adaptations that are the essence of market mechanisms are slow and cumbersome and also clumsy, and the losses that occur because of the snail's pace of responses to market signals are serious. The losses may be the entire holdings of individuals and families.

As a way of seeing this, picture a large corporation that undertakes a project and then abandons it as signals from the market indicate that there is little hope for its success. Engineers and others are assigned to the project by top administrators. They work on it for a year or more, but as prospects for salability or profitability dim, workers are reassigned before losses accumulate beyond a certain point. It is important to note here that the engineers do not lose their salaries for the year because the project lost its allure. The loss is not theirs but the company's, which can better afford it, since it has many projects, some of which are highly profitable. They may be quickly assigned to projects that will put their labors to better use (for the company). In contrast, the independent businessman can lose everything before he realizes that he has made a bad move, and he cannot readily get into something better. The sluggishness of the signal and response is rarely commented upon in discussions of market mechanisms.

Further, there is one item in the market that does not lend itself to increase or decrease in response to signals--labor. Unlike other goods it is not something produced by people; rather, labor is people. No one truly cares if shoes turn out to be available in excess; everyone determines that production of them should be reduced. The shoe itself has no interest in the matter and will retreat to the sidelines without protest. There is no "right to life" movement for foot wear. People, on the other hand are "what it is all about." After all, people cannot just be retired or not produced. No one can raise or lower their numbers to serve some purpose. They *are* the purpose; what happens is good or bad depending on what it does to them. They are the yardstick by which we properly call events good or bad. Moreover, their quantity is fixed. It does not go up or down as does the production of shoes or shirts. When people exist, they exist. We cannot decide to have more of them or fewer of them as need dictates. Put these two things together--that workers exist in reasonably fixed quantity, and that they are the ends and not the means of all decision-making--and it becomes evident that people are quite different from other items in the market-place. Therefore since labor is what workers do, labor, as such, has a twofold nature.

Labor has almost always been available in excess in the United States. Except for the World War II era and certain pockets here and there, there have always been more workers than jobs. Hence, no true market exists for labor. With workers available in excess, the employer always has the advantage. He can replace any worker, but the worker is often unable to replace the job. No true bargaining is possible. In principle, if there are one hundred jobs and one hundred and one workers, the latter have to accept the employer's terms, since any one of them can be the one who has no job. Of course, one will be jobless in any case, but each individual submits to employer demands in order not to be--that one. The answer for the worker is the labor union. The union can, under some circumstances, enable workers to confront the employer "as one man." Even this depends upon some limitation in the supply of workers. Unions have recently become a great deal weaker because that limitation is no longer in force. There is no market regarding labor. There is simply a worker with very little power. His only clout is that if he is paid below a certain amount, he will starve and so be unable to work. He is increasingly unable to demand more than that.

Further, there is the same lethargy in the skills market that there is in every other. A welder does not readily become a nurse, nor can a nurse change into a welder quickly. People make educational investments in lines of work, and these are not readily changed. It does little good to note that "help wanted" advertisements are numerous if the jobs available require knowledge and skills in areas which people are not educated, nor can one blame people's lack of education or training. No one can be trained for jobs in general. Everyone who is trained or experienced has an investment in a particular line of work and in few others. A person cannot be trained for all work any more than he can learn to speak all languages. And even if he makes the investment and retrains, the volatility of the market does not ensure that a demand will still exist in his new field when he is qualified to enter it.

Summary

This chapter on community makes three assertions. First, we human beings are social, and our lives are in essence bound up together. We are not lone individuals who just find it useful or convenient to make contracts with one another. Rather, we are bound together intrinsically and fundamentally. Indeed, our relations with each other are not intelligible on the basis of the idea of contract.

While it may be in people's selfish interest to cooperate with one another much of the time, it is not so always. There are occasions when an individual does best for himself by veering from the cooperative path. By acting selfishly, he will either gain a special advantage or avoid a special disadvantage. So whether the rest of the community is a beehive of communal harmony or a jungle of "every man for himself," a lone individual fares best by acting selfishly. If, therefore, he does not act selfishly but does coordinate his actions with those of others, he does so because of moral motivations. He feels he should; a spirit of community and compassion moves him. A sentiment other than selfish calculation inspires him.

Second, living in community, each person has obligations and rights. Everyone able has an obligation to the community to contribute to the work that must be done if goods and services are to be available. It is not just a prerequisite for receiving goods from the community's storehouses but instead an obligation that stands on its own. If someone fails to do his share of the work, he does not lose the right to enjoy benefits. He loses his good standing in the community. He still has rights--rights to food, clothing, shelter, and other necessities. People have communal rights, not because they work but because they are part of the group. The obligation to work and the right to receive are independent of one another. Only when people's basic needs have been met can surplus goods, if there are any, be used as rewards for people whose activities prove to be of special benefit to the community. Third, community has an extensive division of labor and specialization among individuals. With such a system, coordination is necessary. Each individual performs a very narrow line of work, yet each hopes to receive and benefit from a variety of goods and services. This cannot happen accidentally; administration has to make it happen. Persons or committees (people) may be the administrative coordinators, giving directives to each person in the group. These directives combine with directives given to each other individual to form a coherent plan of action. When each person does his job, goods are produced and distributed, and everyone has what he needs. Alternatively, administration may be by process. Each person sets out simply to get for himself, but he does so within a set of rules; consequently, his selfish actions automatically combine with others to produce a coherent result. With signals coming from the market, each person adjusts his plans and actions so that he can maximize his personal utility. In doing so, he inadvertently does what the community needs him to do. Neither of the two kinds of administration, by people or process, is obviously better than the other. Both have advantages and disadvantages. Actual societies are usually combinations of the two; instances of pure administration, whether by people or process, are nonexistent--although societies differ on how closely they approximate one pure type or the other.

Human beings, then, are communal creatures who have obligations to work and rights to receive what they need to live. They of necessity engage in activities that require coordination. All of this is not news. It is instead "olds;" it is what one easily discerns when the fogs of usual thinking dissipate, and one returns to basic thinking. With that return, people will better understand humanity's plight.

Chapter 4

Justice and the Market

Americans have a healthy respect for *the market,* viewed in
general and abstract terms. As they see it, the market is an arena
where large numbers of buyers and sellers trade money for goods. As
the transactions proceed, innumerable adjustments are made in what
is produced and in prices. As a result of these adjustments, a leveling
occurs in which supplies of goods and prices are stable and serve the
community as a whole. What people want is congruent with what
they have to pay to get it and the work that they do in producing and
marketing goods lines up well with the amount of wealth they gain in
the process. Just as water seeks its own level, so do the components
of the market, with results that are supposedly good for everyone.

However, there are differences in how people fare in the market.
Those who put more in get more out. Presumably, those who perform
better at producing, buying, and selling are better rewarded. That is,
the person who brings forth a superior product and/or sells that
product for a lower price is the one to whom customers flock and is
the one who prospers the most. Such a person has contributed more
to the community, so he gets more back from the community. It is
a process, not a person, that rewards him. In effect, the market itself
gives him his reward. Are, however, the differences in reward fair
and just? May we, that is, accept the outcomes of market processes
as not being only outcomes, but rather as acceptable settlements of
who is entitled to what or to how much of the goods that are scarce?
This chapter goes in quest of the answer.

Feelings or Intuitions Are
The Basis of Value Judgments

In approaching the question, bear in mind that the issues of right and wrong are, ultimately, settled by how we humans *feel* about things. We observe what people do, and we react: we approve or disapprove; we respond negatively or positively. Inner and spontaneous reactions settle issues for us. We may assert that our moral judgments are grounded in an objective source--such as the Bible, the Talmud, the Koran, or some other religious tradition. But careful observation of the judgments that people make reveals that these sources do not essentially determine the contents of our moral judgments. We cite them as endorsement of the distinctions we make between good and evil, but they do not decree where the lines will be drawn. It is rare that someone feels that an action is right and yet decides it is wrong because biblical texts or the Vatican speak ill of it. It is also rare that a person who disapproves of doing something sees that thing as cleansed by the authority of the Bible or Church. When people ask whether the Bible is "for" or "against" something, they usually have a feeling about the thing already, and they simply find confirmation of their feeling in the Biblical texts. The Bible is, we may note, a very large book; it has much to say about many matters, and one can usually find a support for any view on anything somewhere between its covers.

Sometimes, a little twisting of the words of Scripture is necessary in order to accomplish this, but human ingenuity is equal to the task. Supports for racial segregation are a case in point. Even when Scripture is silent on an issue (birth control or smoking for example), enthusiasts are not deterred from saying that it speaks loudly and clearly. The citing of Genesis 38 on birth control illustrates this. And where Scripture opposes what people *feel* is right, they often pass over the offending passages with little notice. The Sermon on the Mount (Matthew 5-7) is especially noteworthy for falling victim to this practice. The fact of the matter is that the *feelings* people have about certain practices being right and others wrong are sovereign. It is they, not Scripture or any other sacred "source," that determine the judgments people make.

Perhaps this explains why Roman Catholics so rarely follow Vatican precepts in such areas as birth control and divorce. They, like everyone else, have feelings about these issues. These feelings arise from their social environment and carry a certain authority or air of "rightness" that repels authoritative claims from ecclesiastical officials. The feelings not only fend off statements about particular issues, but resist the whole Aristotelian natural law framework that serves as the basis for Vatican or Episcopal judgments.

Catholics and Protestants alike base their judgments on feelings or intuitions, and these are, in turn, grounded in the communities in which they participate. As people participate in social life, they feel the force of opinion around them. They cringe as they anticipate disapproval from others, and they bask in the sunlight of approval. Immersed as they are in pools of social interaction, they see reality in ways which are determined by the life that goes on within those social systems. When people in formal positions, such as bishops and popes, offer opinions contrary to societal consensus, the officials are usually ignored. Their views are considered irrelevant. Only a few people veer from the paths to which community-based sentiments lead.

That judgments about right and wrong are matters of feeling or intuition does not mean that they and their applications are clear and simple. In actual life, people make their judgments in an "after the fact" way. That is, they feel that they know what is right and wrong only when they know the facts of a case, when the outlines of situations become clear. Often, a situation is complicated and fluid. It is difficult to understand what it is and what is happening. The perimeters of things are not clear and visible, even when great efforts are made to make them so. When this is the case, a person thinks that if he works at it long enough and hard enough, if enough resources are brought into play, and if others help him in the task, he may be able to understand. He thinks that any day or minute, the situation's outline will become clear, like a ship emerging from the fog and taking on definite characteristics. And as the situation assumes determinate shape, a person thinks that he will "see" what is right and wrong. His ideas may change; what seemed wrong before may seem so no longer, and the content of the "right" may shift as well. There is a certain "fit" between ideas about right and wrong and the ideas people have about situations.

Examples are many. Someone is opposed to "artificial" birth control; he feels it is wrong. But will he continue to feel that way when he sees large numbers of married couples having two or three children in a world threatened by human overpopulation? He considers homosexuality unnatural and therefore wrong. But will his opinion about it persist when he becomes familiar with stable homosexual couples with responsible, faithful relationships? He opposes divorce because he believes that a stable family is the foundation of society. But will he feel the same towards divorce when he sees "best case" examples of families that could not have existed if divorce had been impossible? Situations take on different outlines, and as the lines shift, human feelings about them may shift also. Similarly, by clarifying issues, perhaps this discussion will change one's feelings about what the market is and what it does.

The need to interpret and *re*interpret situations is one reason why judgments of right and wrong are not easy to make. Values are often in conflict with one another. In doing something that is good, the individual at times does something else that is bad. To serve one value, the person may have to sacrifice another. Dilemmas of this kind are endemic to human existence, and everyone has to deal with them at certain times. In the case of the market, people who agree that it involves a significant amount of injustice may yet disagree about the market itself. Some may say that the injustices found in a market setting are a fair price to pay for the availability of quality products at good prices. True, few think that the super wealthy truly deserve the command over goods and services that they enjoy. But some say such superfluity is acceptable because the system which it makes possible is good for the community as a whole. Others, even if they agree that the production is maximized by market operations, feel that a lag in output of goods is bearable if it occurs together with a fair distribution of goods.

Ultimately then, right and wrong are, in this discussion, what we feel and therefore judge to be right and wrong. In philosophy, there is serious question about this attitude. Some philosophers have asserted that judgments about right and wrong are simply reports of emotional reactions. In this view, a person merely feels good or bad about what he sees people doing. But others have argued that good and evil are grounded in reality as such, and judgments about them pertain to substance and not just to feeling. Accordingly, these judgments can be correct or incorrect. It can, that is, be true or false to say that someone should or should not do a certain thing. There is no need to take a stand on this issue here. Regardless whether moral judgments are merely emotions or, by contrast, have truth value, the emphasis on how we feel remains valid. If we hold the opinion that morality is grounded in reality, we may still view our feelings as the means or guides by which we discern that reality. We may think, that is, that an "ontologically" true moral judgment is one that emerges when our feelings are fully clarified. And to the end of clarifying these feelings, we analyze the situations in which we find ourselves; we view these situations from various angles; we note competing values and we see what it is that we feel when all has been taken into account. It is the intent of the following discussion to do this.

Values and Community

The discussion in chapter three of the hypothetical community living in isolation was an attempt to clarify situations. Such a community is like the one in which we live in some ways and not in others. When compared to social life as industrial peoples know it, living in that small society is very simple. Much of what comprises life in an industrial society is missing. The community requires no banks or elaborate devices for assessing who has a right to how much of what, nor are there agencies of social control--police, courts, jails, lawyers. Also missing is the whole sphere of entertainment that suffuses and even defines modern life. A final feature of modern life which one does not find is a well-developed system of social stratification, a system in which a host of symbols is marshaled around a division of people into high, middle, and low classes. All of these are aspects of modern life which are central to the life we know, yet they would not exist in the community of one thousand because no public *en masse* exists there.

Although these features may be important in industrial societies, they do not play a role in shaping human feelings about what is fair and unfair. Indeed, their presence obscures rather than enlightens us on the shape of our own feelings. Fair and unfair are by their nature fundamental categories; they pertain to what is a person's due simply because he lives within a human community. How we feel about what is fair and unfair is shaped in simple terms. When people within a society condemn a condition or practice as being unfair, they are thinking of an individual as not getting his due in relation to others. When they praise a practice as fair, they are saying that people are getting that to which they have a proper claim.

The previous chapter presents fundamentals of what is fair and unfair. In a community-as-such, people have a right to a share of goods available, a share which is sufficient for living in a way which is viewed as decent. The right to a share comes before all others, and it does not depend upon working, though there is an obligation to work. Only after these basic needs have been met might there be special rewards for people who are especially deserving. The belief in the right to luxury is built upon a foundation in which all basic needs of all people are taken care of. When this foundation is laid-- then and only then--something extra in the form of luxury goods and services can be given to those who deserve them. Even when these luxuries are granted, it is not strictly given by right. Rather, the community deems the granting of luxuries to be in its interest because these extras, in effect, promote good production.

Members of any community have an obligation to work, but this communal obligation is not organically linked to the right to have goods and services. People who cannot work retain the right to have and consume, and people who have little need to consume still have an obligation to work. Community membership is the crux; it bestows the right to consume upon people and obligates them to work.

Community members' obligations and rights are intelligible even in a complex society like the United States. When people examine their own feelings and reactions to situations, they realize that they make a significant distinction between necessities and luxuries. Drawing a definite line between the two is not always easy, but the vagueness does not affect the validity of the distinction. People assume, rightly or wrongly, that a person does not lose the right to survive because he owns no resources. If a person's life depends upon medical attention, he must receive it. No one considers that letting him die is an option. Incidents of such deaths may occur, but the usual opinion is that these incidents are rare and scandalous. More often people assume what television programs portray--that any derelict of the street should get treatment. *Trapper John, M.D.* and other programs which show doctors leaping to attention as an ambulance comes into the emergency room present America's values. This prompt attention given to any injured person found in the streets may not illustrate what actually happens in hospital emergency rooms, but it does show what Americans think is *supposed* to happen. It is an accurate indication of American values.

Medical care is different from other goods necessary for maintaining life. It is not only an obvious necessity but is also what we might call an "anti-luxury." That is, it does not push people up from a level of living which is common within a society to a level which is higher in terms of comfort or elegance. What it does, rather, is pull people up from a lower level, that of being sick and disabled, and, where successful, restores them to the common level. No matter what the medical cost may be, medical care promises to do no more (and may do less) than return a person to his normal health status. It removes suffering rather than gives pleasures.

There are, of course, other necessities besides medical care. People cannot live without food, and everyone assumes--again, rightly or wrongly--that people are not left to die of starvation. People may have no right to television sets, and in this sense may be obligated to live a life that is television-deprived, but no one is obligated to die. If he cannot get food in the market, people assume that someone must give it to him. Perhaps the more charity-minded individuals do the giving; but no matter what, he is to get food.

Shelter is a necessity, though people can do without it. But with shelter as with food, everyone assumes that people should not be altogether deprived of it, regardless of their desserts. Homelessness has been a prominent news topic in the United States since the early 1980s; the news media give various estimates of how many people live on the streets. Americans regard it as a national scandal, as something that is not supposed to happen. Everyone assumes that someone, a certain "they," is going to aggressively put an end to homelessness, though not many consider personally undertaking the task. People are quite happy to let George do it. The trouble is that George also expects others to take care of the problem. Thus, nothing gets done, and homelessness continues as an indigestible item in the national psyche. By classifying the homeless as mentally ill or as drug addicts, people can place them outside the circle of normal human beings. They may prefer to think the homeless want or choose to live that way, that unrestrained passionate impulses inevitably result in such an undesirable living situation.

However people cope with the situation intellectually, they admit that hunger and homelessness are *not supposed to happen*. If such horrible situations do exist, everyone supposes, "This is terribly wrong; surely George will take care of it any minute now!" After all, everyone assumes that all members of the human community have a

right to live.   If this is a sincere belief of the community, then
luxuries for the especially deserving must be taken only from surplus
production--the layer of goods above that which is required to
maintain the community at the basic level. The modern industrial
society, then, is not different in any fundamental way from the
primitive-like hypothetical community. When we Americans examine
the crevices of our own feeling and sentiment, we discover that the
same basic assumptions lie in the depths of the cracks.

If the right to live and therefore to have a claim on essential goods
is a component of community life, it follows that work is an
obligation. Work responsibilities are important in modern societies.
In the social arena today, the leisured gentleman is no longer an
honored figure.   In the past, such people probably fulfilled a
ceremonial function similar to a monarch who sits on the throne but
has no power to rule--who does no work but who, simply by existing,
serves as a symbol of national identity. The idle rich played a similar
role.   But today, the person, especially the male, who lives on an
inherited income is an anomaly. He has no place in the community.
Even if he is charming, there is nothing to discuss with him because
he is nothing--or perhaps one should say no-thing. No matter how he
acquired the inheritance, American individualism is too great to allow
him to live off his ancestor's ideological capital, adequate as his
financial capital may be. If he is interested in women, he has no
masculine self to present to them; being a no-body, he is also a no-
male or no-man. Women do not admire his charm, good manners,
and knowledge of how to snap for a waiter. These characteristics by
themselves, if not accompanied by a business or professional aspect,
are not substantively masculine characteristics; they even seem
effeminate. Though no one can specifically define work, everyone is
quite certain that a man has to be doing it to be a man.

As with the right to live, community relations obligate a person to
work. It is not simply a prerequisite for eating, or consuming; it
indicates that an individual is a creditable member of society. People
feel that working coincides with being good citizens, with being part
of a group.

It is widely believed in contemporary society that the rewards one
wrests from the market are fair simply because the rewards (money)
came from the market.   People are willing to pay for things in
measure to how much they value them and to how plentiful they are.
Clearly, the more a person wants something, the more of something

else he will give up so that he can have the object of his desire. If he and others want something very much, that object will command a high price. If he and others want one thing more than another, assuming the availability of the two things to be equal, the object desired more will be more expensive. The scenario works in reverse as well--whatever commands a higher price must be valued more. Assuming availability to be equal, the prices of things are measures of the degree of value which people assign them. For instance, if a hairdresser is particularly good, people value his services and he charges a high price. Value and price are synergistic in the market system.

Why the Market Is Viewed as Fair

It is frequently asserted that people who succeed in getting abundant rewards from the market or through market processes do so because others--people in general--value whatever it is that these people put into the pool of goods. It is therefore fair, since the reward has a "size" (money in a certain amount) determined by this crucial measure of merit, the extent of his contribution; the value others place upon his work and what he can collect in exchange for it coincide. Thus, what a person *can* get from the market is what is *fair* for him to get from it. Moreover, it is often argued that this process is democratic because individuals' personal preferences determine prices and rewards. No elite group decrees that some things are more valuable or more worthy of reward than others. People do. If a good or service commands a high price and so yields high profits for the seller, it is because many people assign it great value. People have "voted" to reward producers of some goods and services more than others.

Situations Which Are Not True Markets

Before taking up the case of the market in its general and abstract guise, note that this discussion pertains only to the market in its pure form. It therefore excludes certain circumstances which affect the market and which comprise its character as market. Among these would be imbalance in the numbers or powers of buyers and sellers, a necessity for business to be rushed so that market processes cannot work themselves out, and the intervention of government.

No true market may exist when either buyers or sellers are few in number. Someone may have a product to sell which others consider to be valuable. But if that producer has many competitors offering the same goods, and there are few buyers, he is in a weak position. He must sell his product for very little if he is to sell it at all. Conversely, when there are small quantities of a product available to be sold, but many customers are offering to buy these scarce goods, the customer will have to pay a great deal in order to avoid being the one who is left out. When producers raise prices drastically because they enjoy this advantage (as with sellers of gasoline during the shortages of the 1970s), their doing so is called "price gouging" and is considered to be wrong. In labelling it "wrong" people recognize that no true market exists, and for that reason the fact that a person is able to demand a certain price for an object does not mean that the price is proper or fair. The fact that people make this judgment is an indication that they consider market prices to be fair only when there is a true market--that is, when there is a certain equality in the powers of buyers and sellers. A similar imbalance would occur in cases where time is of the essence. If someone needed a blood transfusion quickly to save his life, and there were only one donor with the right type who could provide the necessary blood quickly, he could of course demand a high price for it. There might be other potential donors, but if they are at a distance and cannot make the donation in time, the one who can do so clearly enjoys a tremendous advantage. Here also, people would judge that an assessment of a fair price must be made, and this price cannot be determined by the seller's power to demand. It must be based on something else, perhaps on what the seller could demand if he had competitors.

Monopolies play a large role in American economics and history. When sellers are few they do not have to compete. What one charges, the others charge, and they all get more than the market, operating on its own terms, would have yielded them. The sellers do not have to combine in restraint of trade; they need only follow suit. What one does, the others do, and the fair market process flies out the window. Monopoly compromises the free market.

Various government interventions have positive and negative affects on people. Most Americans oppose government intervention when they are thinking in general or abstract terms. But they are commonly less hostile when the interventions hold the promise of improving their personal lot or enabling them to maintain privileges.

This is as true of managers as it is of laborers. Whatever its characteristics, the market as shaped by these interventions is not the focus. This discussion speaks only of the market in its original, untainted form.

Merit and Contribution to Society

Behind the judgments people make about price and value is a truly fundamental idea about justice. People believe that when a person contributes more to the store of goods, he deserves to receive more from society; because he adds more to what is available, he rightly has claim to a larger share for himself. A problem with this belief is that when there is a division of labor, no one can specify or quantify a single person's contribution. Workers do not, as individuals, make things. Rather, they cooperate with others in the production of the things. We cannot, for this reason, say that a certain person has added certain goods to the pool of what is available. We can say only that he *and others* have made that contribution. If, therefore, we wish to assign a value to a person's labors, we must do so on some other basis. What we--what people--commonly do in seeking this other basis is to focus attention on a person's work itself rather than on the resulting product. We say that he has made a contribution of a certain value to the extent that he works a lot, works hard (fast) or works efficiently and well. The moral presupposition is that people who put in more and better work activity should receive extra reward. Work rather than production becomes the center of attention.

Retreating from production to work still does not solve the problem of how to measure the quantity and quality of work. If he has to have considerable experience, people assume that the quality of his work is better. They do not actually see that the work is better, for there is no way to do that. Rather, they take the need for experience to *mean* that the work based on it is better. Also, if he has to devote large blocks of time solely to learning so that he can perform, people assume his work has more quality. Taking the assumption one step further, people also believe that when a job requires deft maneuverability, based on a large volume of background knowledge, the worker labors at an even higher level of quality. While an automobile mechanic has to know much to do his job, a mechanical engineer has to have esoteric background knowledge as well; presumably, the mechanical engineer therefore works at a higher level of quality. People think that those who go to school for a long time contribute more quality than others. People suppose that these learned or "schooled" workers know more; therefore, they work better and are more responsible for the product than others; therefore it is fitting and proper that these well-educated workers are better rewarded. It cannot be demonstrated in any particular case that they make a greater contribution. It is simply taken to be true of cases in general. In effect, the belief is that if one has to know more to perform his part of a task, he in the nature of the case has performed a larger part of that task than have others who put the same time and energy into it.

Despite the public's judgments about what quality work involves, several confounding factors suggest why the correlation falls apart. One deserves special mention--the distinction between private and public work. We note that usually, the private worker receives the larger income. In general, the individual is willing to pay more when he receives goods or services in exchange for money than when he *and others* pay and all receive joint benefit. A person who is in a store that sells television sets, for example, is willing to pay a certain amount for a set. This amount is determined by how much he wants the set and by what other things he is willing to sacrifice in order to have it. But when it comes to goods he will share with others, such as parks or schools, and for which he will "pay" by coming up with money for taxes, he is not willing to make as much of a payment as he would for the object in the store, even if the public park has the same value for him. Willingness is greater when there is a direct exchange of money for something than when the exchange is indirect and communal. This may not be fair, but it is the way it is. And it explains why school teachers, police officers, and clergypeople do not enjoy the levels of income that are characteristic of people in business. There is, however, another side to this difference between private and communal purchasing. This is that people also commonly give more honor and recognition to the public figure than to the private. The public official, the clergyman, and the teacher at any level have a respected identity as a community person that the corporate executive does not. If people think a stranger to be an employee of a commercial firm but then learn that he teaches mathematics at the high school, they often respond with an "Oh" that suggests that their image of the stranger improves. Further, upon hearing that a person is a teacher at the local university, people commonly ask what he teaches; such a curiosity is evidence that the community esteems his work. They are not as inquisitive about corporate executives. The public person enjoys an honor denied the private person despite the latter's greater income. Perhaps the increment in prestige compensates for lack of income. Still, an impoverished high school teacher cannot pay his bills with community recognition, since his creditors require cash. The reward is psychological rather than material. But ultimately, all rewards are of that kind. At a certain point, the businessman's income ceases to make him comfortable and affords him only prestige. So the preacher and the teacher may simply get their kind of reward more directly.

If both money and community recognition are rewards, then people whose careers make studying at length necessary are believed to contribute more to society. People can only make guesses about what is of value to the community, and for this reason can only speculate about who contributes greater or lesser amounts to the group. One might attempt to define "fair" as a return commensurate with a person's contribution to the community, but directly measuring that contribution is impossible; so people measure it indirectly. The public believes it is fair that people whose work requires much knowledge, either by experience or schooling, be rewarded at a higher level than others.

The Market as Game

Examining certain characteristics of the market process may help to answer whether economic rewards gleaned from the market are necessarily fair. Activities within the market are efforts to do something or get something which are carried out in accordance with a set of rules. The rules determine both what a person may try to get and what means he may use to get it. In this sense, business activity is a game just like baseball and other athletic sports, and like cards, checkers, and other games. In all games, obstacles stand in the way of the goal; there are devices for overcoming the obstacles, and there are rules governing what the legitimate devices are. Succeeding in reaching the goal is not a given, no matter what the effort. Indeterminacy is part of playing the game. In part, the efforts to reach the goal succeed or fail because of achievement factors--the player fares well or poorly depending on his knowledge, skill, strength, and speed. But another part is luck, or chance, which may be able to influence the outcome of a game in particular cases. Though one may loom larger than the other, achievement and luck are always both involved in determining victory or defeat. After all, victory merely means having more points than the adversary. The difference between points accumulated by victor and vanquished do not have to be large enough to prove that one team is actually superior to the other. They need only to be more. Indeed, the euphoria of victory which may be observed is hardly affected by the gap between the two scores. In poker, luck would seem to be the greatest factor, though no one seems to doubt that talented and experienced players enjoy an edge in the contest. It is the combination of achievement and luck factors which gives games the indeterminacy which is essential to their charm and interest. People enjoy sports exactly because they do not know how the game is going to turn out.

In contrast to the is a person's effort to move directly to what he wants. If what he wants is out there in the forest, he goes and finds it or catches it. If the natural order does not produce it on its own, he uses elements of the order to cultivate or manufacture it. If others have it, he does whatever he can to get it away from them. In these activities, there are no rules, no man-made determinations of ends, conditions, and means. Instead, the of exigencies of the natural order impose the limits. Seeds do not grow unless placed in the ground and watered; animals do not lie down and submit to being eaten unless overpowered. Humans battle with nature on its own terms. Indeterminacy, which is desired in this direct pursuit of goals, is unavoidable. The farmer is never absolutely certain how his crop will turn out. Even if he enjoys his work for its own sake, his enjoyment is that of the craftsman and not of the gamesman; he likes to know how his efforts will turn out and does not want the anxiety of having to patiently wait and see.

However, the market is a game and not a battle with nature. Even its goal, money, is a "constructed reality," something brought into existence by people talking about it, just as are the touchdown and the victory in football. An employee's reluctance to work, a customer's unwillingness to buy, and a vendor's hesitancy to sell, together with the means for overcoming these obstacles, are circumstances which are shaped and limited by both customary rules and laws. The person who wants to win, and by winning to become rich or to reign as king of a large enterprise, must strive in certain ways to win. He may try to gain fame and fortune by buying things and then selling them (commerce); he may do it by first buying something, then changing it, and finally selling it (manufacturing); or he may achieve his goal by providing services (such as accounting, legal, or advertising services) to whomever needs and is willing to pay for them. All of these are social activities, since buying and selling are entirely occasions of *consent*, in which people *agree* to the transfer of valuables from themselves to others and from others to themselves.

Indeterminacy is present also. Just as an excitement or "tingle" in not knowing outcomes makes people want to watch a baseball game, a certain breathless volatility moves the market to do what it is supposed to do. It moves the market to yield a supply of goods which is adequate in quantity, high in quality, and available at low prices. *Competition*, the indeterminacy of many rival sellers trying to induce customers to buy their products rather than someone else's, keeps the market process lively. Sellers do this by offering products that are better or cheaper than competitors, or they do it by elaborating marginal differences in the product (often "shiny chrome") or by excelling in advertising and public relations. Because the outcome is uncertain, sellers struggle to outdo each other. They are like people playing bridge, chess, or basketball. Their excitements and motivations are those of the gamesman, not the craftsman. It is the "tingle" that keeps them going.

The craftsman is qualitatively different from the businessman, even though his activity is formally a business. He has, in effect, a personal relationship with his work materials and with the product which he brings forth from those materials. If he is making objects such as shoes or violins, he sees these fruits of his labor as expressions of himself--as projections of his personality. They embody the virtue and dignity of his identity as a human being. While he may subsequently sell his products, as indeed he must so that he can obtain what others produce, he does not do so as commerce, for he is not simply exchanging one thing for another (for money). Rather, because his product bears an imprint of himself, he has a personal relationship with the buyer. The buyer possesses a piece of the craftsman's human essence. As the wearer of personally-crafted shoes or the player (or hearer) of handmade violins, he has an essential personal unity with the person who crafted those objects.

Is the Market Fair?

When set alongside the activity of the craftsman, the gaming
nature of commercial and industrial work comes clearly into focus.
Shoes and violins are not produced with the hope that they will
embody an eternal, ideal essence; rather, they are made in an effort to
maximize profit, which means producing as much as possible with as
little effort and expense as possible of what customers in the greatest
numbers will buy. The producer regards his products as factors in the
game; he regards them *impersonally*, just as he regards employees and
all factors of production. Products are marketable rather than good.
As objects, they derive their essence from their attractiveness to
customers who will pay money for them. Their essence is derived
from their role in competition and not from an inherent goodness or
utility. The spirit of the participant in the market is very different
from that of the craftsman.

Of course, we are speaking here of the market as concept. In
concrete situations, the idea of market is always imperfectly
represented. People engaged in commerce, manufacturing, and
services may in many instances have a craftsman-like motivation.
Whenever a worker forgets about marketability, and even for a
moment takes pride in producing something that has intrinsic worth,
the craftsman reappears. Also, in actual market economies,
businessmen avoid the indeterminacy of the market wherever they
can. They do not hesitate to form combinations or to use the powers
of government to increase their profits and make profits more secure
whenever the opportunity presents itself.

The discussion can now focus on whether the hierarchy of rewards
which people glean from the market is simply and by its nature fair.
The person who does well in the market, that is, the person who gets
the monetary rewards it has to offer, is someone who has done well
in the game. He buys something and proceeds to hold, transport, or
change it. He then sells it for more than it cost him, thereby making
a profit. Doing well in the market, as in games in general, results
from the two factors already discussed--skill and chance. The person
who succeeds displays skill in marketing goods and for that reason
fares better than do the clumsy or ignorant. Or such a person has
good luck. Unpredictable and uncontrollable events turn out
favorably for his enterprise. While he cannot anticipate exactly how
many people would want and would be able to buy his product, it

could turn out that many do. What he does is to base his decisions on assumptions about human behavior, simply guessing that if he does certain things, he will have customers. So he makes his guess, carries out certain ways of manufacturing and marketing goods and, by chance, succeeds in accordance with his dreams. He was, as we say, "lucky." It is important to bear in mind that there commonly is this factor of risk and chance. It is why we call participation in the market a "game."

In addition to skill and luck, there is a third consideration---scrupulousness. Legal and moral rules limit the businessman's choices. Certain things he could do to enhance his profits may be ruled out by laws, morality, or simply by a concern for people's welfare. Either a vigorous conscience or a tender concern for what happens to human beings everywhere in the nation and world may prevent some business executives from availing themselves of options that hold out a promise of increased empire and profits. Therefore the enterpriser who succeeds may be the one who breaks the rules, who is undisturbed by pricks of conscience and unbothered by misfortunes befalling human beings in divers places. The person with a lax conscience has a flexibility regarding what he does which makes it likely that he will stay one step ahead of his competitors, when those competitors are limited by moral and humane inhibitions.

Thus, the winner of the market game is the one who exhibits skill, enjoys good luck, and is free of burdensome scruples. The question now before us is whether this victory is fair. Has, that is, the person who "gets" more and who therefore is more able to divert the community's labor resources and apparatus to uses of his choosing in fact contributed more? Has he, in this sense, earned what he has?

There is a certain plausibility to thinking that he has. People do, we may note, choose to buy goods and services. The winner of the market game achieves his victory by offering things for sale that people choose to buy. They bestow victory upon him because he gives them what it pleases them to have. We may think, therefore, that there is an automatic and necessary link between "getting" and "giving." True, a certain observer may not approve of what sellers sell and buyers buy. He may wish that products that are more worthy or culturally uplifting were traded in the market. But if so, his quarrel is with "people," not with sellers, or with the system or the justice of being enriched by market operations.

On the other hand, it may be noted that this is a *deductive* argument. It notes conclusions that can be derived logically from premises. As such, it bears no necessary relation to what actually happens in the world. Events are shaped by all the causal factors resident in concrete situations, not just by those that a process of reasoning takes into account.

Particularly noteworthy is that the market system yields differences in reward that are greater than those that an ordinary person making ordinary moral judgments would see as representing differences in contribution. The estates of the super-rich illustrate this. There are scores of people in the United States who have personal estates in excess of one hundred million dollars. A few are worth a billion dollars or several billions. If these mammoth accumulations of money are viewed simply as such, people take them for granted as being the facts of life. But if stated in terms of claim on goods and services, or ability to direct resources to desired or approved purposes, matters are different. The ordinary person will say that there is no possibility of a person making so great a contribution that he is entitled so great a reward. True, he may have played an important role in the construction of great enterprises. And these enterprises may have much to do with why we have what we have, including automobiles, airplane travel, televisions, smog, and water pollution. But the person did not "build" these enterprises. The labor and intellect of thousands of people were employed to that end. He only played a role or did a part in the process. Yet his reward is a very large multiple of theirs. No, ordinary moral judgments will not call this fair. The most they could do is to call it tolerable, given that this is an imperfect world and that the excess wealth of a few arose from the operation of a system that serves all. Letting them have so much, that is, might be thought to be a reasonable price to pay for what the rest of us have.

Sometimes the way to answer questions is by observing results such as this. If there is something wrong with a result, there must have been something wrong in the original process that gave rise to it. Thus, if a sharpshooter misses his market three hundred yards from where he is shooting, there must have been a tiny inaccuracy in the aim of the weapon, possibly one too small to see when looking at it. Or, an automobile engine may be adjusted after being driven a few hundred miles, because inaccuracies too minuscule to measure even with instruments are magnified many times over as the vehicle is driven. So if it is wrong that a few people have mammoth fortunes, there must have been something wrong--that is unjust--about the process that produced those fortunes.

At the other end of the income scale, it is also and obviously wrong that innumerable people labor hard for wages that could not possibly support them. They are doing work we want done; our society is able to provide all its members with a decent living; therefore, it is clearly unfair that some must labor so much for so little. If we were not accustomed to the "McJob" that pays minimum wages, we would easily see the injustice of this low pay.

Unfairness of the Market as System

We may now proceed to see how this is the case. When a person participates in the market, he engages in exchanges with others. He gives goods in exchange for goods or for claims on goods--money. Or he gives claims in exchange for goods, or he gives claims in one form in exchange for claims in another, as when he buys or sells stocks and bonds. His exchanges are not direct; he does not give someone a thing that the person wants in exchange for something that he wants. Rather he and the other person are part of a much larger network of exchanges or an exchange circle. This is what is called the "market." This network of exchanges is not directed by anyone. No person or agency controls it in the interest of any given purpose. Rather, it consists of innumerable person-to-person exchanges in which each individual is striving to "strike a deal" which is good for himself. He could do so because the trading partner thinks that the "deal" is good for him also.

Notable about this mass of exchanges is that the nature and shape of the entire mass and the consequences of its operations are not designed in any way. They are, instead, determined by the purposeless outcomes of a very large number of actions in which participants strive only to do as well as they can for themselves. Precisely because self-service is the only intent of each trader, the outcome is, so to speak, "blind." It is a "how things turned out" that is not determined by any person nor shaped by any purpose. It is, in this sense, *a*moral. It is not by its nature either good or bad. It is not by nature, in fact, any particular thing.

Thinking deductively--that is by pure reason without resort to facts, the people who assert that the market is fair say that the outcome has to be benign. They argue that since people buy voluntarily and on the basis of an intelligent assessment of what pleases and serves them, exchanges must result in people getting out of the market the same value that they put in. The man who emerges wealthy, then, must have made a contribution to the pool of goods and services which is of a size comparable to the riches he got from it.

Such a deductive line or reasoning is not, however, as certain and air-tight as it appears. Actually, it is false. The fact that some emerge super-wealthy is a clue that something is wrong. We are now in a position to see what the error is. When each person engages in an exchange, he does not gain objects that he wants for pleasure or utility from the exchange. Rather, he obtains a claim on goods, one that he calculates is the best possible in his particular circumstances. And his calculation is based not on what a person can give him in exchange for what he may give the person, but on his conception of the *entire market as a system.* He takes the whole mass of exchanges into account as he forms his guess of what will serve him. That system as a whole has a certain structure, and it is this structure that determines what the individual will do. It is itself a product of what the individual, together with many others, did. But once it has come into existence, it "feeds back," so to speak, and shapes the behavior of those who gave rise to it. What a person does and what he acquires, then, are not *exchange* in the usual sense of the word. They are not, that is, a back-and-forth in which one person gives to another and receives from him. Rather, they are a negotiation with a *system* that has its own structure and determines events in ways that are qualitatively different from two-person exchange. The most important feature of this difference is that there is no longer a correspondence between what a person puts into the market and what he takes out of it.

Certainly, such is the case with the man who accumulates a billion dollars through business. This man played a role in a massive change in the commercial landscape. He served as financial and managerial leader of a corporation that arose from the dust and became a massive enterprise. He did not get his billion dollars because someone thought he deserved it or believed that the community would benefit by his having it. Rather, everyone with whom he had dealings was looking out for "number one," for himself. These people sold him things, built structures for him, and worked for him directly as employees of his firm. Each was getting the best deal he could under the circumstances. As a result, he accumulated results from the large number of deals which totaled over a billion dollars. With that money, he can of course buy everything he could possibly need or enjoy. And when he has bought them, he still has almost all of his billion dollars left. With that, he can only buy prestige or power over what people do.

Why, we may ask, did the many people with whom he had dealings not demand more for themselves? Since they were essential and he could not have made even a modest fortune without them, surely they could have struck a better "deal" in which he was well rewarded but they were also and the difference between them was not so great. The answer is that the system as a whole did not leave them in positions to do so. Had they been a single mass able to act as a unity, they could of course have done that. But in fact they were like the sand of the seashore, divided into many grains, while he was one person. Each of them, then, acting simply as himself/herself, was in no position to demand a just due. That is how he got to be so wealthy.

The belief that the market has to be fair because people can get wealth from it only by providing people with what they want is fundamentally wrong. It assumes what we might call a two-person model. In this model, a person trades with one other person. He gives that person certain objects of value and receives objects of about the same value from him. He does so because what he gives is excess to him, while what he receives serves him in positive ways. Each participant emerges from the transactions with a collection of goods that is unchanged in total value but which consists of items which are more suitable to his needs. Matters are altogether different when what is at hand is a system instead of a pair-in-exchange. The system has its own nature formed by the aggregate effects of innumerable self-serving decisions by innumerable persons. These decisions are all made in response to situations and in view of a necessarily limited set of options. And thus formed, the system makes it possible for some to take out much more than they have put in, while others must be content with much less than they contribute.

Further, there are people who gain (and lose) fortunes through nothing other than buying and selling. They buy stocks and then sell them, and they buy real estate and then sell it. They do not change what they buy; they merely hold it for a time, often a short time, and then sell it. Their affluence derives from the fact that sellers are willing to sell them things--either goods or claims on goods--when it would have been profitable to hang on to them and sell them later. Perhaps the seller did not know the value of what he had, while the buyer did. Perhaps the seller had a more desperate need for cash that could be spent. Perhaps the seller was engaged in other games that made the sale seem at the time to be profitable. In any case, the buyer ("speculator") exchanged goods and/or claims on goods and then exchanged again, emerging with a claim on goods (money) for which he made no contribution. He is living, then, and often living quite well, off of the labor of others.

The Labor Market and Fairness of "Market"

One feature of the market that deserves special attention is that of the relations between employer and employee. Whether the employees of a company are being paid as they should depends on whether there is a true labor market. Assume, for the moment, a simple model of enterprise with an owner-manager and a corps of workers. The workers are partners with the owner in the enterprise, for the owner could not run a business without them. It is not just the owner or manager who buys, changes, and sells things; it is he and they together who do that work in a joint operation. The employees therefore are entitled to a fair share of the profit, whatever it may be. Assuming that ability-to-get-from-the-market and fair are the same thing, one would think that a fair share for the workers would be what the owner must pay them for their labor in a true market situation; a true labor market must exist.

But what is a true labor market? It is one in which employers are in competition with each other for workers, just as workers compete for available jobs. The number of workers is just as limited as is the number of jobs. There is in this sense a rough equality between employers and workers. Being left bereft of necessary help is a threat to the owner in a measure equal to that of the menace of unemployment imposed on the worker. In such a situation, an employer who is anxious to assure the adequacy of his labor supply will do so by allowing the workers a rather generous proportion of the enterprise's earnings. Once the employer does this, other employers are under pressure--market pressure--to do the same. Those who fail to do so are in danger; they may find themselves without workers, and so without a product to sell, and consequently, without profits.

As an enterprise's profit swells, so does its payroll. The owner-manager may reap an abundant reward for himself, but the extent of that abundance would be held in check by the need to have the pay roll grow along with it. For example, the late Sam Walton, owner of Wal-Mart, was one of the richest men in the nation. Yet his personal fortune might have been more modest, though still large, if he had to compete for workers.

This picture of a true labor market is of course fanciful. Where in the real world can we find instances of it? The trouble is that employers are few while workers are many. One owner-manager deals with thousands of laborers, each of whom deals with a sole employer. In negotiations between owner and workers, the owners are threatened with the loss of one worker at a time. Each worker is but a tiny proportion of the work force and so cannot threaten the employer with a significant loss. It is different with the worker. For him, the loss of a job is the loss of his entire livelihood. The contest unfairly places the worker at a disadvantage. Because workers lack leverage, they have formed unions. If the employer can bargain as one, then workers should be able to do likewise. Labor unions attempt to unite workers so that they can confront management as a unity and so assure that the bargaining is fair. The manager needs no union because he already is a unity. By himself he *is* a union. Once workers have unionized, the potential for real negotiations develops. If a labor union exists, owners cannot ignore workers' demands, especially if there is no vast sea of unemployed workers waiting at the factory door to serve as replacements (scabs). Without workers on the job, the owners cannot continue operations, and their mammoth investments will be of no value to them. The vehemence, and frequently violence, with which owner-managers have countered unions ever since the beginning of the industrial era reveals the vulnerability employers face when unions organize. Of interest here is an image of what would be if employers had to deal with unionized workers bargaining as a unit, with the employer having no recourse to non-market coercive instruments (goons) and no unemployed people anxious to take the place of striking workers. Certainly, no one would expect workers on the factory floor to receive salaries equal to managers, but the differences in their incomes might be lessened a good deal.

There has almost always been a surplus of workers in the United States. Indeed, we could even say that labor surplus is an endemic condition of industrial societies. Apart from a few special eras, such as that of World War II in the United States and the postwar era in Europe, industrial societies typically have more workers than jobs. This is not the only reason why employers do not have to bargain as equals with workers, but it is certainly a major factor. In recent decades, the increased ability of corporations to site their operations outside of the country has exacerbated the situation.[16] What was a sea of available labor has become an ocean of virtually unlimited manpower, resulting in powerless laborers.

What potential does exist for justice in a market economy, then, lies in there being relationships between employer and worker in which the two bargain as equals. In such a relation, the worker would become more of a partner in an enterprise and less of a "factor of production" who can be treated in accordance with rational calculations. Most notably, he would get rewarded more handsomely. While his wage would not equal the manager's salary, it would be closer to that salary than previously. Moreover, *all* enterprises would have this worker-manager relation, so no competitive advantage or disadvantage would be involved. As long as this is not the case--as long as, that is, managers have an advantaged position in dealing with workers, no one should expect their respective incomes or conditions of life to be fair.

Dramatization of Unfairness of "Market"

As a way of dramatizing or bringing into clear focus the unfairness of the market, we may imagine the hypothetical case of a person who holds large investments. He has accumulated five million dollars, or its equivalent. Invested at six percent interest, he would have an income of three hundred thousand dollars a year in perpetuity. Because his holdings are of stocks that represent capital goods, both the value of his estate and the income derived from it will rise with inflation or sink with deflation. His "real" holdings and income remain, that is, the same. He can go on forever with his very large income. He cannot, of course, live forever, but his descendants can, and they can continue to reap benefits as though they were he. In the person of his descendants he goes on with his generous allowance indefinitely. To think this, we would need to imagine that he has two children, and each of his children and their descendants continue to have two children. Moreover, each of the children and grandchildren marries someone of similar inheritance, so that each person, in effect, inherits the entire estate. There is no subdividing. If, then, society continues essentially unchanged for a thousand years, the original tycoon's descendants could still be receiving the three hundred thousand dollars per year, without any of the intervening thirty generations having done any work at all. Now one might wonder if it was fair that the first man got the five million dollars. But even if that does not bother us, what about this wondrous extension in which he--in the persons of his descendants--continues to claim a handsome share of available goods and services without contributing anything at all to it? Even if the first man made a truly marvelous contribution to society in the process of earning the five million, the contribution was finite. Yet there is no limit to the claim on goods and services that can be made thereafter. The annual income paid out because of his venture could go on for centuries; indeed, it could go on forever. No one expects that to happen; we think something is bound to happen to the man, his dynasty, or the society. That does not matter here. The purpose is to examine principles, which come into clearer focus when we make such simplifying assumptions. Whatever the tycoon did to earn five million dollars enables him to lay claim to goods produced by others' sweat until, potentially, the end of history.

Property Is the Monkey Wrench

Property is, by the common consent, central to the whole idea of the market. When a person gives something that is his in exchange for something else, he gains full rights to use, control, and disposal of the item he has purchased; these rights are his for as long as he decides to hold onto the item. The moral sentiments of society grant him the rights and at the same time obligate others to respect those rights. The law enforces and endorses what morality decrees. All of this is an assumption of the market. Without it, there could be exchanges of things for use and consumption; but there would be no true market.

That property is thus crucial for the market does not mean, however, that it shapes justice. Being in possession of property does not of necessity imply the making of contributions to the pool of goods and services. When the man bought a field and later sold it for many times the price he paid, he was able to do so because of changes that took place around his field. Business and industry flourished, and the field--which became important to businesses-- underwent an increase in value. People were willing to exchange much more command over goods and services (money) for it than they were before. This increase in value occurred because others effected changes; the man who owns the field did nothing to make the land command such an increase in worth. Events just happened to unfold favorably for him. Why he in particular benefitted from these changes has no definitive answer; he simply happened to be ideally situated--that is, he held, or had, a piece of property at the right time.

When thinking about what is fair, people imagine a community in which each person makes a contribution to the store of good things available to the rest of the community. Each person then receives a portion of that store of goods, the portion necessary for surviving at a certain level of decency. If after such portions have been distributed, there remains a stock of goods, the community may use it to reward those who have made special contributions, either in qualitative or quantitative terms. And since they cannot separate one person's contribution to a concrete process of production from the contributions of others, everyone equates *contribution* with the skill and knowledge a person must acquire to do a job. Notably lacking in this picture is any notion of *property*. People exchange and distribute goods and services, and they use and consume goods. However, people do not pin the goods down and decree that lands or buildings are now theirs with all that implies in the present and the future. Such pinning down would be a confounding factor, like a monkey wrench in machinery. Counter to much that is sacred to many Americans, property claims stand in the way of the processes of give-and-take through which justice is achieved, as Reinhold Niebuhr explained in his *Children of Light and Children of Darkness*.[17] Further explanation of property is therefore necessary.

Property itself has positive functions. In a market context, it provides some protection for the weak against the strong. Those with power could gather everything for themselves, leaving little or nothing to those with no power, but they are prevented from doing so because certain things *belong* to the less powerful. Houses and lands are a poor person's property, and this is a bulwark against total domination by the more powerful. Where justice is not otherwise enforced, property affords some assurance of a minimum level of living for the poor. Certainly it does not assure enough, but it does to some extent.

Also, property allows fixed points of reference that enable people to plan their activities. If a person is to conceive and carry out plans, either in production or consumption, he must have such fixed points as the basis for his planning. A farmer cannot plant, cultivate, water, and fertilize crops unless he can assume that he controls what happens in a certain field. The office worker must have facilities, equipment, and stable responsibility and authority in order to carry out a plan. Thus, from the standpoint of justice, property is a good thing.

One can analyze investment similarly. Think of the person who has an ability and inclination to work. He devotes some of his efforts to the production of tools. These tools afford him no pleasure nor fulfill any basic needs. Instead, these capital goods serve only to enhance his production of other goods. They are very valuable because they help to speed production and to improve the quality of other goods. The labor invested in making the goods is latently stored in the tool and released when someone uses the tool. Thus the person who makes tools for others' use contributes to the community. Others produce more and more efficiently because of the tools even though the tool maker himself produces nothing that can be eaten, worn, or lived in. The toolmaker is the primal investor.

A man making sharpened stones, plows, canoes, and other functional items is very different from the Wall Street investor who accumulates his portfolio. Nevertheless, the principle of investment is the same. Productive efforts are stored in tools, or in claims on the tools (money). If the person who has these tools or money in hand then consents to their use by others, he enhances the productive output of those others; he contributes to the total pool of available goods. Since justice means that those who give should receive, it is fair for him to receive in return. He could even be producing for consumption at the same time that his earlier work is working for him. Since he is thus working double at any given time, he is also earning double. If what he has as a result of his early labor is money (or claim on goods) then his money is out there working for him while he does other work or possibly no work. His early work is gaining claims on goods for him; what he receives is measured by what he contributes. Investing can contribute just as labor can. Indeed, investment is labor stored in a box and then let loose

Both property and investment, then, have a place. Owning things helps to assure a person a share of the goods available; and investment--storing labor in a class of things called tools--enables a person to make indirect contributions to the pool of goods. However, note that once the matter is stated this way, its limitations as well as its extensions come to the surface. Property supposedly assures a person a share and provides some fixed points of reference; it is not supposed to enable people to dominate others or enable them to control the pool of goods (have wealth) to a degree which exceeds their contributions. Investment is supposed to enable people to make indirect contributions; it is not designed to allow people to lay claim to more than they have contributed.

Property does enable certain people to dominate others and to take out of the pool of goods and services more than they have put in. This fixed point of reference is not supposed to be so inflexible. If someone totally owns his property (perhaps a piece of land), he can use it for whatever purposes he wishes. If he sells his piece of land, he merely changes the form of his personal estate; he changes the form or location, but not the amount of his property. While it was land, it may now be transformed into stored-up goods (money) or into something that money can buy. It is like a piece of cardboard attached to a surface by a thumbtack. The cardboard can turn in a circle, but the thumbtack stays stationary. Likewise, the owner can do much transferring and changing with his land, but that he possesses property is an invariable point.

In the hypothetical community developed in Chapter Three, property was not mentioned, for no one expects it to have a place in a community's life when the community is struggling for survival. Nevertheless, distinctions of what belongs to whom would still be a part of life. One would expect that if someone in the group builds a house or produces other goods which he then exchanges for the house, the house would be his in which to live. However, the right to live in a house is different from the individual's right to rent houses and thus receive an income from them forever; the justice of granting this right is questionable. It seems more reasonable that a person who leases a home which he owns to a leaseholder should only receive rent for a certain amount of time, after which ownership of the house passes to those paying rent and living in it; at some point the owner should be required to sell (possibly for rent already paid) rather than rent the house. Limits to the amount of compensation the builder-owner receives should be set. The house should not be his to rent forever.

The same applies to investments. The person who invests may be a tool-maker who allows others to use his tools, or he could be someone who uses money to buy stock in corporations. In either case, he creates stored labor which enables others to produce much more than they could have otherwise. It is certainly fair that the investor reap some harvest from his investments. Yet we must also acknowledge that limits are necessary. A person's estate should not be a hydrogen balloon that rises indefinitely. Sooner or later, the property invested should become community property to be divided among the people who comprise that community.

It is easier to understand this if one thinks of property in terms of land. Where a few families in a nation own most of the agricultural land, it is easy for one to see that such owning by a few is unfair. The lands ought to be divided among those who actually work them. Agrarian reform of this sort has occasionally occurred, but more often people merely recommend it without taking action. Just as lands should ultimately become the property of those who till them, so factories should cease to belong to shareholders and become the property of those who labor in them. In general, ownership should be tied to *use*. People should own what they live in and what they work in or on.

As strange as it may sound to the contemporary American, such a system is not far from what Americans envisaged in the early decades of the nation's history.[18] America was to be a land of owner-operators. Most people, founders assumed, would be farmers; they would own the land they farmed, and farm the land they owned. The few who were not agrarian laborers would be owner-operators of various kinds of small shops. "Democracy" meant that people who worked the land also owned it. No large landowners living in elegance off the aching muscles of a corps of agricultural laborers were to exist. For early Americans, to own something meant to use it for production or consumption. Ownership was not an abstraction that provided a fixed point by which the owner played the game of multiplying his wealth. Conceivably, the United States could have preserved that concept of ownership.

However in the United States, and elsewhere in the world, people now view property as sacred, and seeing it so, they think that to abridge property rights in any way is a serious matter. Such a perception implies that people accept property as an abstract, fixed point. And with it, they accept the whole capitalist order and the vast differences in wealth to be found within it. There is a certain intellectual slight-of-hand involved in such thinking. The original idea was that families were to work and live, and that they were to *own* the lands, buildings, and equipment that they used in the process. Ownership pinned down, so to speak, their rights to the land and objects used in working and living and therefore their rights to work and live. The affirmation of property was actually an affirmation of people. The people, after all, were what was important. Their ability-- and right--to live and find fulfillment in living was the prime concern. And since to do so they needed fixed points of reference such as fields and houses, their right to retain these items was raised to a high level of importance. "Property" is actually nothing other than these rights. It is for this reason that a certain sacredness attaches to the idea of property. It is a sacredness of people and life.

In contrast to this people-affirming view of property, people today have defined property itself and *in the abstract* as an ultimate value. They have wrenched ownership of property from its context and made it itself to be the important thing. In so doing, they brought about the metamorphosis by which the property rights of corporation managers and large stock holders have attained the same sacredness as originally given to owner-operators. "Property" has come to mean the opposite of what it originally meant; while it began as a way of assuring that each person would have his share of materials and dignity, it now allows some to rise way above others. The image of the farm family enjoying dinner together after a hard day's work on the land they own has been projected onto the owner of a huge mansion having cocktails brought to him by servants while he reads the *Wall Street Journal* and makes plans to expand his corporate empire. The sacred aura which hovers over the former descends upon the latter. The corporate manager is now the ideal instead of the independent farmer. The manager's right to superior riches and power is assigned the dignity that is properly the birthright of ownership of small properties by individuals and families who earn their living from those properties.

The transformation did not take place by accident. When some Americans did well and became wealthier than others (which happened immediately), they wanted everyone to consider their property rights to be sacred, for that assured and justified their privileged position. Since the wealthy were (and still are) the powerful and vice versa, they succeeded both legally and ideologically. Before long, the idea of democracy came to mean the abstract concept of ownership and the free market economy.

The answer to this chapter's original question--whether what a person gets from the market is fair since it was from the market that he obtained it--is "no." "Fair" means congruent with contribution. It is fair for someone to get in proportion to what he contributes. It is fair for a person to receive a handsome reward if the rest of the community is better off because of his being in it, even if he withdraws a large portion for himself. The ability to get from the market is not the same thing as having contributed to the market, i.e., to the community. Property conceived as an abstract and totally fixed point prevents it from being so. Exchanges from people do have a tendency to grant rewards according to how much people have contributed. But property steps in, removes part of the exchange from its natural setting, and thus separates the notions of fairness and contribution from each other. As a result, the winners of the economic game get much more than they give.

Winning the game is one thing; giving or receiving justice is another. If we want justice, we must concern ourselves with the true meaning of justice. We cannot just promote the market.

Chapter 5

Individual and Community Decision-Making

Human beings are always busy doing things. Some of these things are pleasant or "fun," or are, as the people see them, good and worthy. Others of the things they do serve a purpose; they are not good in themselves but because of what they accomplish. In either case, people make decisions. They determine by an act of will that they will do something in particular. When we look at the human scene, we see a mass of activity. We see people running to and fro. But we also see structure and pattern, since people are not just moving but are doing "things." They are making decisions and acting on the basis of them.

Among the decisions that people make, some seem to those who make them to stand alone. A person decides to do something because he enjoys doing it or because he wants what his action gets for him. These are the only considerations. His actions may, of course, have many consequences, some of which affect the people around him for good or ill. These are not, however, his concern, at least not at a certain time. He decides to do something and that is that; consequences that may affect others are off in the distance somewhere, and he does not feel that he should worry about them. For example, when he buys a power lawn mower, his purchase of that item may result in a reduction in the availability of nonpower mowers, since such mowers did not sell well. The few who need them may therefore have to do without or pay a high price. But the person buying the power mower does not feel that this is his concern.

It is different with other decisions that people make. In these cases, people are well aware that their decisions combine with decisions made by others to produce a single effect. They decide in favor of certain actions in order to produce this effect. Voting in an election is an example. We will refer to the decisions that stand alone

as *individual decisions.* Those that people make with an intent that
they combine with decisions made by others we will call *community
decisions.*

Individual Decision-Making

Individual decisions are those that a person makes because of
what, in a broad sense of the term, he wants. He does not concern
himself with decisions made by others on the same matter. What
others do does not interest him or is not "his business." There are
certain words that we use in talking about such decisions. The words
are "buy," "sell," "employ," and "be employed." These terms have to
do with exchange. A person has in his hand an object that has little
value for him but which does have value for someone else. That
second person similarly has little use for what he possesses, but does
want the object that the first person has in hand. So, the two trade.
Each then possesses what has value for him while being rid of the
object that does not. Fundamental to the exchange is that each
individual is concerned only with the value that objects have to him.
In his deciding to trade, he determines that doing so will result in his
possessing what will serve him. The decision has this and only this
meaning to him. He does not see his choice as taking place alongside
similar decisions made by others.

The same thing applies to employing and being employed. A
person employs someone because what he must pay that person is of
less value to him than the work that person will do for him, while the
employee accepts the work because the leisure he gives up would
serve him less than does the payment made to him. Again, the
decisions stand by themselves. People are either customers who buy
the labor of others, or they are salespeople selling their own. Whether
buying or selling, each is acting entirely for himself. If something
happens because he and others make parallel decisions, it just
happens; it is not his concern.

Nevertheless, very often a person's decision does combine with
others, and an aggregate effect comes into view. A lone tourist
wandering through a national park picking up arrow heads and other
artifacts left by early Native Americans may have no discernible
effect on the park; but many tourists doing the same thing everyday
will eventually denude the park of all evidences of aboriginal society.
For this reason, the park authorities prohibit the taking of these items.

The artifacts, as they put it, are "of interest to the American people" and so must be left where they are. They consider it important that archaeologists will have access to the items for their research. While the lone tourist can have little effect by himself, he is asked to understand that he is one of many and thus must behave in certain ways because his actions in combination with those of others have certain effects. While each may see himself as just one person, he is in fact one of many.

Indeed, sometimes a "snowball" effect occurs. For example, a city has a fine system of public transportation, mainly buses. But as private ownership of automobiles increases, people decide to travel by car instead of by bus. They think only of the relative merits of bus and automobile travel on each occasion. Making a comparison, they note that if they go by bus, they will not have to worry about parking and can read the newspaper during the trip. But if they go by car, they will be able to travel when they choose, will be able to go wherever they want, and will be able to go from where they are to their destination without having to walk to and from bus stops. They will be able to carry more things with them and will not have to share a space with just anyone who may choose to be there. Very commonly, the latter considerations win, and they decide to go by car. The automobile wins out over public transport. Many people make this decision.

As a result of this chorus of decisions by individuals to go by private automobile, there is a decline in the number of passengers on the buses. That drop-off results in a lessening of the money taken in as bus fares. Having reduced funds to work with, the bus service is compelled to curtail services. It determines that there will be fewer bus routes, and the buses will pass less frequently on the routes which remain. Fares, of course, have to go up, since there are fewer passengers to share the cost. With bus services reduced and prices raised, people are even less inclined to use the public services than they were at first. They decide in favor of their automobiles even more than they did before. This results in further diminution of bus services. The downward trend continues until it reaches a point from which it can go no further--either no bus service exists at all, or a minimal service exists for those who do not drive cars.

Obviously, individual decisions do have aggregate effects. Continuing with the transportation illustration, innumerable instances occur in which a person finds it more convenient to go someplace by car than by city bus. In each case, the person is concerned only with the relative merits of the two forms of travel for himself. All these instances combine into a single effect--very little bus service is available, and automobile travel is necessary even for those who would prefer to use buses.

There are consequences of these changes that are not readily foreseen but which are very real. If going by car is convenient in certain cases, it results in a loss of convenience in others. Many car-lovers will discover that they now have to provide chauffeur services for children and for handicapped persons who cannot drive but who could go by themselves on the bus if the service were available. Whole trips will thus be added to their itinerary when they could have been free to lounge at home while others in their family went about by public transportation. When Mother and Father decide to hop in the car and go to work, to the store, or to Grandmother's instead of taking the Main Street bus, they do not think that they are setting themselves up to have to make car trips that would have otherwise been unnecessary, but in fact they are. And in addition to bringing this burden on themselves, they are also reducing the independence of the people who cannot drive. Children who are too young to get their licenses, the elderly who have diminished speed of response, and the handicapped may be confined to where they are because reductions in public transportation have made the service inadequate for their needs. And further, even drivers will find themselves immobilized when their cars are sick and "in the shop," or they will avoid this fate only by having multiple cars per family at great expense. These are consequences of the many, seemingly unimportant, decisions to go by car instead of by bus.

What defines a decision as individual, then, is not that it does not have aggregate effects, for it frequently does. Rather, it is an individual decision because the person making the decision does not *intend* it to have such effects. Quite commonly he is unaware of the causal connection between the decisions that he (and many other individuals) makes and other events that take place. And even if he is aware, he regards those consequences as natural or inevitable and thus not as proper factors in his decision. Indeed, in the world view of pure capitalism, it is a matter of principle that decisions be so viewed. A person is supposed to be busy making individual or "business" decisions, and it is considered right and good that he let the market processes take care of the consequences. If the family farm disappears, for example, he does not evaluate that outcome. Instead, he views it as "natural," since it is a result of the processes of buying and selling.

Community Decision-Making

In contrast, community decisions are those which people make with the intention that they combine with decisions made by others to produce a single effect. Here also there are words which we use in speaking of the decisions. Among them are "vote" and "contribute." These words suggest that decisions and the actions based on them are by their nature of the community type. When citizens vote in elections, they perform an act that has no effect or meaning in itself, for its meaning derives from what occurs as a result of its being combined with a large number of others. When a person prepares to vote, he sees himself as being one of many who will also be making voting decisions. Though his single ballot is extremely unlikely to affect the outcome of the election, he feels that he *and others* can determine the outcome by voting in a certain way. He sees himself as representing a type. In deciding to vote as he does, he sees himself as choosing not only for himself but also for others like him. Perhaps it occurs to him that he could save time and energy by not exercising his right to vote, but he also reflects on what would happen if not only he but also others like him decided to refrain from voting. Actually, of course, if he does stay home, others will most likely vote, and the outcome of the election would not be affected by his lack of participation. He will for this reason bestir himself to leave his home and go to vote only as a result of thinking of himself as acting in tandem with others, as swimming in a social current. Only so will he make the sacrifice of time and effort necessary for participating in the voting process.

It is the same with contributing money, except that the moral element is stronger because there is more pain to overcome, since contributions involve surrendering money in one or another quantity and not just taking a few minutes to go to a polling place. Perhaps a person contributes money to a political party or an organization which serves a specific cause. He knows that his contribution is minuscule relative to the needs of the organization or the demands of the cause which it serves. But he believes that if he puts in his pittance and others donate theirs, the combined effect of the meager offerings will be enough to make a difference. The individual's decision costs him in this case because he could have made good selfish use of the money if he had not contributed it. He clearly hopes that, in donating something from his limited funds, he will be joined by many others and that the cause that he and they support will therefore prosper. An extreme example of community decision-making occurs when a soldier decides to go to battle. He knows that he runs a risk that he may get killed. He also knows that in accepting this risk and in serving in the armed forces, he provides a very small portion of the country's whole effort, certainly relative to the task of winning a war. If he is killed, he makes a sacrifice that is very large indeed for himself and his family, but one that is very small relative to what is called the "war effort." Both his actions in the battle and his death make no more than a minuscule contribution to the victory to which his country aspires.

Considering these two factors--the largeness of his personal sacrifice and the smallness of his contribution, it is problematic whether he can throw himself enthusiastically into the battle. To do so, he has to imagine himself as being two people simultaneously: a lone soldier, a person whose whole world consists of himself, those around him, the task assigned to him and them and the danger to which they are exposed; and an officer looking at the soldiers--at "the troops"--from a position outside and above them. As the officer, he sees the importance of the action in which he and all the other soldiers together engage. As the lone soldier, he sees himself as moved by the importance of performing his tiny part of the larger task and, possibly, of accepting his sacrifice. Only by this dual view of himself is he able to pursue energetically and courageously a course of action that really makes no sense from his standpoint as an individual. Community decisions are by their nature moral decisions. A person who focuses on the community makes decisions because he feels a sense of obligation; he feels he *should* do certain things. And these things are not what serve his own private interest. They cannot do so. Without the "should," a person would be simply "reasonable," and would busy himself with his own pleasures and comforts. Nothing would compel him to exert the effort or make the sacrifices required for doing what is good for the community. Being sensible, he would shirk his responsibilities to the community and would use his energies entirely for his own benefit. In the meantime, the others around him would be doing the same. Each of them could remain inactive or preoccupied with his own "good" while hoping that a certain "they" would do what is in his--and the common--interest. Here, as noted in Chapter Three, is where morality comes to the rescue. People act for the good of the others around them or of the community as a whole because they are driven by sympathy or by conscience--by sentiments of obligation--and not by calculations of what will do the most for "number one."

In recent decades, many economists have tried to paint a picture of humans as beings who, by their nature, act rationally in their own self-interest. These economists assert that this is the way people do and also the way they should act. But try as they will, there is a gap which they cannot bridge without assistance from (non-economic) morality. The only way in which one can see acting as part of the community as being in an individual's interest is to incorporate a person's moral sense into that interest. That is, one must see morality as integral to a person's selfhood and therefore to what is "good" for him. Asserting this will not, however, save the day for the view that human beings act entirely in their own self-interest. That a person acts on the basis of his sense of obligation is a moral matter, and to see him as doing so is to part company with the view that human beings are rational calculators. It is to see people as naturally social and communal, as Chapter Three has already noted. In seeing people in such a light, we radically change the concept of interest. We change it so much that "interest" is probably no longer the word that we want.

Organs of Community Decision-Making

Community decision-making is almost always carried out through one or another type of organization or agency, or with its help. Such an organization may be said to function as an *organ of community decision-making*. It is a social entity that facilitates the process whereby members of the community make decisions as a community. Through it, people can coordinate their individual actions to achieve what no one of them could achieve by himself.

It is possible, in principle, that people within a community may make decisions spontaneously without the help of an agency. One could imagine, for example, that a certain retail store, perhaps a grocery, includes pornographic magazines among it wares. Many people take offense at this and decide on their own, without consulting others in the community, to refrain from patronizing the store. Perhaps so many people decide to stay away from the grocery that business suffers and the manager decides to remove the offending magazines from his shelves. The people then reward his change of conduct by resuming buying at his store. It clearly takes a large number of buyers to bring about such a result. The manager's objective is to realize a profit, and it is in his interest to remove the undesired magazines, at least assuming that he has no moral opinion of his own on the matter. The decision of one customer alone will not affect the store manager's decision, but many people refusing to buy at the store will compel the manager to act. In a sense, the people who take their business elsewhere are making community decisions and taking community actions; they have made what we may call a *spontaneous community decision.*

In contrast to this arousal of wrath and the action which it engenders, the great majority of community decisions have to be made through one of the organs of the community. Only with the help of an organized group can people bring about the necessary coordination. The group or agency serves as a center to which people come to discuss what to do, with the intent of assuring that the actions of each of them will combine with the actions of the others to produce a single and desired effect. Every person who does a certain thing performs his action with an expectation that others will do the same thing or will do things that fit with it.

Of the many organs of community decision-making, government is the most important. Indeed, the word "government" refers to a special organ of community decision-making. A government is communal, and by definition, is assumed to have special responsibilities relative to the community as a whole. Its top officials, whether kings, presidents, or *caudillos*, take it as their task to worry and fret about issues that pertain to the entire community and not just to a person or group within it. The Chinese officials who presided over the construction of the Great Wall, for example, were presumably worried about China as such. While they may in fact have been thinking about their own royal grandeur, the *assumption* was that they were concerned about the nation's welfare and that this explained why they undertook that massive construction project.

Government also has powers and privileges usually not possessed by others. This includes a pervasive aura of legitimacy and an ability to use coercive force under the glow of that legitimacy. In a word, it has *authority*. If a government appears to its subjects to exercise force without concern for the community as a whole, it will lose the legitimacy it had enjoyed and will appear as pure amoral power. When this happens, the government is called by a special name: it is said to be a tyranny.

Because the people who run government frequently exercise power to exalt themselves rather than to serve the community--they act as tyrants--Americans are suspicious of government. This suspicion is seemingly justified by information given on every page of all history books. Yet it is important to recognize that when government is not tyrannical, government serves as the primary organ of community decision-making. It makes it possible for people to decide matters as a community and not just as individuals. Government enables people to control the aggregate effects of individual decisions and actions. This is important to keep in mind when people deprecate government, as Americans often do.

While government is the major organ of community decision-making, organizations of all kinds also serve a similar purpose. Labor unions enable workers to confront managers as one body instead of simply as a very large number of individuals. This gives the workers far greater power, a matter which is of great importance since rarely do human beings voluntarily treat the less powerful fairly. As with government, a union can easily become more concerned with itself than with the purposes it was intended to serve. This, unfortunately, is true of every organization, but one should not let this flaw obscure his view of the value which organizations such as unions have when they do act in accordance with their proper reasons for existing.

Churches and voluntary organizations of all types are also organs of the community. Churches serve this purpose when they reach beyond their own liturgical and educational activities and undertake various social welfare projects. Both national and community-based voluntary organizations enable people to make community decisions that would otherwise be impossible. Many of these issues pertain to social welfare; others deal with cultural and scientific causes, and still others serve various professional and avocational purposes. Many exist to protest or to support social and political causes. That people find it necessary to create these organizations indicates how necessary organs of community decision-making are. A special example of such an organ is Saul Alinsky's Industrial Areas Foundation. Originating in Chicago, it undertook to organize poor residents of urban neighborhoods to act cooperatively in improving their areas and therefore their lives.[19]

The American Emphasis on
Individual Decisions

American society emphasizes individual decision-making and action so much that people view community decisions as unreal or, at best, as marginal to the serious business of living. The nation's people accept all sorts of community actions and facilities, but these are not considered to be of first importance. They are instead viewed as context or as the furniture required for what is really paramount: the lives that individuals live as they carry out their individual decisions. This often means specifically the lives that people live in or on their own personal property. And this property consists, of course, of items that are obtained through individual decisions and actions--that is, through buying and selling. In this sense, television sets and other consumer items are viewed as really real, while the services of government and non-profit organizations are denied that title, or are, at most, seen as having a secondary reality. This is a great part of what is meant by saying that America is a "consumer society." Possession of items which one purchases, including automobiles and microwave ovens are viewed as endowing life with vibrancy and substance, while the ability to read and write offered by teachers and the security of person and possession provided by the cop on the beat are just a haze in the background.

Certainly there exists an irreducible realm of community decision-making. This realm consists of those features of society and government that provide the framework for individual decisions. It is the framework for business and commerce. It involves creating and enforcing laws as well as maintaining the entire monetary system. The community acting together determines that it will provide these things; otherwise there can be no playing-field in which the more treasured individual decisions can be made and carried out. Commonly, however, such community decisions are so taken for granted that people see them as the terrain on which activities take place rather than as themselves being activities.

In the framework of government, education is a special case. Early in our nation's history, Americans decided that state and local governments would not only provide schooling for all children but would also compel parents to send the children to school. With "reading, writing, and arithmetic" being essential for commerce, universal education can also be seen as part of the framework which undergirds business, just as are law and law enforcement. A consequence of this massive community undertaking is that Americans have tended to see people as divided into two occupational "kinds": those who teach school, together with those who police the streets and provide other public services, and those who are engaged in private enterprises intended to make profits.

Also irreducible is infrastructure, those goods (such as roads and bridges) which by their nature necessarily belong to everyone. After all, everyone who travels does not need his own road. Once the community establishes these commodities and services, it can deal with "reducible" items--those items that the community could decide to have or not to have without changing its basic character.

Community Decisions and Determination of Value

Basic to the individualist view of people and society is that individual decision-making determines the value or worth of objects. People acting singly decide what they want and how much money they are willing to pay for it. As the desire for an object increases, so does the willingness to do without other goods in order to have it-- that is, to "pay" for the object. From the standpoint of the individual, the price is determined by how much he wants an item, how much he wants other objects for which he could spend his limited funds, and how readily available (or scarce) the object is. As a large number of individuals make such decisions, objects come to have determinate prices. That individuals make the decisions privately and entirely in their own interest is the presumed beauty of the process. Americans tend to consider the individual to be an independent entity or "atom" who lives alongside of but in mutual indifference to others. And he, together with the other atoms--persons, comprises "the people." Accordingly his--and their--purchasing and selling decisions sanctify as completely "democratic" the determination of value (prices) as an aggregate effect of individual decisions. This view of value is incorrect. While people certainly do have individual tastes and desires, the very idea of worth is social in nature. In making judgments about the value of things, people collaborate with others in making joint judgments that will be the property of a group as such. They wish, that is, to make community decisions about what is "worth"--how much.

This is especially obvious in regard to one kind of merchandise to which it would seem that the individualist determination of value does not apply--*vice.* This kind of product deserves attention because it reveals something about American values, particularly about how Americans determine the worth of goods and services. The word "vice" refers to a zone within the array of goods which does not come under the sovereignty of the consumer. It includes certain drugs, together with gambling, prostitution, and pornography. The community--that is, people--consider these to be outside the galaxy of goods whose value is to be determined by the market process. Because they are outside, their sale is condemned and often prohibited regardless of how they are valued in the market, that is by people--by people making individual purchasing decisions.

Why does a society otherwise so committed to people determining value as individuals make an exception with these items? Why, that is, does the community intrude in an area when in every other way the individual reigns supreme? We cannot say that it is because these items are illegal; actions and objects are not viewed as bad because they are illegal. Rather, they are illegal because the community defines them as bad. So, acting through government, the community declares them taboo and then prohibits anyone performing certain actions or providing certain objects on pain of being penalized. Notable here is that the sovereignty of the goods purchaser is abridged. It is subject to limits, just as is the authority of a constitutional monarch. Individuals determine value only in certain ways and to a certain degree. If the community can enter the decision-making at one point, it can enter at any point. Once again, humans are social, like it or not. Value is, in the final analysis, what "we" say it is. The community as community determines what has value. The community may allow individuals who make purchasing decisions to assign value to certain goods. This is, however, a *specified* and therefore limited allowance. It is one that is made in certain cases and not in others. And it is the community that decides where the allowance will be made and where it will not. Prohibition and its repeal illustrate this drawing of boundaries, as does the recent and more limited frowning upon tobacco expressed by the disallowing of TV advertising of cigarettes.

What happens is that the community labels a certain array of goods as "merchandise," and in so doing removes the goods from the realm of social evaluation and opens them to individual determination of value. It flattens the goods out, so to speak, and establishes them as having an undefined and therefore equal social value. In so doing, the community allows prices to vary as buyers express preferences in offering money for goods. This is, however, an allowance made only in certain cases. The fact that the allowance is made only in these cases makes it clear that, in final analysis, the community is who determines *value*. Indeed, we could view "merchandise" as the exception rather than the rule, with the rule being the determination of value by community consensus.

Just as some community decisions define what goods and services are vices, they define others as having *more* value than that which the combined effect of individual decisions would grant them. These consist of items to which the community gives special honor and approval. Among them is an array of objects or presentations generally described as "high culture," including classical music, painting and sculpture, drama and poetry. People view these as having value above and beyond what would be derived from selling such items to individuals--that is, from the market. Because of this, some people contribute funds to make the items available. These donations greatly exceed what the donors would pay for private access to objects. They see themselves as "doing something for the community" in supporting a symphony orchestra, a local theater, or an art museum. People also do this by voting to have governments use tax funds for similar purposes. In addition to this support of fine arts, scientific, humanitarian, and religious causes are also endowed by people who define themselves as acting for the community and not just for themselves. Church members who contribute "according to their means" commonly do so with the idea that certain services-- perhaps those of the pastor--will be available *to people*, regardless whether they personally want those services. Those who contribute (or seek to induce government to contribute) to humanitarian or scientific causes often have no way that they, as individuals, could benefit.

We should be clear about what is involved here. Certain items, perhaps displays of art or sculpture, do not "sell" in the usual sense that the people who could benefit from them will be willing to pay for their individual servings of them. But the community as a whole or well-endowed persons within it make a judgment that it is good that people have these servings and therefore are willing to make sacrifices so that people can have them even when those people will not pay for individual packages of them. The people would not, for example, pay a high enough entrance fee to a museum to support the museum, but wealthy individuals or governments support the establishment because they think it *good* that the people have that access even though they will not pay for it at all or will not pay enough. The museum has, that is, an aura of "goodness" that stands in direct contrast to the badness of drugs and prostitution. If the latter are called "vice," perhaps the former should be denoted "virtue." In both cases, there is a social determination of value that is unrelated to the processes of the market. And there are goods and services that are totally distinct from what we call "merchandise."

Areas of Community Decision-Making

Though each person can acquire much of what he wants individually, not everything that he desires can be obtained that way. An agreeable and healthy physical environment is very desirable; yet the single individual cannot possess it alone, for the environment surrounds human communities and affects all of the people in them simultaneously. Everybody has clean, sweet-smelling air, or no one does; if foul breezes impose themselves on one person, all are likewise afflicted. It is the "we" who have an environment, not you, me, or George separately.

Just as the environment itself belongs to everyone, so does the task of doing something about it. Decision and action to prevent or reverse degradation of the environment is the responsibility of the community as a whole. "We" are beset by pollution of land, water, and air, and "we" must do something about it.

Not everybody agrees that the community as a whole must act together. Because pollution is commonly a result of commercial operations, many economists argue that the processes of the market place can correct it. They assert that if a certain corporation spews forth noxious substances into the air, people have something that they can do about it--they can refuse to buy that company's products. And if that company has a competitor who avoids polluting, people can give that particular company their business instead. People can punish one corporation while rewarding the other. If many do that, corporations will find it in their interest to treat the environment kindly.

Since it is buying or refusing to buy a company's products that exerts pressure on the company to stop polluting, the argument is that citizens would be operating entirely in terms of the market. The government is not involved, for government officials would not threaten company officials with fines or imprisonment if they do the wrong thing. Nor are there religious (sacerdotal) sanctions, as would be the case if a bishop held out the menace of excommunication. The only reason the company would have for acting as it should is that its products will not "move" if it fails to do so. They have the same reason to stop polluting that they have to improve the quality of products or lower product prices. They must control pollution if they wish to sell what they produce.

This analysis is, however, incorrect. It fails to note a fundamental feature of the market--that it is an arena of individual decision-making. People buy and sell as individuals and not as participants in a group. Each person makes decisions designed to benefit himself and not to benefit the community. He does not do so because he lacks community spirit. He may either lack it or have a great deal of it. But the decisions he makes for himself are big ones; they have a large effect on him, while those intended to benefit the community are very small; they do not serve the community interest unless they are combined with similar decisions made by many others.

To see this, consider the following illustration of self-interested decision-making. If I want to buy a lawn mower, I consider two things: the quality of the product and its appropriateness for my needs, and its cost, which includes the price of the lawn mower together with projected expenses for service and repair. These are the only things I think about. I may possibly be concerned that the company which produces the lawn mower is polluting the atmosphere. If it has competitors who are not doing so, I may take notice. But if the company's product is really best for me in terms of quality and price, there is a good chance that I will restrict my decision to those considerations. After all, the superiority of the first company's lawn mower is more important to me than is the contribution I would make by refusing to buy it. If I *and others* refused to buy it, the combined effect might be a great matter. But I feel that my decision alone cannot make much of a difference, so why should I fret about the tiny support I give to the polluter by purchasing his product?

To state the matter another way, I might assign a value of *ten* to the greater worth to me of the one lawn mower over its nearest competitor. I then note that my refusal to buy that mower because of the bad pollution record of its manufacturer has a value of either one or zero. It is small, or it is nothing in the sense that it cannot affect what the company does. So my sacrifice in buying from another company is excessive. I gain at most one while losing ten. On the other hand, If I *and others* make the decision to favor non-polluting companies, our combined influence might bring about a real reduction in pollution. That reduction might have a weight of ten or more for all of us--for the community--but it also has that great weight for each of us, since we all breathe the same air. But this would be a communal, not an individual action. Where the market reigns supreme, there is no possibility of punishing or rewarding corporations on how well they treat the environment and the community.

Such selfish motivation is integral to the *market*, the set of processes which take place as people make decisions to buy and sell entirely on the basis of their own interests. If a person knows what people's circumstances are and can see what lines of action will yield them the greatest profit, he will be able to predict what they will do. And if he can control features of the circumstances and therefore what actions promise the most, he will be able to control what they do. If he could change interest rates, for example, he could make people invest their money in certain projects rather than others. The market retains its character only as long as people act on the basis of individual decisions, for hordes of these decisions comprise the market.

Certainly, there are occasions when people, sometimes in large numbers, do make purchasing decisions on the basis of what they approve of rather than what will serve their selfish interests. But when they do, the market no longer exists. Processes with a different character go forward in accordance with different dynamics. Community rather than individual decision-making occurs, and events take shape as a result of purposeful actions rather than impersonal processes of the market. No longer are people simply buying certain products rather than others; in this situation, they are voting by making purchasing decisions. People can boycott, that is, refuse to buy, a product. With the introduction of a new word, "boycott," into the discussion comes a new item in the menu of actions from which people choose some to perform.

However, to boycott effectively, people have to organize, either *ad hoc* or permanently. Through the organization, people agree that they--many of them--will not buy a certain product. They do so for a specific purpose which all understand. Perhaps it is to induce companies to stop polluting the environment, or to influence a corporation to behave in some other way that is good for the community as a whole. They make use of an organ of community decision-making. It would be virtually impossible to elicit the necessary cooperation without it. Organizations ask people to make a sacrifice in the interest of the community, to forgo individual benefit to obtain a benefit which would not be theirs privately, but in which everyone would share. The sacrifice might not help the individual, but it would help others or serve a cause of which they approve. Individuals are likely to make the sacrifice only if they feel they are a part of a large group of people doing the same thing. Hence, the organization is necessary.

Once introduced, the organization pulls the processes even further away from the dynamics of the market. First, people who make purchasing decisions in the interest of supporting companies that do not pollute veer from the path of private or individual interest. They no longer act on the basis of what serves their personal wishes and their desire for low prices; and for that reason, the aggregate effects of their decisions no longer move in the direction to which selfish motivations would direct them. It would be a purposive, rather than a market, process. Organizations can combine people's actions in the interest of specifically stated goals, such as reducing pollution. Like an army on the march, people setting forth goals and seeking to realize them shape events. It is the extreme opposite of an impersonal market process.

Community decision-making is necessary for dealing with problems such as pollution. It has to be the community, not just individuals, that decides and takes action. A boycott, refusing to buy from offending firms, may accomplish their goal. Though boycotting is an action that is part of the market, it is only so as part of an action-in-concert of many people.

Government and Community Decision-Making

Also definitely communal is the use of the government as an instrument for fighting pollution. It has an ability to deal far more directly with the sources of pollution than do the organizations that institute boycotts. Government has the power to establish laws and enforce them. Thus, it can force corporations to reduce their output of pollution and to manufacture products (cars, trucks, tractors) that pollute less. Because of government's directness and completeness, this kind of community action is potentially more effective than any other.

Though community action is more effective than individual action, it may still fail to induce companies to reduce pollution because it places them at a competitive disadvantage with their rivals. To do well, indeed to survive, companies have to offer products whose quality and price are as good as those of others. The devices which reduce pollution are, unfortunately, not part of the quality. Those affecting the output of factory smokestacks are totally invisible to the consumer, and some of those that are placed *on* the product are not much more so. For example, the exhaust fumes that come from cars may annoy someone standing behind the vehicle, but the owner-operator of the car is not affected; for this reason devices that reduce those fumes are, to say the least, unimportant. It is the general public, not the car's owner-driver, who benefits from them. And if a company were to install such devices voluntarily, it might get "points" with environmentalists, but not from potential customers.

Thus, a manufacturer who has community spirit and wants to take measures to protect the environment may not be able to do so and stay in business. The steps he will have to take will be expensive, and he will have to absorb that cost in one way or another. He may pass it on to the consumer, charging more for a product which must compete with similar items produced by rivals who lack his concern for community. He is unlikely to get sympathy from customers, since they are busy making decisions entirely for their own individual benefit. Or, he settles for realizing smaller profits, which might lead to a decline in the company's stock and ability to attract investors. It may also shrink funds available for internal investment, and so stand in the way of development of new products which might provide a competitive edge in the future. In general, the public-spirited manager must repress his communal and altruistic urges in order to stay "competitive."

Government, with its ability to regulate, enters the scene at this point. It tells both the community-minded manufacturers and those interested only in the "bottom line" that they not only may but *must* take steps to keep pollution down. This regulatory burden is not, of course, a hindrance for corporations with community spirit; it merely requires them to do what they wanted to do anyway. But for those companies that were willing to damage the environment in the interest of profits or empire, the regulation is burdensome. All firms have to obey the regulations; thus, the profits-first manufacturers lose their competitive advantage, while other more environmentally responsible managers shed their competitive *dis*advantage. Government regulation bestows the ability both to do right and to succeed upon those who want to do as they should; it does so by *requiring* all to do as they should. This is something to keep in mind when government is deprecated.

Decisions and the Military

There are in the United States certain productive activities that should be--or will have to be--radically changed. Either they are unnecessary and should be reduced or eliminated, or they do not in their present form serve the community. Among these are military activity and equipment, energy production, and certain kinds of insurance. Military expenditures include both the armed services themselves and the industries that provide them with their equipment. In general, military production has been very important to the American economy ever since World War II. Though billed as taking place for the sake of defense, the role of the manufacture of armaments in American economic life (the "battle with society") has been of far greater importance than has been its role as a bulwark against aggression from the outside. America's economy cannot work unless its productive powers are used. Failure to use them affects not only the people in the industries but the nation as a whole. If one sector is idle, the multiplier goes to work. Since some people cannot sell, they cannot buy, and the vicious cycle continues. The military is necessary to keep productive capacity alive. It is well equipped to do this; it can eat up any amount of productive power, an ability not to be taken lightly. In the years following World War II, Americans were well aware of the depression of the 1930s and were very much concerned to prevent anything like it from happening again. Maintaining a large military machine seemed to serve that purpose well. Americans have not, as a rule, been aware that they have kept their economy "going" by engaging in what is in fact a highly wasteful use of productive capacity.

A large military has its dark side. Military power, once developed, tends to get used. If no real enemy exists to give it something to do, one is invented. In one way or another, bad guys will appear on the horizon, and the military will take measures to counter them. Note that the collapse of the Soviet threat did not occasion any serious reduction in American military power, as it might have reasonably been expected to do. Enemies are replaceable; Americans can always find another. If Communists are not available, "drug lords" or "terrorists" will take their place. Evil always lurks in the background, and it affords a stimulus to make actual and tragic use of military power.

We may also note that military power serves one immediate purpose--to kill and destroy. This is a hard fact that no amount of bugle calls and well-pressed uniforms can gainsay. It is of course argued that the violence for which soldiers are trained and equipped has a humane objective a bit further down the road. "Our guys" are doing battle with tyranny and brutality and are supporting freedom and democracy. Shooting and bombing are just a means to an end, a "lesser evil" that serves a larger good. The enemy, in the meantime, has a similar view of *his* use of violence. Yet we should never fail to recognize that the only effects of military action that are definite and "for sure" are death and destruction. We cannot be certain of anything else. Greater evils are not always greater, and larger goods are not always served. Democracy, like a person held hostage, can be destroyed in the effort to rescue it. A nation using military power to counter an evil that is not truly worse than its own is without moral defense. The violence it inflicts on people and communities, no longer credibly cloaked in humanitarian purpose, is left naked. The horrors are exposed and clearly seen.

Also, unless military power is needed, and needed in a certain magnitude, it is, in productive terms, wasted. The nation devotes a segment of its total productive power to the military; thus, the country subtracts productive power from other areas. Of course, that power might not be used for other purposes; even if not dedicated to military equipment or activity, it might just go unused. But in either case, productive power is not used to generate goods and services that benefit people; it is wasted. The populace is no better off than it would be if the level of technological advancement were lower and if productivity were less.

What is important for present purposes is that *if* it appears good to reduce military production and to either devote that productive capacity to other things or to allow people more leisure, doing so could only occur as a result of a community decision. People making individual decisions would never bring it about, for too many people have vested interests in military production; too many are in a position in which continued military expenditure is what affords the greatest personal and immediate benefit. And it is all too easy to invent enemies when they are needed. There is no way that the market, crowned as King, can deal with an excessive military. No amount of buying and selling will cut the armed forces and related industries down to size. Only the community acting *as* a community would be able to do that.

The people, acting through their government, would have to set up alternative employment (public-type activity, as is the military itself) for people previously engaged in military production. To be sure, additional consumer items might be invented and put on store shelves; new ways of imprinting money on goods might be found, so that people "have to have" things that they do not know at the moment that they have to have. Advertising and marketing these objects could also eat up many hours spent in labor. Clearly, however, many Americans are already at the saturation point when it comes to purchasing goods. Where people could use more of something is in another realm, that of public goods. These are items to which people have access but do not own, such as roads, parks, schools, and libraries. These, as John Kenneth Galbraith pointed out in *The Affluent Society* are the kinds of goods that could add to people's enjoyment and fulfillment.[20] These, therefore, are where workers not needed for production of fundamental commodities should be employed. These can issue only from community decisions. Again, the market is impotent in the face of truly awesome problems and genuinely hopeful possibilities. The community has to act as a community.

Many companies do business in areas that would be better served by a public enterprise; insurance companies are a case in point, and health insurance is probably the most notable. If it were ever determined by Americans that the country should have a single payer health care system, one in which health insurance were separated from employment and coverage were universal, a problem would clearly exist, for hundreds of insurance companies provide health coverage. The kinds of coverage insurance agencies provide vary tremendously, as does the adequacy of their services. Like businesses, they engage in shiny chrome marketing where services appear good but are really shoddy. What matters is that these companies still exist, and the people who work for them have the same right to a living as anyone else. If the community shifted to a single-payer system, the community would have to determine how to do justice to the companies and their employees.

The same applies to corporations doing business in petroleum and gas. These very large and powerful organizations resist any measure that threatens their markets and profits, yet sooner or later something will have to be done, for the products they market will one day be exhausted. That day may be further off in the future than has sometimes been believed, but supplies are finite and cannot go on forever. More importantly, in the interest of the environment, shifts from petroleum, coal, and gas to other kinds of energy are necessary. Wind, solar power, water and other renewable, clean resources of energy could replace those on which people now depend. Petroleum companies could initiate the transition, but every indication suggests that they will hold onto the reliable sources of profits they now possess for as long as possible. As long as they are engaged in a market operation, they will not do otherwise. Therefore, it is certain that only community action will instigate the change, as well as help to ease the transition for all people involved. Actually, whenever it is in the community's interest--sometimes a very vital one--to make major shifts in productive activity, only the community can do so.

There is a need to qualify the statement that Americans are saturated with privately-owned consumer goods. There are many poor people in the country who, by definition, do not have as much of these goods as they want or as people in general would assume they need. In this sense, there is a potential market for more goods and so more employment for those who produce them. But here also community decision-making comes to the fore. Only by a community action can these poor be better rewarded. There is no prospect that their current employment by fast-food chains and other low-wage employers (in "McJobs") would give place to better jobs or better wages for the jobs they have.   People do not have to pay more for hamburgers, and fast-food establishments do not have to pay more for labor, so why would they?   Clearly, it is only by a community action of some sort that people in the low-wage sector could gain access to more goods.   But if they did, the full saturation of the goods market would be postponed until these deprived members of society catch up with their better endowed neighbors.

Community and Justice

A final topic in this discussion of community decision-making deals with the issue of justice.   There are many instances where individual decision-making and fairness go together.   People think it fair that a worker who works harder, better, and faster be hired first or promoted in preference to others; and commonly, the employer does hire or promote such a person.   Obviously, the employer finds it in his self-interest to do so.   Similarly, the manufacturer who offers merchandise which is of better quality or cheaper in price usually succeeds where others fail because customers, making individual decisions, give him their business.   It is not their intent to reward him; they merely want products that are of higher quality or lower prices. But they have, in effect, rewarded him by accident.   Thus, it seems fair that he succeed; fairness and individual decision-making appear to go together in certain cases.

This, however, is by no means always the case.   There are many structures and relations in society that the community--that is, the people--will not consider fair.   As noted in Chapter Four, some people get more than is their due, while others are deprived of what is properly theirs.   "We," as a community, often make judgments about this.   Injustice is a zero-sum game in which one person's loss is another's gain.   Those who benefit by unjust distributions, whether of goods or honor, do not see the injustice readily; profit has a way of blurring the vision.   Those who are treated unfairly see it far better since victim status does wonders for sight.   So, concern about justice is virtually always a struggle within society.   Those who favor action on behalf of justice are on one side of the battle line, while those who oppose it are on the other.

Still, the concern for justice is a community concern.   In declaring that something is unfair, a person does not render a private judgment comparable to his tastes in various kinds of ice cream or clothing. Rather, he speaks for the community as a whole. He is like the first person to clap his hands at the end of a musical performance: such a person expects others to do the same and so to produce "applause." A person who makes a moral judgment makes it with an anticipation that others will join him in the judgment. If some others fail to make the same judgment, it may not be because they do not share his definition of fairness, but because self-interest has clouded their vision of the moral character of things.

Perhaps the best example is racial discrimination and civil rights. The United States has historically defined itself as a land of freedom in which "all men are created equal." Yet at the dawn of its history, slavery and racial oppression were present like a worm in the middle of an otherwise healthy apple. The matter becomes clear when stated in terms that do not refer directly to race: early in the nation's history, one American in five was a kidnap victim who had been brought to the country against his will and made to live as a servant with no hope of ever being anything else. Democracy and its opposite existed side by side, both as fact and as idea. This contradiction has been ever-present in the country, and Americans have never been able to either deny or resolve it. The community certainly judges it unfair, but discrimination against African-Americans continues, in part because many white people benefit from it, and in part because those who do not benefit do not see it as their problem. Also, discrimination continues because it is built into the pattern of life. Many white people (Euro-Americans) do the discriminating, not because they believe in it but because they think others believe in it, while those others are thinking the same. The restaurant owner who in the past denied services to African-Americans might have thought he was doing right; or he could have believed he had to reject them to retain his other clientele. So, Americans have had to live with contradictions at the very core of their national self-consciousness.

If racial discrimination is a part of American history which still affects contemporary Americans, so also is the Civil Rights Movement. Rarely in human history has a people undergone such a social cataclysm because of a belief about justice. Rarely has a people been so torn by an inability to either embrace or deny its own views about what is fair. The Civil Rights Movement did happen, and it did make a tremendous difference, even though it certainly did not accomplish all that was hoped for. Unfair differences in jobs and incomes remain, and race-related hate crimes continue. But the America of today is vastly different from that of half a century ago; there is more opportunity for people of all races than there was.

The change took place as a carrying out of community decision. There was, indeed, little possibility that it would occur as a result of separate individuals making innumerable independent decisions. Racial discrimination was too much of a social fact, of the community's way of life. An employer of fifty years ago who wanted to hire a capable Negro to fill a demanding and high-ranking position would be prevented from doing so by two factors. He would feel the "heavy hand of custom," and he would realize that others would disapprove and might well treat him badly; notably they would not patronize his business. The many Southern white people who wanted to treat their Negro neighbors fairly could not do so singly or on their own. In the nature of the case, racial discrimination could be ended and justice achieved only by a community action. It had to be an action in which *all* people had to stop discriminating against people on the basis of race. The actions were boycotts carried out by voluntary organizations, and laws implemented by governments. In either case, they were community actions.

While this is by no means the only example of a community making a judgment about injustice within its own borders, it certainly illustrates community decision-making effecting change in a situation where the individual alone is helpless. The organs of community decision-making, by making it possible for people to act as a community, contribute to human freedom.

Community Decision-Making and Freedom

Americans are not accustomed to thinking this way. Often they consider the idea of freedom as equivalent with individual decision-making. They think they are free only when they make individual decisions, or when they freely, of their own volition, cooperate with groups. Americans see persons who buy and employ, or who sell goods or their own labor through a pure contract with others, as the truly free people. Indeed, sociologist Peter Berger in *The Capitalist Revolution* asserts that the private entrepreneur is the ultimate individualist; he is the epitome of the free American.[21]

The concept of freedom is complex and tricky, and it is beyond the scope of this book to analyze it in detail. It must suffice to say that a free person is one who is able to make determinations that pertain to his own fulfillment. Stated this way, the concept of freedom requires no assumptions at all about institutional, governmental, or economic systems. A person can be free or enslaved in a society with no government as well as in a system where government controls everything. He can be free or enslaved in a capitalist, socialist, or communist society. He can even be free or enslaved in a secular or religious society. Other aspects of how people govern themselves, make their living, enjoy their leisure, or worship their deity determine whether or not a person is free.

Critical here is that to be free, people have to be able to make community decisions. If community decision-making is ruled out, if organs for making decisions are weak or controlled by certain sectors of the community that are hostile to others, or if people fail to see the importance of joining together in deciding matters, they will not be free. The entity that will enslave them may in the end be themselves as individuals, controlled by the consequences of their separately-made but similar decisions. These effects are, to be sure, not intended, but they are nonetheless real and capable of influencing people's lives. We need a name for this. We will call it the *tyranny of aggregate effects*. It is a tyranny that can be just as fierce and can render people just as miserable as can dictatorial rule over a person or small group. It may mean, for example, that people cannot do anything about pollution, even if each individual wants to. Because each makes purchasing decisions based on his own immediate interest, he renders himself and his community helpless.

It seems that if people cared enough about an issue such as pollution, they would make purchasing decisions in concert with others designed to achieve the goal. However, humans are as a rule "rational" when they make purchasing decisions. They see that the benefit which derives from the purchase of the best product at the best price is greater than the benefit--to them--of making an infinitesimal contribution to the community when to do so they must make a second-best choice of product to buy. That is, people are selfish when it comes to market decisions, and immediate self-interest takes priority. American culture itself encourages individual decision-making rather than concerted community decision-making. People who buy microwave ovens on the basis of quality and price feel that they are doing what is best for their families; thus, they feel they are doing what is right. Only when the organ of community decision-making comes into play do people begin to realize that they act as part of a movement that can use purchasing decisions as votes to boycott companies whose activities they consider harmful.

It is fundamental to the nature of individual decisions that people cannot control their choices' aggregate effects--what results from the combination of each individual's similar decisions. While people do not control the effects, the effects may control people. For example, the lack of good bus services will determine much of what some people can do, and pollution affects the environment in which all live. To be free, therefore, is to be able to join with others in making community decisions. The organ of community decision-making, in this sense, gives freedom; it does not take away. While a strong government may compel or coerce people to do things they do not wish to do, it can also do the opposite. It can enable them to do as they wish or to act on the basis of their moral convictions. It does this by requiring all to act rightly so that no one can gain from doing wrong and therefore no one will suffer from doing right. Stated simply, we are more free when we can and do engage in community decision-making.

Chapter 6

The Individual-Group Problem

Though similar to community decision-making, the individual-group problem has attributes of its own. Attention focuses on practices or policies that serve the interests of an individual as compared to those that serve the community as a whole. The individual could be a person in the usual sense or could be an organization that acts like an individual in relation to others. It could be a corporation or other entity that owns property, buys, sells, and performs other actions. The community is really just a large number of people, though it has the character of being a "whole," an entity which embraces all who belong to it. The contention is that there frequently are differences in what serves or benefits an individual and what serves or benefits the larger number of people, the community.

For example, imagine a barber who lives and works in a community in which there are about a dozen other barbers. Because he has many competitors, his income depends in part on how his own ability to attract customers compares with theirs. This in turn depends on a number of factors, notably his price and how well he cuts hair. But one of the factors may be how accessible he is, or, more specifically, how many days he keeps his shop open. Since Monday is the customary barber's day off, it occurs to him that he might fare well in the competition if he worked on that day. He knows that some men may, for various reasons, want haircuts on Mondays. Consequently, he will get more business than he would have otherwise.

However, the barber is taking a chance, for the other barbers, aware of the threat to their businesses, may follow suit and open their shops on Mondays also. If they do, the first barber will have sacrificed his day off for no purpose. His number of customers will return to its previous level, and he will be confined to his shop on Mondays, where he will spend more of his time sitting and waiting for the customers to come. All he has gained for his pain is--pain. Had he stayed home on Monday as do his colleagues, he would have had the same amount of business *and* the day off. As a group, then, barbers benefit by taking Monday off, but if they definitely do take it off, any one of them would profit by working the extra day.

Consider the situation in abstract terms. An individual who is part of a group has two options, A and B. If others are certain to do a certain thing, it is to the individual's advantage to choose A. But if he and others choose B, both he and the others will fare better than he does when he chooses A. If, then, it turns out that it is not certain what others will do, or if there is a possibility that he may influence what the others do (even if just by making his own decision), the individual would do well to choose B. Thus the barber does best by working on Mondays only when he is certain what the others will do. If he knows that they will *not* open their shops on Monday, he does well, for he purloins some of their customers. If he knows that others *will* work on that day, he also serves his own interest by doing the same. In the one case, he seeks a special advantage. In the other case, he tries to avoid a special disadvantage. By contrast, *all* are better off if *all* decide to stay home on Mondays.

Individual-Group Problem and Depression

The world of social and economic affairs has individual-group problems of many kinds. Among the best examples are those found in the phenomena of economic depression and inflation. An economic depression, as Chapter One has explained, is a failure of communication. It is similar to what happens when a man and a woman want to have a love affair, but cannot do so because they are unable to convey their sentiments to each other. Both want to be romantically linked, but each is afraid to tell or even hint about his or her feelings to the other. They both fear the humiliation and emotional devastation of being rejected. With both wanting the relationship but neither daring to communicate his or her desire, the seed of a beautiful romance cannot blossom. It remains dormant, until one of them decides to brave the storm and raise the subject.

Exchanges of goods and services are far more mundane, but the principle is the same. Two people could potentially profit by exchanging things with each other. Perhaps the first has an excess of canoes, for he can ride in only one at a time, and if he has several, he is in no better condition than if he had only one or two. The second person has horses. Since horses do tire on occasion, he benefits by having more than one, but having half a dozen horses is excessive. The canoe rider can profit from having horses (since he sometimes wants to go places by land), and the horseman can benefit from having a canoe (since he needs to take trips along waterways). An exchange would therefore benefit both, but before they can exchange things, they must talk--communicate. If they cannot do so, neither will profit from the exchange. Whatever the cause of the communicative failure, its effect would be the same as that of laziness, ineptitude, or lack of resources, for all result in the failure to get hold of the things that one wants. It is the same as though one had been unable to deal effectively with nature.

A depression occurs when communication between several millions of people, instead of two individuals, breaks down. Exchange moves not by a direct giving and receiving of objects, but by going around in a circle, with each person giving to one while receiving from another. Communication becomes far more complex than when only two people are involved. Here is where money enters the picture. By using something--bits of anything--to represent the desirability of things, people can give and receive in complex patterns. They divide labor, each producing specific things and exchanging them for many things. The things they use to symbolize desirability are called "money," which we may view as a communications device.

Like other such devices, money can fail to serve its purpose when not enough of it exists, or not enough of it is being exchanged (circulated). The resulting depression occasions widespread misery. It gives rise to a condition that is not different from the state of affairs brought about by lack of technology, scarcity of resources, plundering by an enemy, assaults by drought, flood, locusts, or storm, or even simple laziness. Simply stated, it is the same as defeat in the battle with nature. However, it is different from the other afflictions because it is a community problem which community decisions, as discussed in Chapter Five, could solve. Money can be added to the mix, or government could decree that all prices and wages must go down simultaneously. Either of the two measures would increase the "muchness" of money.

All of this explains why depression is an individual-group problem.   An individual who is caught in a society undergoing a downward spiral has certain options.   Assuming that he has some money, he can (A) hang on to it, or he can (B) spend it. If he takes what the rest of the community will do as a "given," that is, as unaffected by what he does, the sensible thing for him to do is to hang on to his money.   It is characteristic of depression that money increases in value relative to goods, while goods decrease in what they are worth in terms of money.   To spend, if one does not absolutely have to, is to leave a seaworthy ship for a sinking one. As time goes by, money will be valued more, and goods will be valued less.   Therefore, the intelligent thing to do--from one's own, personal standpoint--is to hang on to money. What would be extremely smart to do is to hold onto it until the moment before trends change, assuming that others are not quite so smart, and then spend it when its value is greatest and is about to start spiraling downward.   That way, one would acquire a maximum store of goods which would benefit him if (and only if) he has use for them.

Acting in this way would exacerbate the depression.   The downturn spiral started because of a lack of money in circulation. The person who holds onto his cash is therefore making matters still worse. Yet it is the sensible thing for him to do, as regards his selfish economic interests. This is an individual-group dilemma. If the rest of the community is definitely spending or not spending money, any lone person does well--for himself--by hanging on to what he has. But if, as a result of a community decision, everybody spends money, more money would circulate; the depression would moderate, and the lone person together with all the other persons would be in better shape.

Individual-Group Problem and Inflation

Inflation is the opposite of depression (or deflation).   Money is worth less in terms of the goods it will buy, and goods are worth more in terms of the money they command.   Inflation takes place because sellers perceive that they will profit more if they demand more for their goods.   Many sellers then raise their prices, and elevated costs become characteristic of the economy as a whole and not just of specific goods or transactions.

Inflation occurs for three reasons. First, it takes place as a result of scarcity of goods and is a way in which a community spontaneously copes with a lack of the things that people want. When there are not enough of certain goods for everyone to have all he wants, prices go up, and those who have money and are willing to spend it get theirs while others do without. Or, the people who want certain objects more than others do will devote limited funds to obtaining them while doing without other merchandise which they value less. Those who crave orange juice will pay the price for it and so do without the vegetables that others, free of citrus addiction, will prefer. This is one of a number of ways of coping with insufficient supplies of goods. Another is the "first come first served" approach in which prices are held constant and goods are sold until they are gone. Everyone can then go home, some emptyhanded. Those with the greatest desire will line up at the shops earlier than others. Or, a community could deal with a scarcity of goods by initiating a system of rationing. People could be allowed to buy only limited numbers or amounts of the goods that are in limited supply. During the Second World War, this device was used and was widely accepted by people. Sugar, meat, coffee, and gasoline were available only in limited quantity because of the war, and everyone regarded it as fair that each person would get a portion. There was an attitude of crisis and community-mindedness in that era that made this kind of sharing possible. Of course, allowance had to be made for people who needed to have more, as when doctors were allowed more gasoline than were others.

Second, a surplus of money can also cause inflation. Perhaps a government simply prints more dollar bills and spends them, thus putting more cash into circulation without increasing the supply of goods which can be bought with it. Or, money which was inert as savings can be brought out of hiding, so to speak, and put to work pursuing goods. A change in mood in which people want more things can also bring about this effect. Or, it can happen because savings are put to work--that is, loaned--so that they circulate when before they had been merely waiting. This happens when the government spends in excess of its revenues and so must borrow or when anyone borrows more than he had before. Money may also be brought out of hiding (savings) and used to pay people to produce goods that are not part of the existing shopping list. They build roads, fight wars, educate, or the like. As a result, there is more money chasing the goods that are on that shopping list. It is also possible that money is brought in from outside. Goods are exported, and those who buy them pay money only; they do not send goods, with the result that there is more money in the country relative to the supplies of what people buy with it. Whatever the reason, more money is in circulation; thus, sellers are able to demand more for what they sell.

The third cause of inflation is an increase in the costs which sellers must meet before they can offer goods for sale. Sellers strive to set prices at a point that will maximize profits, the point at which the profit-per-sale multiplied by the number of sales is a figure greater than it would be if prices were lower or if they were higher. Quite naturally, if costs to the seller who manufactures and/or retails an item go up, that figure (the price) will also rise. Sometimes, increases in seller costs occur as a result of a specific economic shock, such as a sudden rise in the price of oil in world markets. That increase then reverberates throughout the economy in the form of general inflation.

In contrast to depression, inflation does not necessarily hurt anyone. Scarcity of goods can of course do so; but if it does, scarcity is the problem, not inflation. A citrus crop ruined by frost is usually considered bad because the prices of oranges will go up. This is a good example of usual thinking. In contrast, the basic mode of thinking sees the problem as a scarcity of oranges. The rise in prices is not the problem but is, instead, a way of resolving it. The people who want oranges more than they want other things and/or who are wealthy will have their oranges. Others will have either fewer or none. This is hardly an ideal resolution, but then this is hardly an ideal world. Apart from scarcity, inflation causes suffering, not because of its intrinsic nature, but because it takes place in an unbalanced way. Some people have their wealth in the form of money, while others possess less liquid holdings, such as buildings and land. When inflation takes place, the people who have emphasized money--a claim on goods and services--as a way of preserving their material well-being are the ones who lose. Their money will buy them less than it did before. On the other hand, those who changed their cash into property, especially durable property, will win; they are likely to have more than they did before, and are likely to come out ahead. Money can simply be held, or it can come in regular payments (pensions) in which the agency that pays has no obligation to deliver *claim on goods*, which is what money is, but only specific and unchanging dollar amounts. What happens, then, is that the economic seesaw moves up and down. People with goods have more power to demand the things they want and need, while those with money have less of an ability to do so.

In addition, some prices go up more than others. People often say that inflation hurts them because their salaries will not buy as much as previously. Yet salaries are prices also; they are what it costs an employer to buy labor. That a salary buys less indicates that certain prices went up more than did others. The result is that those people whose offerings within the market rise more will do well economically, while those whose offerings (whether of labor or goods) rise less or not at all will suffer. Inflation is therefore a reshuffling in which certain sectors of the populace can demand a larger share of the pool of goods and services while others are forced to claim only a smaller portion. In inflation, as in depression, an individual-group dilemma exists. Since money goes down in value, it is in an individual's interest to change his money into goods as soon as possible. He will get more for his money today than he will tomorrow, and some goods can serve as stand-ins for money; they are salable, and because they rise in the amount of money they command, they serve as a way of preserving demand on goods and services. But if an individual does rush to spend his money as soon as he receives it, his doing so will worsen the inflation. By offering money for goods, he encourages sellers to raise their prices even more than they would otherwise. His contribution to inflation may be small, but in combination with many other people doing the same thing, he makes the rise in prices grow especially large. Were members of a community to act as a body, they would realize the smart thing to do when the clouds of inflation gather is to stop spending. If many people did this, money would go into hiding (savings). It would no longer be present in the quantities which exceed the goods it is supposed to buy. Once again, the individual and the group are at odds. The person who vigilantly pursues his own interests will spend his money, while one who is solicitous for the community will refrain from spending. However, if one individual, worrying about people in general and not just about himself decides to hang on to his money, he succeeds only in hurting himself. In a severe inflation, he could lose everything, while his contribution to slowing the inflationary spiral is minuscule. Thus, in the absence of government or community action, the smart thing for an individual to do is to change his money into goods (spend it) as quickly as he can.

Depression and Inflation are Spirals

These considerations explain why both depression and inflation are spirals. When a depression is under way, it is in a person's interest to spend less, making the depression worse. When inflation threatens, the intelligent thing for a person to do is to spend his money, an act which intensifies inflation. Both intensify and deepen the disaster which has befallen the community.

It is important to note that these two disasters have nothing to do with how well human beings are faring in their battles with nature. Available resources, technology, and (willing) human-power are sufficient to provide food, clothing, shelter, order, and TERM for everyone. But the same is not true of our ability to manage relations and associations among people. Problems in balancing concerns of individual and group, especially, are obstacles standing in the way of efforts to make life good in material terms for lots and lots of people.

Corporate Cost-Cutting

More dramatic forms of the individual-group problem occur in cases in which "individual" refers to a corporation and "group" means the rest of the community. A corporation is in legal and economic terms a "person" because it owns, buys, sells, and does all that individuals do in economic relations. It is a collective person. There is one way, however, in which it is different from an entity that is unified or "single" and which makes decisions on its own. The difference is that it is managed by human beings. These individuals are mindful of their own career interests, and often make decisions designed more to serve these concerns than those of the corporation. The analyst of corporate behavior should have this in the back of his mind, but not too far back, as he does his work.

Corporations may have to compete with each other, and when they do, they fare well by cutting costs. Sometimes monopoly (often accomplished without actual collusion) allows them a certain tranquillity about how their offerings compare with one another. But monopoly is often far from complete. Though they may not compete in certain ways, perhaps in price, they frequently must seek to outdo their rivals in other ways. They may elaborate special or marginal features of their products (cruise control on a car), put on superior advertising campaigns, or the like. Whatever it is that they choose to do, it is likely to cost money, and cutting costs will help smooth the way. If what they spend can be reduced at one point, it can be increased at another, more strategic point. They can use the freed funds to add those special features of products, or offer those special "deals" which lure customers from their rivals or prevent them from being lured by the rivals.

Competition is not carried on only between companies that produce the same products. Often, businesses must try to outdo corporations that provide alternate ways of meeting certain needs or desires, as when grocery stores compete with restaurants or automobile travel does battle with travel by air, railroad, or bus. And there is also the option of nonconsumption open to the buyer. If the coupling of product and price does not suit him, he may decide to do without. Many demands are made of sellers, and cutting costs is virtually certain to be of help in meeting those demands.

Among the devices for cutting costs, trimming the payrolls has a prominent place. The number of workers who must be paid may be reduced; the salaries given them may be lowered by one artifice or another; or benefit "packages" may be eliminated or made more modest. Americans are by now accustomed to the hiring of part-time or "temporary" workers as a device by which these reductions are accomplished--or at least explained. Or, expenditures on the work place can come under the knife. Less can be devoted to making the office or shop agreeable, healthy, or safe. In general, what is spent to get necessary work done may be reduced. Corporate leaders will always hope that this can be accomplished without failing to get the work done or sacrificing quality or certainty of the company's performance. Sometimes this hope will be realized; sometimes it will not. But the hope always is to get those costs down.

Of concern here is that in corporate cost cutting, the laborer who earns low wages, who has no benefits, or who is dismissed and then exhausts (as is said) his unemployment compensation will not be able to buy the company's product. He cannot buy any other company's product either, but that is not the concern at the moment. In the possibility that he cannot purchase the corporation's output lies the germ of a corporate crisis: by cutting its costs, the company could also be cutting its throat, in the sense that it weakens or reduces demand for its output even as it seeks to court that demand with its better, cheaper products.

Because the work force of a company is only a tiny proportion of its clientele, the corporation does not suffer an immediate, bitter fate. The wages it does not pay because it spends less on each worker or employs fewer of them include, in the aggregate, a large section of the corporation's costs. But the workers' purchases are a small, even negligible, part of the consumer demand that is "out there" in the great, wide world around them. So dwarfed is their own work force by the larger populace of nation and world that the managers do not see it as a factor at all. From their standpoint, they have cut costs without significantly sacrificing demand. An important feature of the corporate manager's world view is the vision of a national and international buying public which extends indefinitely in all directions without limits. It is like the Western frontier at the dawn of our nation's history and like the furthest seas.

This mammoth clientele may, however, get cut down to size when many other corporations join in the cost cutting. For instance, customers' demands for seat belts in automobiles may be cut only a little bit when the company that makes them reduces its payroll. But that little bit will be combined with similar little bits resulting from reductions of what is paid to work forces by manufacturers of television sets, VCR's, living room furniture, automatic transmissions in cars, and innumerable other items. Just as a wealthy man who loses pennies will, if he loses enough of them, become a poor man, so the company whose clientele is reduced by enough small amounts will cease to have a clientele at all, or will at least discover that its product is in less demand. Certainly there are people who still want it, but they cannot pay for it--which is the same thing to the company since, it means that the company cannot sell what it produces.

The individual-group problem again comes into view. Assuming that the rest of the corporate world is going to behave in a given way, a way that will not be affected by anything managers of a certain corporation do, the corporation will profit by taking a certain line of action. It will do well for itself by using any artifice available to reduce its labor costs, regardless of what the fixed policies of other companies may be. If other companies do not cut costs, the first company may gain a competitive advantage. If they do, the first company will avoid a *dis*advantage.

If, however, the managers' colleagues in other corporations are amenable to influence, and thus likely to act according to their managers' commands, matters will be different. Here, they profit by paying their workers well rather than poorly and by hiring more of them rather than trying to squeeze more work out of fewer. In doing so, they will maintain a level of demand in the general public for their product. True, the increment in their payroll which they award to their workers will do little to enhance demand for their product. In this sense, they are sacrificing more than they gain. But because other corporations are enriching their workers at the same time, they get many small pieces of demand which, if sufficient in number, add up to a large demand. If large enough, this demand may generate profits exceeding those the company would have made by minimizing its payroll. The policy of paying workers well, then, serves the corporation's interests when it is done simultaneously with other corporations.

This will be more evident with some companies than others. The firm that produces luxury items will be the least affected. The people who buy expensive automobiles, high-fashioned clothing, fine jewelry, and home security systems have money and will buy these items in any event. But demand is more problematic in the cases of those companies that produce more mundane goods which sell to the rank-and-file members of the buying public. Such items as the ordinary car, the less flashy clothing, and the Timex watch will sell or fail to sell depending on how much money the vast numbers of ordinary people have in their hands. The corporations (or branches of corporations) producing these goods will therefore profit the most from what might be called a communal maintenance of demand. They will profit most if they and others pay workers well and so maintain a high level of demand.

There is a question that cannot be avoided: is not the number of a company's workers determined by the work to be done? If so must we not suppose that a company cannot dismiss workers without sacrificing the quantity or quality of its product? Or, by contrast, do we think that "Parkinson's Law" has been in operation, and companies have had far more workers than they need? If the former is true, we would think that a company that cuts the size of its work force will necessarily reduce the scope of its operation and therefore the size of its profits (assuming constant demand). If the latter is the case, eliminating people from the payroll would only reduce "featherbedding"; it would cut labor costs without sacrificing the firm's output. It is not possible here to answer which of these two--or which combination of them--is true. What we can note is that *in fact* American corporations seem to find the trimming of work forces and the reduction of workers' status to be effective ways of cutting costs and of maintaining or improving profits. They find this to be more the case now in the 1990s than they did before.

Corporate Surplus Production

Corporations, even those with extensive horizontal integration, are specialized, producing just one or a few items. They do so believing that these items can be thrown into space and, boomerang-like, will return as many things that people want. They participate in the division of labor, just as do lone persons. Like those persons, moreover, they question whether there are others out there in the world who have the things they want and will exchange these things for those that the corporation has in excess. The usual way of referring to this is to say that there is or is not a *market* for the goods one has to offer. Without that market, work and production are of no value; one could possess willingness, knowledge, resources, and the apparatus that the job requires and still achieve nothing. If the corporation produces fishing boats, its managers, employees, and stockholders can use only a few of them. The bulk of the output will be useless--will be non-goods--unless someone wants them and will give them things of value in exchange for them.

The required market will not exist unless the people in the surrounding society have good things to give in exchange for the fishing boats. They rarely have the right things, so in practical terms, what they must have is a claim on goods and services, rather like the gift certificate one receives and decides to use in combination with others to purchase a more expensive item. So the fishing boat company's customers give them claim--money.

However, whether the residents of the nation in which the company is located have money and the consequent ability to demand as well as a desire to buy fishing boats, there is still a possibility that the supply of boats may be excessive. After buying a certain number, people have all the boats they want and will buy no more, even if they have the money. The local market may be "saturated." Fishermen need no more than one boat apiece, and some may not want a boat at all. If the production of boats goes past the citizens' level of demand, the company must look for markets outside the country to find more customers. It will be able to do this if there are people in other countries who want its fishing boats and who have claims on goods that can be transferred across national boundary lines. That is, they must have a sufficient quantity of money so that when exchanged at official (or black market) rates it translates into enough to buy the boats. Simply stated, the company must find markets abroad.

Important to notice here is that it is the company that has this need for foreign markets. It is not the American people that are so burdened. It is a unit within our society that has the need, not the society itself. When matters are viewed from the standpoint of the entire society, they appear to be very different from what they look like when seen from the perspective of the unit, that is, the company. This is an individual-group problem. Neither Americans nor the people of any other nation have need for markets elsewhere in the world. There is no such thing as a "need" to export. If there is a need, it is to import, not to export. Importing gives people things they need, while exporting only gets rid of objects. Because of climate, natural resources, apparatus, and technology, then, peoples are sometimes incapable of manufacturing what they need and so must either import it from elsewhere or do without it.

Importing is necessary, or at least quite desirable. But because people do not give others objects out of the goodness of their hearts, a country must export so that it can import. A transfer, or exchange, between nations occurs. Yet as stated in Chapter One, Americans *see themselves* as having a need to export. They think that they have to have markets in other nations, and gaining "access to markets" in places where people have money is a prime objective. But from the standpoint of the community, the only true need is to import. The truth of the matter thus contradicts people's image of reality in which the basic need is to export.

To better understand the seeming contradiction, observe that it is only the corporation that has the need to export, not the people of the United States. The larger community needs to export only in the measure to which it needs to import. For instance, the people need bananas, coffee, and other items. In the interest of inducing farmers and processors in Brazil and Costa Rica to give them these things, people in the United States need to find something that they can produce which those Latin Americans want and need. By giving them these things, Americans persuade the other countries to ship the required bananas and coffee to the United States. Thus, exporting is a means to an end, the end being acquisition of bananas and coffee, items that induce the world to continue turning on its axis and that, in general, make life more pleasant.

While there is a need to import, and therefore to export, it is limited. The United States is really quite self-sufficient. Americans have vast amounts of territory which contain many natural resources. They are blessed with a climate that enables them to produce food and fiber in excess of what they need. Apart from a few esoteric items of technology, they have all the knowledge they need, and they have the apparatus and infrastructure that make it possible to produce. The nation is diverse; it has regions that are different from each other, and it has people in almost every conceivable specialty. Americans are, in general, able to produce enough for their needs and to produce things in sufficient variety to give all the people what they want. The enduring problem in the nation is overproduction. Americans cultivate and manufacture too much of almost everything. Its farms and factories can supply its needs, assuming that possession of money and therefore of demand is sufficient, and the country's productivity can also take care of peoples elsewhere in the world.

With this in mind, consider the functions of exporting for the individual, or the corporation as legal individual, and for the community as a whole. As far as the community is concerned, there is very little function because there is very little need to import. There are only a few things that Americans cannot produce but which they need or want; there is, therefore, a need to export only a little in exchange for the little that needs to be imported. Of course, the country could always export for humanitarian reasons. Moved by the needs of other peoples, Americans could ship out food, medicines, and other items with no intention of receiving something in exchange. If we can assume that doing so does not distort local markets in those countries, there is nothing wrong with that; indeed, there is something right about it. But that is a separate matter, for it would mean exporting because of someone else's need instead of America's own. Again, being so close to self-sufficiency, America could export just a little and import just a little.

This is not so with the corporation. It does have a need to export, since it cannot sell all of what it produces in the United States. It--

the managers, the employees, and the stockholders of the company--
cannot change the items it produces but does not need into items it
needs or wants but does not produce. The corporation therefore seeks
markets outside of the United States. It looks for people in other
countries who will exchange money for its fishing boats or other
items. If it finds them, it will then export the boats to them and will
import money. In importing cash, the corporation presumably does
so as a participant in the exchange circle. It receives money first and
then uses it to claim goods or services. These goods can come from
anywhere, either from abroad or from the United States.

While the corporation can thus benefit from its exporting, the
American community does not. It is not able to benefit because it
already has most of the goods and services it needs. Apart from a
few items, such as coffee, bananas, and petroleum, America produces
enough and more than enough for its own use, and for this reason
cannot have more. To add more would be simply to increase the
excess; it would merely augment the store of goods people cannot
use, making these things non-goods. Just as one cannot add water to
a glass that is already full, he cannot increase supplies in a country
that has more than it can use. In this sense, there is no possibility
that the exporting of those fishing boats, television sets, or other items
would benefit America as a whole. It may benefit individuals within
the country, but not the country itself.

Effects of Exporting

To understand this, examine the matter from a number of angles.
For one, the members of the corporation may receive money from the
sale of goods abroad and spend it for goods from abroad. They use
it to buy clothes from Hong Kong or Thailand, cars from Japan or
Korea, and computer parts from many Asian sources. They then
bring these items into the United States where the products join
similar supplies that are already more than enough. In doing so, they
crowd out other units of the same kind of goods. Clothing and
automobiles perhaps are not sold or used, in which case they retire to
the status of non-goods. They may just as well have not been made.
Perhaps the foreign competition hits the American market before the
birth of American versions of products; thus, American workers never
even make the product. The worker is laid off, so to speak, before
manufacturing of the superfluous items begins. He is idle, and the

day's work he would have done had he been employed is lost forever. He may work at some point in the future, but he does not get the chance to work *that* day, nor does the community receive what he would have produced. Even more, capital goods such as machines and buildings remain idle, losing their productivity for the time being. Investors also lose out, since their investment is unemployed just as is the labor of the worker. Clearly, with goods being non-goods and with work and the use of capital equipment being lost, the importing of clothing and other goods from abroad has not added to the pool. The community has not benefitted. It has, in fact, suffered while a few people, those in the corporation, have been enriched.

Alternatively, the members of the corporation may spend the money derived from sales in this country. They buy clothing and cars made in the United States, creating a flow of money that other Americans lap up. These others, however, may then buy goods made abroad, and the result may be the same as it was in the first case. The only difference is that the status of being importer, along with the money, transfers from the members of the American corporation to certain others.

If this does not happen, if the money continues to flow within the fifty states, matters develop differently. The most significant consequence of selling goods abroad is that sellers end up with a larger share of the total amount of money held in circulation in the country. They have a larger claim on, or a claim on a larger portion of, the pool of goods available. They are therefore able to determine the uses of more of the goods within the pool than would otherwise be the case. They can appropriate more for their own pleasure, comfort, or notoriety than they could if they had not exported. Or they can decree and approve what purposes more of the objects and services will serve, as when they donate funds to political, religious, artistic, or humanitarian causes. Whether for selfish or unselfish purposes, whether for good or bad causes, they will direct the uses of a larger piece of the total of goods and services in the pool. This is perhaps the strangest outcome of exporting: because corporations send goods abroad, they can claim more of what is in America.

However, the picture may not be quite so grim. The corporation may be dumping money into the cash flowing in the nation. Perhaps it has employed workers who would otherwise be idle. It pays them for their labor. They then spend that money, and the multiplier goes to work. The economy is stimulated, if ever so slightly. As far as the nation is concerned, this labor is make-work like any other. The supply of goods within its borders is not greater than it was before; there is merely more money. Or perhaps the members of the corporation, having more money, spend more for goods made in the U.S.A. This has the same effect. The sellers have more money which they spend, and the multiplier is again busy. No goods have been added to the pool of things available. Still, the addition of money is a serious matter, for depressions do or do not happen depending on the quantity and velocity of money in circulation.

There is a possibility that the total store of goods will be increased as a result of exporting. Because the members of the corporation have more money, received from their foreign customers, they buy more goods in the United States. They draw more goods, so to speak, from the pool, thus leaving empty places where the goods originated. Additional goods may be manufactured, then, to fill these places, like water rushing in to a place from which some was drawn. The fact that labor and apparatus have gone unused is what makes this possible. Workers and machines come out of hiding to begin producing. So there are as many goods at one point as there were before and more at another point. The place where there are more is populated by luxury goods, those the corporate wealthy wanted, with the newly utilized labor and capital replacing the ordinary goods for which the luxuries substituted. What is more important about this scenario is that ordinary people are not more deprived. The fact that the wealthy have more luxuries is one that can be regarded with indifference. Thus, this is one of the more fortunate among the possible outcomes of exporting.

In the event that inflation grips a country, exporting for money has less happy consequences. Here too, money is added to the quantity of cash that is flowing, but that quantity is already excessive. Too much money is chasing too few goods. While money has been added, goods have not, and inflation is made worse. Sellers will be able to raise their prices even more. And here also, more goods will flow toward the people who did the exporting.

While the consequences of exporting vary with the conditions in the country, they always include giving the exporting company a greater claim on goods and services. After all, that is what motivated the company to find foreign markets and export goods. However, this enriching of the members of the corporation often, though not always (as we have seen), occurs at the expense of other people within the society. The size of the pool of goods is not changed by the exporting, and when certain people are able to claim more of it, others are able to claim less. The member of the corporation increases his share and, as a result, someone else will have a lesser share. This is what happens when the corporation uses its foreign earnings to buy foreign models of goods that are also produced in sufficient quantity in the United States. This happens more often during inflationary periods than during depressions because the additional money in circulation alleviates the depression and can result, for that reason, in an increased pool of goods.

Clearly, this is the individual-group problem in its starkest form. When people act as individuals or become members of corporations that act that way, they promote the interests of a unit within society. In doing so, they often act against the interests of society as a whole. They, of course, are also part of society as a whole. And while they may prosper because of actions which benefit only the unit, they also suffer because of similar actions taken by others who are in other units, mainly other corporations. Being both a member of a society and of units within society is part of what makes it difficult to be a human being!

Purchase of Imported Goods

The individual-group problem also arises in the case of private persons buying foreign goods. For example, someone decides to buy a Toyota because he thinks it is a better value (in quality and price) than Chevrolets, Fords, and other cars produced in the United States. His thoughts are entirely selfish, but are not generally disapproved. On the contrary, the community around him encourages him to think that way. The numerous advertisements to which he is subject assume that people like him make decisions based on self-interest. When people talk about making choices, they assume that a person should consider only how an object serves him and how much it costs him. The idea that one should use his purchasing decisions to vote for conditions that he considers good for the community seems strange and distant. Instead, people assert that if American car dealers want people to buy American cars, then let the dealers make cars that people *want* to buy! Excluded from the self-interested individual's consideration is the impact of his decision on the community of which he is a part. His decision to buy a Toyota may cause an American car maker to lose his job, at least if made simultaneously with similar decisions by several other people. But that is not the concern. He is not cold-hearted, and he does worry about that laborer's welfare, but he does not believe that such a concern should influence his decisions about what to buy. In doing this, he is failing to recognize that the worker who makes cars is also a customer, and ultimately, his customer. Whatever it is that he sells, whether goods or services, he has to sell to others who have the money to buy because someone bought whatever they sell, and so on. Sooner or later, the effects of his purchase return to the car buyer. He is messing up his own economic environment when he buys the Japanese car. He is, however, messing it up just a tiny bit, while he gets the (presumed) large benefit of the superior Japanese car. Obviously, his is an individual-group problem. If others' actions are given, he does best to buy the Toyota. But if he and a large number of others in the United States buy American-made goods, he and those others will be in a better condition.

Solving the Individual-Group Problem

Resolutions to the individual-group problem are at hand, though they are not items on the current menu of plans for dealing with the economic problems. By definition, they require community decision-making. People can act in the interest of the group only when they are participating in the determination of what many people will do and not just in what they, as individuals, will do.

The major feature of a resolution is that the world should be divided into more or less self-sufficient economic communities. The exchange circle should exist and be activated within these communities; the people who comprise them should buy and sell with each other. As each person buys from another, he transfers claim on goods to that other. The other in turn buys, with that claim transferring to still others, and the process goes on. Ultimately, it comes back to the first person. So everyone produces, and everyone receives what he needs to enjoy life.

Further, with both the production of goods and claims on goods circulating within the community, some of the productive prowess will be used to produce capital goods, those that are not themselves enjoyable but which can be used to produce those that are--what we broadly define as "tools." As these capital goods accumulate, people are able to produce more with their labor. A tool is stored labor in the sense that a person who works with it manufactures more than he would without it.   Such accumulation is what observers call "economic development." Further, since the community acts well as a community, it will also do well building and maintaining infrastructure--those tools that the community (government) must produce and which everyone uses.   Every person may be an individual, but he is part of the group and thus benefits from the group being given its due.

There is of course a question concerning what the boundaries of an economic community should be.   For Americans, the unit consisting of the fifty states seems obvious; it is already free of boundary difficulties such as tariffs, contains a diversity of climates and terrain, and exhibits a certain cultural homogeneity. Yet someone could ask whether smaller, self-contained units should exist. Perhaps each state could be an autonomous community, or the nation could be divided into four or five regions. Going in the opposite direction, a larger unit could comprise the economic community. Instead of the United States alone, the community could include the United States and Mexico, as envisaged in the North American Free Trade Agreement (NAFTA).

Outside the United States, problems become even more severe. If we do not think that Wisconsin should be an economic community, what about Luxembourg? What about Nepal? Many nations seem to be too small and so would have to be linked to others. Other nations, whether small or large, are too specialized. Both England and Japan are so industrial that one would think they need an agricultural partner to be a community, whereas largely rural countries such as Bolivia and Thailand would need industrial partners.

Clearly, there is no ready answer to the question of just what expanses of territory and what groups of people should comprise economic communities.   Nor does this discussion provide one. It merely suggests, in general terms, how that boundary should be drawn: the community should be large enough to have an extensive division of labor that includes both industry and agriculture and which yields a wide variety of products from both, and it should be small enough to contain a genuine exchange circle. Such a circle exists when people both give (sell) and receive (buy) within a community. That is, one person gives a product to another who gives to another and so on until in due course the process returns to the first person.

There is, so to speak, a high density of exchanges taking place, and for this reason all of them together may viewed as comprising a single thing--a single *market*.

Stated negatively, an exchange circle is a reality when companies do *not* export as a financial machination, that is, as a project in which they accumulate money paid them by foreign customers without receiving goods in return. The occurrence of a "trade surplus" with another nation is in itself indication that an exchange circle does not exist. No one gives without exporting to receive in return. But individuals (corporations) may give when what they expect to gain by doing so is a larger share of what is in the domestic pool of goods rather than a return from their buyers or their buyers' customers. They expect, that is, money. In this sense, the community has given goods "for free"; only the individual--the company--has been "paid" for what was offered. And it is the rest of the society in which the company is located that does the paying. Where a true exchange circle is in existence, there could not, in principle, be such a thing as a trade "surplus" or "deficit."

In other words, the community should be large enough and diverse enough so that no more than a small proportion of exchanges need to be with individuals outside its boundaries. Exports and imports should be few--it ought to be possible for them to be few. Perhaps five or ten percent of all exchanges could be exports and imports. Those numbers make allowances for things that a community cannot make for itself (as with America's need for coffee and bananas) while assuring that most trade will take place within the community.

The Poorer Nations and Exchange Circles

Many countries, and even groups of countries, cannot be as self-sufficient as the United States. Often smaller, they do not have the expanse of territory or the variety of terrains and climates. Nor do they include both the rural-agricultural and urban-industrial sectors that are to be found in the United States. With these lacks, they are not as able to have complete exchange circles within their own borders. Nor do they find themselves in a position in which they already have what another nation might offer them.

Quite apart from size, resources, and variety, however, is the fact that many nations are not able to produce much of what they need and so are dependent on those who do. The world's poorer, nonindustrial nations do of course offer agricultural and mining goods. These they have and can exchange for the apparatus produced by the factories of the industrial nations.   But they are not in an equal relationship with those nations. We cannot say that the apparatus they want is "more" than the bananas and other produce they are able to provide. For who is to say that a certain quantity of one thing is "more" (of more value) than a quantity of another?   But there is little question that the poorer nations are more suppliant than their industrial neighbors; they are in no position to bargain as equals.

One needs only to wander through Nicaragua or Honduras to see why this is the case. The roar of cars, trucks, and buses is to be heard everywhere and constantly; lights shine at night from streets, houses, and businesses.   On a hill at the edge of Tegucigalpa, Honduras, one can see houses, mainly of the poor, scattered over the steep slope. If it is night, lights flicker throughout the scene. Near the top, and clearly visible at night, is a large lighted sign which says COCA-COLA.   It assures the doubtful that American civilization has arrived!   In addition, the streets of the city are full of evidences of advanced technology.   Computers are everywhere, as are FAX machines. If any conclusion can be drawn from these observations, it is that these nations have no intention of carrying on without the things the industrial world has to offer. And just this is what makes them dependent; they have to have what they cannot produce. They "negotiate" with industrial nations the way a diabetic negotiates with the person who has the only insulin that is available.   Whoever has the greater power sets the terms of the negotiations.

It could be otherwise.   In the 1840s, for example, the Mormons traveled West and settled in the state of Utah.   There they built communities and began to prosper without the apparatus most Americans now take for granted.   They clearly could not carry those devices in covered wagons, and even the railroad, when it arrived, had its limits. Much of the apparatus had not been invented yet anyway! So houses, farms, towns, and a host of institutions arose on the western prairie in what would appear to contemporary Americans to be a technological vacuum. [22]   They managed to prosper without a large supply of "inputs" from others.   What is significant is that nobody anywhere in the world considers it possible to repeat that performance.

Also obvious to anyone wandering in Central America, among other places, is that there is a great deal of wasted labor. Everywhere there are people trying hard to sell things, most of the time in vain. For example, a man with an armful of watches walks up and down past a line of people waiting to get on a bus. He hopes to make a sale and will probably be unsuccessful. The people work hard, but they get little for their efforts. The abundant apparatus from industrial nations, then, coexists with tremendous waste of human labor. Labor is what they have in quantity.

Accordingly, we note that there is an individual-group occurrence here. Honduras does not have that much need for many of the goods the industrial nations have to offer. It has abundant labor and so does not need labor-saving devices. But *individuals* within the country need, or at least want, these devices. It is individuals who want and acquire such items, not the Honduran community. And as long as they make individual decisions--or as long as they do *not* make community decisions, it will inevitably be so.

Truthfully, no one would recommend that such nations dispense altogether with modern apparatus and build "from the ground up" as the Mormons did. If in nothing else, we would want them to have modern medicine and the equipment required for its practice. But they could come a lot closer to that way of dealing with their problems than they do. After all, the apparatus they have does not profit most of them anyway. They are just as poor, or poorer, with it as they would be without it. Again, it is a set of individuals who profit, not the community--not, that is, the larger number of people.

Perhaps the most dramatic illustration of the relation of poor to wealthy nations occurs in the case of Vietnam. North Vietnam and its Viet Cong allies performed a mighty feat. They defeated the forces of the world's strongest military force and did so despite the latter's incredible fire power and domination of the air. And then, in the aftermath of that victory, they in effect came hat in hand looking for foreign investment; they went begging for apparatus of the sort only the industrial nations could give them. Here we see clearly that developing from ground zero, even to the degree that the Mormons did, does not appear to be an option.

In principle, however, the poorer nations could. Making community decisions, they could determine that they wish to produce more for their own consumption and rely more on what they create to take care of their needs. More of their agricultural output could be devoted to domestic consumption, with more emphasis placed on basic grains and less on commodities intended for export to the

United States and Europe. A significant reduction in what they need from the industrial powers would bring about a similar reduction in need to follow the lead of those powers. In his 1980 book *The Poverty of Nations*, William Murdoch suggested that healthy development within a poor nation should be mainly internal. That is, one sector of the society, perhaps the agricultural, will produce a surplus that will then serve as capital for another, possibly the industrial. Initially, labor-intensive industries should be developed. Then there will be a back-and-forth between the sectors until the total apparatus has built up to the point where people can produce more with their labor and their standard of living rises.[23]

While this process is taking place, the majority of the people may have to live at a level which Americans would see as very modest. Their homes may be very humble indeed; they may have latrines instead of bathrooms; their diets may be unvaried, and they may get around by public transportation rather than cars. But this, we may note, is by all indications going to be their lot in any case. Only the wealthy among them have prospects of a material existence that can compare with that enjoyed by the majority of people in the industrial nations. And, while modest, their access to goods may actually be better without an abundance of industrial blessings than with it. If non-industrial nations do not import as much machinery, they also do not have to export as much. They may for that reason be able to keep more of the fruits and other products that they produce. Because they import less, they export less.

What about the Corporation?

Acting through its government, a nation's people could make a community decision to take matters firmly into their own hands. Corporations, we may note, are not primal realities; they exist only because the community endorses their doing so. They own their property, but property is what society says it is. Just what belongs to whom is determined by what the government, acting as the agent of the people, decrees and decides. Those decrees are usually made in the interest of preserving existing arrangements. That is, people own what they *have* owned or what they have acquired by highly specific forms of transfer. And it is usually assumed to be good that people have stable points of reference (such as, "This building is mine") so that they can make production and consumption decisions. But in the final analysis, decrees about ownership are made in the interests of the community as a whole. This is why we have eminent domain, among other things. Making decisions on that basis, the government can do certain things. It can decide that corporations will keep their operations in the country. It does not have to allow them to wander around the world looking for cheaper labor. And it can require people to buy and sell within the nation. "Buy American" campaigns are fine but probably of minimal effect. However, government could pass laws which compel everyone to do just that. It can determine that all or any of a given proportion of exchange will take place within a country. This may sound restrictive, but we should remember that part of freedom is the ability to make community decisions. If Americans *as a community* felt that they would fare better in a more self-sufficient economic community, being *free* would mean being able to establish such a community.

Some may object that making the community self-contained would sacrifice the interests of individual consumers. If the Japanese automobile is better than its American competition, should I not be free to buy it? After all, American companies can get busy and produce cars as good as those coming from across the ocean. By restricting imports (and exports), are Americans not putting chains on the consumer and stalling those competitive market processes that generate good consumer items? This is a point that must be, in part, conceded. But there are many tradeoffs in this world, and the benefits of the self-contained economic community may well offset the sacrifice of a bit of automotive quality. Having to drive a Ford instead of a Toyota may be a fair price to pay for possessing an exchange circle that is good for all people.

Making the United States more of a self-contained economic community might also seem unfair to poorer nations. If Mexicans and others work in *maquiladoras* for long hours under terrible conditions for wages that are a tiny fraction of even low wages in the United States, there must be a reason why they do so. It must be the case that such labor, horrible as it is, is better than available alternatives. Would they, then, not be hurt if the wealthy nation insisted on being more self-sufficient?

The answer is no. What is hurting them is the entire export strategy. This is the strategy in which nations abandon production for themselves and strive to produce for others, with the idea of importing more of what they need. This is a project which, as we have seen, benefits American exporters and domestic elites, but leaves the ordinary people of nonindustrial nations worse off than they would be otherwise. The reason why self-sufficiency in the United States would not hurt them, then, is that it would encourage them--or give them permission--to become self-sufficient themselves.

Human beings have the ability to provide goods for themselves and each other. The battle with nature is not the problem. What stands in the way of the good life for all is the individual, the single unit. It is the person or the corporation who chooses, among the available options, lines of actions that serve only his or its own interest and not that of the group. The person may seem to be serving himself, but he is not. For he is part of the community, and he suffers when the actions of others are as self-serving as his. If everyone would do what is best for everyone, everyone would be in a better condition.

Chapter 7

Capitalism and Human Beings

Corporations, as noted in Chapter Five, typically make individual decisions. Owners act in ways calculated to benefit their organizations without regard for the larger community in which they live. Often, when a certain company acts as a solo performer, it indeed benefits, though people outside the company do not. However, if the company carries out policies as part of a chorus of firms doing the same thing, matters may be different. Now the many corporations, acting in the same way, collectively hurt themselves. They dry up demand for their products through their cost-cutting stratagems, and by emphasizing exports, they confound the exchange circle that enabled them to come into existence in the first place. Mired in individual decision-making, they cannot make the appropriate community decisions.

The corporations do make community decisions. They decide and act in concert. Yet they do so to preserve their ability to continue taking the individual option. They become communal for the purpose of remaining *individual*. While they could use their abilities to cooperate with one another to retain work forces, keep wages up, and promote the general welfare of the labor sector so as to assure that demand for products continues, they instead continue cutting labor costs and cooperate with one another in using government as an instrument for doing so. Paradoxically, they cooperate with one another in order to act singly.

Given that corporations put themselves in danger when they act in ways likely to reduce demand, this may seem strange--especially if they are acting in concert with one another, for it is the simultaneous deeds of many companies that have the most pronounced effects. Is one to think that managers do not understand this? Are they so committed to individual decision-making that they do not realize that their cooperative gestures are merely efforts to preserve their individual prerogatives? Are they like bacteria that destroy their host and so ultimately themselves?

The Managerial Culture

To answer these questions, one must first realize that there is a *managerial culture.* Corporate managers constantly talk with one another, and as happens in any group, they begin, as Peter Berger would say, to construct their own reality.[24] Their conversations determine how the world is, for them, formed and shaped; a map of the world is drawn, as it were, complete with both tangible and intangible realities. This image of everything that exists includes a dynamics, ideas about what-causes-what and why it is that certain things happen. In addition, it has definitions of what is right and wrong, noble or evil. Because this constructed reality appears in conversation among managers, it may seem strange and alien to outsiders, but to those on the inside, it seems quite normal and even self-evident.

Among the features of reality as envisaged in conversation among managers is the sanctity of the individual decision. That a manager is doing right when he struggles to reduce labor costs becomes obvious; it takes on the character of a moral axiom. Reducing labor costs cannot be wrong, for "everyone knows," (or at least all the managers believe) that it is right. To think otherwise is to be a wet blanket. It is to fail to be "in" and often occasions the shocked look with which people regard others who say strange things. Thus, arguments to the contrary, assertions about maintaining demand cannot get into the conceptual corral. They may seem valid to an intellect who regards them in solitude, but they do not have the dignity of being generally accepted, even for discussion. Perhaps they are not accepted especially for discussion, since the truer they are, the greater is the danger that they will appear true and so dim the warm glow of group belonging. For this reason it may be necessary to push them away.

A major feature of the managerial culture is the tacit acceptance of the axiom that the future will take care of itself. We Americans concern ourselves with acting so that we can prosper immediately. Or, more accurately, we believe we need to act so that the corporation prospers. After all, such behavior taps into the basic laws of nature, we think. The market is nature in its pure form, and by acting in accordance with its logic, we Americans feel assured that nature is on our side. Our actions are in this sense healthy and bode well for the future. They are more certain to bear fruit in the long term than would be actions based on any other kind of rational calculation.

If this seems difficult to believe, recall that managers commonly take the same attitude towards the environment and problems of pollution that they take towards the plight of workers and the need to maintain demand. Consistently, they oppose government regulations that pertain to pollution (or anything else) and they consistently favor locating their plants in parts of the world that either have no such regulations or are lax in enforcing them. Certainly, a lone company could hurt itself by going to some expense to spare the environment while its competitors fail to do so. But if the others are forced to do the same, that company could slow down its polluting without suffering. Thus, it is blatantly evident that companies that oppose regulations are acting together to preserve their ability to act individually.

Managerial independence also manifests itself in the incredibly cold attitude managers take towards workers and, in general, the masses of people. It is part of the managerial culture to be unconcerned with how policies affect human beings. The dismissal of a worker is, in the manager's view, no different from deciding to retire a machine from active duty. Workers come and go, and managers see them only as resources that help to run operations. It is not necessary to think that the managers are particularly callous people. Very likely, most of them are glad to help a stalled motorist start his car and are kind to dogs and children. But the view within the managerial culture is that the manager cannot worry about helping individuals when he makes decisions. Indeed, he can even be proud of his cost cutting achievements, not thinking that he made them at the expense of living human beings.

It is not only the managers of particular corporations who seem to lack concern for people. Beyond that narrow zone is a larger world of lawyers, economists, and other intellectuals who have similar views. These people are consultants to managers, both in the United States and elsewhere. As such, they represent that part of corporate life that transcends particular companies. They are, in effect, the essence of the corporation incarnated in particular people and professions. And they, too, see the welfare of ordinary people as

outside their concern, regarding it as all right that people may be left
without resources for living decently and possibly even without a way
to survive if serving corporate interests happens to have that
consequence. If asked, these intellectuals would most certainly point
out that people cannot prosper unless businesses do, and thus it is best
to think only of business and postpone attention to the people's
problems, perhaps indefinitely. They believe that people
automatically benefit from business prosperity in the long term, even
if not in the short term.

Individualism and the Worker

In the meantime, each individual among the millions of ordinary
Americans is expected to engage in the same individual quest for
prosperity as do the corporations. In the past several years, hundreds
of thousands of Americans have lost their jobs. One newspaper report
after another speaks of massive layoffs by commercial firms. Only
occasionally do the media tell us about any mass hiring of workers,
and in the few cases where such an event happens, it is often a calling
back of workers who had been "laid off." Newly created jobs are
generally low-paying and include few or no benefits. Anyone
standing back and looking at this state of affairs would say that
America has a problem. It is not just that certain persons are beset by
them; it is that the nation as a whole is. Yet neither political party
nor any political or other kind of leader of stature has any plan to do
anything about the problem. The American perception seems to be
that the country can no more *do* something about the impoverishment
of its people than it can control the weather. Very likely, anyone who
suggests plans for real change never becomes a respected national
leader, for Americans tends to see such a person as outside the circle
of normalcy.
    Suggestions for helping people that are set forth are individualistic.
Often speakers advocate training and educating people better so that
they can get jobs--that is, get one of the few good jobs that still exist.
Each job-seeker, it would seem, is to be interested only in solving his
particular problem. Instead of thinking about whether he together
with his neighbors and fellow countrymen can have a good life, he
should think only of how *he* can do so. He is not to see himself as
one of "the American people" who have a problem of unemployment,
but as a lone individual who happens to be without a job--or a good

job. A way of saying this is that the individual is left to *improvise* solutions to his own very personal problem. The objective features of the world around him, such as available jobs, opportunities for business, and facilities for training, are the materials with which he will work. They are not themselves up for discussion; they are the rocks and ridges the person must maneuver in and around if he is to get to safe haven.

What is wrong with this view of matters can be seen in an analogy. A musical performance has been scheduled. The hall in which it will take place will accommodate only one thousand people when double that number wish to attend. Announcers, aware of the situation, tell people that they should "hurry up and get their tickets." One would think from hearing such counsel that if everyone would hurry, everyone would get a ticket and would get in! Yet it is obvious that this is not so. If everyone were to hurry, only those who hurry more than others would get the tickets. Since there are one thousand tickets, one thousand people will get in regardless how quickly or slowly the two thousand people act in the effort to obtain them. The advice, then, is individualistic in the sense that it is appropriate only if it is beamed at one or a few persons. Any one person can, by hurrying, get to the box office and buy a ticket. But the two thousand people cannot.

Similarly, when a nation or large community has a problem of unemployment, it is the community as such that has the problem. Any one person might, by getting advanced training or education or by doing a vigorous and expert job of looking for work, be able to find a position he could not have obtained otherwise. But if he does, it will be he rather than someone else who got the job. The number of people left jobless will not be affected. When unemployment or underemployment afflicts a community then, advice given to persons to pursue training, to learn how to interview for jobs, and all the rest is, from the community's standpoint, irrelevant. It has no bearing on unemployment itself. And to offer such advice is to counsel people to improvise solutions if and however they can. It is not to deal with the community's problem. In basic thinking, it is always the community's problem that matters. We are, after all, social creatures.

Social Class

When people act cooperatively in order to establish their right to act *un*cooperatively, a new reality appears on the scene--*social class*. Calling it "new" does not mean that it is a recent development. Karl Marx first wrote about it over a century ago, and his critic, Max Weber, refined the ideas in the early decades of the twentieth century. Still, social class is new in the sense that it comes into being when wealthy businessmen join forces to protect what they consider their interests.

Both Marx and Weber wrote that class appeared first as a collection of people who owned the apparatus of production and depended on that ownership for their wealth. They may also have worked, but if so, their labors gained only a part of their income. The other or unearned part was essential for maintaining their basic style of living. Often, they labored mainly to manage their properties, and not infrequently did not need to do even that. In the contemporary era, this translates into the class consisting of those people who own shares in a company. These people receive dividend incomes; they neither work nor exercise control over income-earning property. To be truly part of the class, the dividend income needs to be large enough to afford a luxurious or wealthy ("seignorial") style of living.

Also among members of the class are managers. These people are like workers in one respect, which is that they work for their pay instead of getting it from property. Their income, however, is much greater than that of workers lower in the hierarchy, and it is so for good reason. The managers provide special services, not simply to the enterprises from which wealth derives, but also to the owners as well. They do the administering which is essential for maintaining and enhancing the owners' positions. They have the owners' class position in their hands, so to speak, and serve as its defenders. Unearned income as such depends upon them. In this sense, they are more in league with owners than they are with workers. While they share with workers the condition of working for their pay, they are really more like owners than like workers. Thus in speaking of class differences, we put owners *and* managers on one side and workers on the other side.

In all social organization, people at the top have to have allies among groups beneath them. Only so can they maintain and extend their power. Police forces are in many cases an example of such allied groups. But so are managers of corporations. And because they offer special services to owners, they are given a special reward. The reward is well worth it from the standpoint of the propertied, because by it they gain allies who will use judgment and ingenuity to maintain the class structure in which they, the owners, have such a privileged position. In this sense, a manager is part of, or at least allied with, the owning class, even if he himself owns nothing and depends entirely on earned income.

It is not, however, simply obvious that corporate owners and managers who are identified with the corporation comprise a class. Nor is it simply self-evident that they would see themselves as having common cause with all owners and managers. We could imagine that instead, solidarity and a disposition to act together would occur among people who are associated with a specific corporation. The stockholders, managers *and* employees of Ford Motor Company might reasonably feel that it is they who should stand together against a common adversary, that adversary being their corporate competitors. Because they are rivals of Chrysler and General Motors, it could be these companies that are "the other guy" rather than different ranks within their own organization. Do not Ford Company owners, managers and workers all benefit when people buy Fords instead of other cars? Are they not all under threat that customers will prefer products put out by their competitors? In view of the apparent reasonableness of these ideas, it is remarkable that such does not seem to be the case at all. Identifications are in fact by class and not by company.

Evidently, managers seem to have a certain idea of their interests and the challenges to their interests. Their interests lie in making decisions in which the worker employed by a company is simply a factor of production. To the manager, the worker is like buildings and machines and is so in at least two ways. First, the company cannot possibly produce and market goods and so realize a profit without the laborer. He is indispensable. Second, if profits are not only to be realized but also increased, managers must be free to deal with workers on the basis of rational calculation. They must be able to hire and fire as need dictates. They must be able to get maximum use of a worker for minimum cost. Restrictions preventing them from dealing with workers in this way should be few, if any.

The worker, united with others, forms another class with objectives that sharply contrast those of the managers. This class came into being because of the birth of the owner-manager class. It appeared early in the industrial era. At that time, peasants from the countryside flocked to the rapidly growing cities, either pushed by rural hardship or pulled by promises of prosperity in mines and factories. They became workers, a rather new kind of actor on the economic scene. Because they found themselves considered to be factors of production, and because they deemed their lot hard, they too had a sense of common cause.

Managers against Unions

Workers, in general, soon realized that they deserved a greater share of the largesse received by their employers. They wanted higher wages, safer and more pleasant working conditions, and greater job security. To attain these items, they formed unions and threatened to use their only weapon--the strike. The strike was a challenge to managerial interests, for how can someone charged with managing a factory do so if he has to contend with demands from the factors of production? The center and core of this challenge lay in any tendency among workers to achieve unity and to engage in community decision-making and group effort. Striking, of course, was the supreme group effort. Workers thus threw down the gauntlet before the owner-manager class.

Evidence clearly reveals that mangers took unionization very seriously. They did not regard it as trivial, nor did they wait long before taking action. Most importantly, they did not accept unions as in any way right and proper. They did not wish to bargain with them about wages or other matters. Managers held steadfastly to the view that workers should decide and act only as individuals. To prevent unionization, managers fired workers who organized or joined the unions and hired "goons" to inflict violence upon workers who tried to organize or strike. If workers did strike, the strikers were treated as individuals who, having failed to show up for work, could be fired. Managers hoped to encourage workers who had little room for financial maneuvering to remain on the job or return to it. Whenever possible, managers hired people off the street to do the jobs of the strikers. Union advocates referred to such replacement workers as "scabs." Managers also used government whenever they could, which was often, to break up strikes. All of this indicates that managers defined themselves as a class over and against the working class.

It was the workers who started the war between the managerial and working classes. The managers did not want to start anything, for they had control over hiring, firing, and wages from the beginning. The only limits on their power were the points at which workers would starve and so be unable to work, and the possibility that at a certain time there might be a shortage of workers, which would force employers to compete for the workers who are available.

The story of struggles between labor and management forms a rich and complex history, one full of events, heroes, and villains. It will be sufficient here to note that, according to Strobel, a high point for the laboring man came in the 1930s under the presidency of Franklin D. Roosevelt.[25] The rights of labor gained far more respect than ever before. Government established by law that workers had a right to organize and form unions; they had a right to negotiate wages, working conditions, and benefits; they had a right to strike if negotiations broke down. All of these rights enabled labor unions to strengthen and become important parts of the social and economic scene. Managers ceased to think about how to defeat or crush unions and devoted their attention, instead, to how to bargain with them.

With some retreats in the late 1940s and 1950s, labor achieved an unprecedented, higher level of living in the 1960s. Workers in a number of major industries were making wages that enabled them to live in a comfortable, middle-class lifestyle. Automobile workers and others had incomes sufficient to buy houses, cars and in general, to live the good life. They worked comfortably short weeks--commonly forty hours--with leisure time in the evenings and on weekends, something which their ancestors knew nothing about. They also had protection against arbitrary firing and the "speed ups" that would make the working day unpleasant. The corporations were doing well also.

As William Domhoff asserts in *The Power Elite and the State*, people (voters) were able at that time to take a more demanding attitude towards firms and the corporate world. There was a tight labor market; the civil rights movement was disturbing the order of society, and "hard hat" support for the war in Viet Nam was needed. Corporate managers felt for these reasons that they needed to make some concessions to the lower and middle classes. Then too, people tend to demand more of corporate management when the firms prosper.[26] With both labor and management doing well economically, things seemed to be going well in the United States in the 1960s. America's prosperity at the time explains why Lyndon Johnson handily won reelection to the presidency in 1964. The country seemed to have settled into a modified capitalist economy in which labor unions were strong, public assistance prevented people from skidding into poverty, and the government was ready to stimulate the economy if depression threatened.

The New War against Labor

In the 1970s, however, the battle between the managerial and working classes heated up once again. This time it was the managers who started the war. They sought to undo the gains achieved by ordinary people in the previous decades. According to Domhoff, a major factor leading up to this battle was the passing into history of the wave of social protests that occurred during the 1960s. The Civil Rights Movement, undertaken to establish racial equality, especially for African-Americans, lost its punch. The Women's Liberation Movement was tamed; it continued to hold conferences and produce literature, but did little in the way of actual social disruption. The Antiwar Movement also faded from the scene with the end of the Vietnam Conflict.

According to Domhoff, the upper classes have little reason to fear political elections, for they are well able to manipulate them, mainly with financial contributions. What does get the wealthy's attention, Domhoff says, is social disruption. The protests against the war in Vietnam were particularly potent because the corporate elite wanted the war, at least for a time, and they needed "hard hat" labor support for it in the face of protests by college students. With the ebbing of the tide of social protests in the 1970s, the business classes were once again inclined to test their muscles.

Another factor in the new management-labor war was one which Domhoff mentions and which Robert Ross and Kent Trachte make into a major theme in their *Global Capitalism: The New Leviathan.* They suggest that the ability of corporations, made possible by advances in technology, to locate their operations in other countries was the basis of a new battle. Instead of producing goods in the United States for sale within the country, the companies could "site" their plants elsewhere, employ the much cheaper local labor, and then ship the products back to the United States.[27] According to Walden Bello, corporations are always in quest of cheaper labor. They begin with countries like South Korea, Taiwan, Hong Kong and Singapore. When labor gets too expensive in these places (despite the repression of unions), they move on to Indonesia and Thailand. When wages rise or prove too high there, they reach the ultimate destinations for cheap labor--Vietnam and China.[28]

The savings which managers achieve in this way derive from a couple of sources. The obvious one is the large pool of labor in those other countries which works at a very small fraction of what it takes to satisfy an American worker. But equally important is that American managers can always threaten to move their operations elsewhere, even if they have not yet done so. In this way, they are able to "discipline" the worker, showing him that he is lucky to have a job at all and thus should not be complaining and trying to get higher wages and better conditions. For that matter, they suggest that he should not try to prevent reduction in wages and the worsening of conditions. Presently, their intimidation is working: union membership is down; and unions, in general, are in retreat.

Employers have had recourse to various artifices in cutting costs at the expense of their employees. Since the law requires firms to provide benefits as well as wages, but only for full-time employees, companies have made it a practice to hire a large number of part-time workers. They do not need to provide health insurance, pensions, and other benefits to these employees. In some cases, workers are all dismissed and then rehired on a part-time contract basis at a lower cost to the company. These new employees then replace workers with seniority who earn higher wages; obviously, cost reductions are the companies' focus. Across contemporary America, the bugle has sounded retreat for employees as a class--in other words, for most Americans.

The Decline of the Middle Class

In *Upward Dreams, Downward Mobility*, Frederick R. Strobel documents the gradual impoverishment of what he calls the "middle class," a designation he uses to refer to most Americans, those who are neither very rich nor very poor. More wives work today, he says, because they must work if a family is to live at the same level as they did on a single income earlier.[29] Ironically, this has happened simultaneously with great advances in technology. Such advances, one might assume, should enable people to produce more in any given period of time spent working. Because they can produce more, one might think that they would have more. Increases in production can mean increases in the supplies of those things that make people's lives comfortable, pleasant, and safe. However, just the opposite has taken place. With advances in technology, production becomes more dependent on apparatus and less dependent on labor. People can own apparatus, unlike labor, and owning it enables them to claim for themselves more of what it produces. In claiming more of the product, they deny to workers the proportion of the product which they had before.

There is no really good reason why people who have wealth should want to claim still more for themselves, for they already have as much as they can use and enjoy. So why not share the abundance of goods with one's partners in the processes of production? However, this rhetorical question ignores what Chapter Two discussed: by using money to represent the value of things, people subject all goods to a single standard of "more" and "less." Money, unlike goods, exhibits upward linearity. It goes up infinitely in a straight line. No matter how much a person has or how well off he is, he can always have more and be better off, for by imprinting money on goods, the objects shed their limitedness-in-value. Thus, it is possible for those who own apparatus and therefore can claim more of the product to actually do so. Some have luxuries, while others do not have what it takes to enjoy life.

Confusion reigns here. If one thinks that increasing production or productivity (goods per hour of work) will result in people having more of what people need and want, one is thinking in terms of the battle with nature. In that battle, the better an individual's tools, the greater his knowledge and skill, and the more effort he puts forth, the greater will be the supply of goods available to him and the better the material aspect of his life will be. But this is not a battle with nature; humans have already won that struggle. People now have the ability to feed and clothe everyone well. All could live in three-bedroom, two-bath homes with barbecue pits and boats in the back yard. Everyone could also have generous servings of TERM. Despite having this productive prowess, many Americans are poor, and many are becoming poorer. The battle is no longer with nature but with social and economic organization (with society). The whole concern with productivity, so characteristic of our era, is an irrelevant digression from the serious issues. Or worse, it is a retreat into purely individual decision-making in which each person is supposed to improvise his own way of surviving in a setting which affords very limited opportunities. In doing so, he abdicates his position as a member of a community who can join with others to solve everyone's problems and who can find fulfillment in doing so.

American Capitalism

Like all peoples, Americans have notions about the way their social, economic, and political lives are organized. These ideologies or theories are simply thoughts. From the 1930s on, the dominant thought in the country was *modified capitalism*. The economy is basically capitalist--that is, people who have wealth use that wealth to make more wealth. They have a claim on goods, but they use that claim to obtain goods that are of no value in themselves but which serve to make other goods that are. For instance, with his claim on things-of-value, a man buys a building, machinery, and raw products. With the machine and the building, he changes those raw products into something else; perhaps leather is transformed into shoes. He then sells this other thing--the shoe--for more than its share of everything he spent to produce it. The difference between the sale price and the share of production costs is his *profit*. It is his income, what he depends on as a continuing claim on goods. The people who buy the products view them as necessary for living; their incomes, whatever the sources, enable them to lay claims. In its concrete form, capitalism is much more complicated than this, but the basic principles remain.

As a way of organizing economic life, capitalism is distinguished by an extensive division of labor and by the preeminence in social life of the claim on goods. The division of labor, for one thing, sets capitalism apart from what went before it, a subsistence economy. This is a system in which people produce for themselves and depend upon what they themselves produce. Medieval feudalism, characterized by a very unequal relation of lord and vassal, was a special form of this system. Both lord and vassal lived very mediocre material lives; the lord no more than the vassal had the amenities that we consider necessary today. His only luxury was people, that is, his servants. The combination of technology and its apparatus with division of labor makes possible a material existence for most people of far greater luxury than anyone had previously. Though not frequently praised, the modern bathroom is a good symbol of this advancement in the everyday quality of life.

The claim on goods as a central feature of social life also sets capitalism apart from systems in which government plays the central role. These include mercantile systems and certain kinds of socialism. In them, economic life is managed by governments or by other, less centralized sources of power in the interest of one or another value. The value may be the exaltation of nation and monarchy (mercantilism), or it may be an idea of justice in the relations among people (socialism). Capitalism, by contrast, is a system in which the use of capital to achieve profit serves as the organizing principle for the provision of goods and relations among people. This quest for profit initiates a process that plays itself through, by intention undisturbed by other factors. Capitalism happens, and it is the center and core of the society.

American capitalism, however, is a modified capitalism. Qualifying the system are certain compromises of the autonomy of the capitalist enterprise. The processes of buying capital goods (investing) and selling consumer goods for a profit take place in, and are central to, social life. But their autonomy is abridged in various ways in the interest of making the economy work for the majority of people.

The encouragement and promotion of strong labor unions is one of these modifications. This is achieved partly by the unions themselves and partly by legislation. Whatever the source of its strength, an active union serves to enable workers to negotiate with management as a body and therefore with strength. It establishes something more like a true labor market. The union bargains with management on the basis of equality, as when a buyer and seller negotiate the price of an item that is for sale. The outcome of the bargaining is a market outcome, just as are the prices on which the buyer and seller agree. Such bargaining depends on the relative strength of each, which is determined by the fact that they need each other. Laborers have no jobs without management, and management has no product without laborers. Their need for each other moves them to a level of wages and benefits which each finds acceptable in view of the strength of each party.

In this sense, the activities of labor unions are a market phenomenon and a true part of the capitalist system. There need be no government intervention and no intimidation by violence or threats of it. Only bargaining about the sale of labor to a buyer is essential. The union allows for a one-to-one negotiation instead of the one-worker-at-a-time encounter. Managers actually depart from market operations when they have recourse to their accustomed ways of fighting unions. They use spies, police repression, and the firing of competent workers who engage in union activities as non-market devices, indicating managerial unwillingness to play the bargaining game by the rules. Of course, such a concept of the union's function is based on the assumption that a union represents all workers. If it restricts admission to its membership and therefore to certain occupations to people of certain races or ethnic identities, it fails to functions as it should.

Behind the seeming bad sportsmanship of the manager, however, is an understanding of the market economy that is more restrictive. In this conception, only buyers and sellers of goods (corporations) are the proper players in the capitalist drama. The worker who sells his labor is not part of it. Or, if he is, it is as a player in the subplot which should not affect the unfolding of the larger story. That larger story is the negotiation between buyer and seller, a process which is supposed to be played out on its own terms without assertive laborers being a confounding factor. This can be done if workers do not organize and do not try to bargain as a unit.

A second way in which capitalism has been modified in America is in the establishment of the *social wage*. This refers to the number of ways government at any level acts to provide what people cannot provide for themselves--what they cannot glean from capitalist processes. Among them are benefits which people are entitled to under specific circumstances. Examples include benefits to which people have a right, such as social security and unemployment compensation. Others are assistance designed to help people who cannot help themselves--food stamps or Aid to Families of Dependent Children. These programs attempt to soften the harsh blows of the market. Advocates have argued that they should not be seen as charity but as justice, since market processes unfairly deprive some people of their due; however, this is a matter of interpretation. What remains definite is that the community, acting through government, makes payments to, or on behalf of, certain people.

The third way in which capitalism is modified in America is in the action to keep the exchange circle--the economy--functioning properly. An economy is a system by which people are able to communicate in a way that enables them to exchange goods in a circle. Each is able to produce one thing but receives many. If the communication (monetary) system breaks down, people do not exchange and so are deprived of goods. The situation is an exact replica of a defeat in the battle with nature, though it is not nature that is the adversary.

Actually, the social wage is a major device by which the continuation of the exchange circle is accomplished. Because of entitlements and assistance, people who would otherwise be in desperate straits have money. They spend it and so a seller is able to move his goods and realize a profit, and the multiplier goes to work from there. Unions may have a similar effect. They protect laborers' incomes and may even get those incomes enhanced. Strobel argues that money in the hands of ordinary people provides a more dependable source of demand than it does when held by the wealthy.[30] The latter may demand luxuries, a demand which could have the same effect on the economy as the purchase of ordinary goods by those who are not wealthy. Yet such a demand is not a stable indicator because the wish for luxuries is more volatile than the need for food, clothing, and shelter. Strobel further suggests that the United States' successes in its bouts with depression are due more to the increased equality of incomes than to anything else.

The alternative with which Strobel takes issue is the Keynesian idea that government does battle with depression primarily by deficit spending. When it spends more than it takes in, increasing its debt, it releases money into the economy and so gets the exchange circle going. In Strobel's view, the efforts of the Roosevelt administration in the 1930s were inadequate and thus did not defeat depression. Only the far more massive "Keynesian" measures of financing World War II defeated the depression, as did the Cold War expenditures in later years. It was, Strobel believes, the prosperity of ordinary people that kept things going.

The Idea of "Pure" Capitalism

It is necessary to emphasize the "modified" in the expression "modified capitalism" because the United States economy operates under such a system. In the early 1970s, modified capitalism seemed to be the form that would last for ages to come in America. Some wanted to modify capitalism more, some less, but few took issue with the general idea. Both Republicans and Democrats seemed to accept it. The unmodified capitalism of fond memory seemed to recede further and further into the past. The few who continued to advocate it seemed to be anachronistic, or even extremist, ideologues disconnected from reality. Now, however, matters are drastically different. The idea of the pure market economy has surged into prominence once again. It is now hale and hardy and has become high fashion. Its advocates are exuberant and are joined by many who would not have held such views twenty years ago. Economists, sociologists, clergymen, and other professionals have jumped on the bandwagon. The whole movement has an aura of power and inevitability. It appears as a wave of the future that cannot possibly be stopped.

Central to this trend of thought is the idea of the pure or unmodified market economy. While much of what people say may seem to laud the general idea of market and proclaim the benefits of market processes, it is the market *as freed from the modifications* that has the place of honor. It is not enough simply to have a market with its processes; it is essential to have a market which is uninhibited. This perspective of market economy equates it with the destruction of those structures that were set up to soften the system's harshness and to make it work for people.

As with all political agenda, advocates must sell their propaganda to people. It is a clever trick if it can be done, since most people depend upon the economic edifice scheduled for demolition. Advocates sell the agenda by speaking of market and market mechanisms. They extol the market mechanisms and cite facts that suggest that their market plan holds out the greatest promise for prosperity and a pleasant life for people. Fundamental in their argument is the *incentive*. Because people under market conditions have maximum reason to produce good products and offer them at low prices, advocates of the free market assert that large numbers of people will begin producing. These people will necessarily employ workers, thus creating jobs. Whatever the merit or demerit of this argument, note that it pertains to the idea of market and market dynamics, not to the market economy in the specific sense of one freed from all modification. Logically, the one does not imply the other, and in this sense, the agenda is a hidden one. To say that market mechanisms can do wonderful things without mentioning the destruction of labor unions and the reduction or obliteration of benefits is truly deceptive. It is like speaking to a patient in the hospital about the wonderful healing processes that go on in the body without mentioning that the patient will not get the surgery or medicines he needs. It is one thing to say that the process has salutary effects, and another to announce that all other supports are to be removed.

Also hidden behind the rhetoric of the market economy is an insistence that all decisions are to be individual, as distinct from community decisions. Individuals are to decide and act on their own behalf. Advocates of the market suggest that a full market economy promises a blossoming of vigorous economic activity. Managers and executives will promote their enterprises with such energy that they will increase prosperity not only for themselves but for others as well. With the success of their businesses will come better paying jobs and more and better opportunities for other businesses. But underneath the words is a hidden message, the true one, which only the acute listener hears. This less obvious message says, "We are sorry that there will be fewer jobs and that those that remain will pay less. But take heart. If you train well, work hard, and meet the employer's other demands, *you* may not be one of the unemployed. Others will, but *you* will not. If your wages buy less, you can work longer hours, get a second job, or get more people in your family to work." Note that the message assumes that the individual is concerned only with improvising solutions for himself. The urgency of doing so dissipates any concern he may have for people other than himself. To the extent that a person is concerned about the community and not just about himself, he would find this message to be a digression. Giving it to him would be like telling a woman on a sinking ship who is upset that many men, women, and children may lose their lives at sea that there is reason to take comfort: there is room in the life boat *for her*.

Why did such an intellectual turnabout happen? Why did styles of thought take such a twist to what most people call the political "right wing"? It is remarkable how infrequently people ask this question. Perhaps the sovereignty of style in our society makes it seem unnecessary to ask. The tendency is to see "the times" as having an objective character; and if it is thought that "the times are changing," people assume that one must accommodate to those changes on pain of being left behind by the march of history.

Why Did the "Turn to the Right" Take Place?

Among the possible answers, some would assert that critics of capitalism have always been wrong. Perhaps the horror stories of the mistreatment and exploitation of workers a hundred years ago are all in error. The low pay, grisly working conditions, and job insecurity are all figments of someone's imagination. Or, they may have been things that happened, but only to a few people. Other employers were far more fair, and their workers did better, but no one hears about them because they are, like the airplane that lands safely, not news. So, the argument goes, people err by taking some cases of mistreatment and generalizing them. Or, perhaps moral confusion reigned then. Maybe workers of the nineteenth century suffered deservedly because they were lazy and ill prepared, thus condemning themselves to miserable ways of life. Perhaps the early labor leaders were just greedy or power-hungry. Possibly socialists were simply mesmerized by the prospect of government power, which they hoped to share. The Christian "social gospel" advocates may have had clergymen, professors, and other church folk who were hard-pressed to find a cause to serve or were moved by an idealism that had no relation to reality. In general, it is possible to justify capitalism by asserting that it was never as bad as it is often depicted.

Another way of answering the question is to suggest that early capitalism may have been grim, but that the dark side of the system was in force only in those early phases. This explanation suggests that as capitalism and the industrial society matured, things improved for everyone--including the industrial workers. Past situations do attest to this phenomenon. Even when labor unions are severely repressed, as in South Korea, there is a tendency for wages to go up over time. Further, one can argue, as does Milton Friedman in *Capitalism and Freedom*, that the improvements in the lot of workers in the United States have not been due to labor union activity.[31] This position suggests that granting workers higher incomes as time goes by is an intrinsic characteristic of capitalism--even, or perhaps especially, when capitalism is free of government interference.

However, once these arguments are on the table, it is easy to find their vulnerability. The harshness and the heartlessness of early industrial capitalism are too evident to deny. Efforts which ignore this reality serve only to establish the point. Regardless whether they had solutions, the critics were right in condemning several aspects of capitalism. Regarding the movement of industrial capitalism from its earlier to its later or mature phases, it is not possible to make a definitive statement. The change over the years did not take place in a vacuum. With the passing of time came a depression, pro-labor legislation, and active labor unions. It is not easy to say what the capitalist order would be like *if* there had never been either a union or a social wage. History, it has been said, does not reveal its alternatives. However, note that American workers achieved an unprecedented level of prosperity in the era of strong unions, whereas people in general seem to be faring poorly as the American economy inches nearer to the pure capitalist model. Strobel documents this fact quite well in *Upward Dreams, Downward Mobility.*

But are the sufferings just dislocations which are to be expected when government interference in the economy is reduced but the dynamics of the free market have not yet had a chance to take hold? Many have argued that this is the case, both in the United States and elsewhere, notably in Latin America. To cite an analogy, surgical patients are commonly in worse conditions immediately after surgery than they were before. Yet in most cases they are well advised to undergo the operations, for when they recover from surgery, they will be in better condition than they were earlier. Similarly, there may be difficult times while waiting for the free market to get moving, but better times will surface later. The problem with this argument is evident. Certainly there are many examples of actions that make a situation worse at first yet which promise to make the situation better over time. Surgery is just one of these. But it is possible to say *why* the situation will change from being worse than it was before to better than it was in the first place. Physicians can explain the processes of healing and the course these processes will take as a result of the changes effected by it, such as the excise of an offending organ or by the sewing up of previously separated tissues. To believe in the salutary effects of surgery, it is necessary to be able to specify these processes.

What then is taking place in the American economy or in Latin American countries that promises a life better than the ones people currently live and better than they had in the eras of government intervention? Are workers laboring to produce capital goods rather than consumer goods? Once those tools are available, can they be used to manufacture things that make life better? This would be a reason why life might be difficult now but better in the future.

However, this clearly is not what is happening. Rather, what is taking place is simple *un*employment. Workers are not producing tools or anything else. Another possibility is that when business is freed from all inhibition (government interference, labor union demands), it will begin, even if slowly, to prosper. And as it does, it would provide both goods for consumers and jobs for workers. Here too there might be an initial period of hard times ("dislocations"), but in due course the patient will heal and will be better off than he was before. The trouble with this expectation is that there is nothing to indicate that it will be realized. No preliminary blossoming of business, employment, and increased income takes place with promise of more to come. All evidence suggests that workers are increasingly deprived. Wages are less; benefits are fewer; working conditions are worse; and job insecurity is greater. When speaking frankly, business leaders acknowledge that this situation is the whole point of the rightward turn, for with it, businesses prosper by cutting labor costs. And of course, it is hard to cut labor costs and pay workers higher wages at the same time. Nor is there any reason to expect a change in business management practices in the future.

By the early 1980s, all this had become evident. Thus, one can conclude that the rightward shift of the last two decades is not truly due to Americans changing their *opinions*. There was no accumulation of evidence that forced people to change their minds. To change from a belief in modified capitalism to an acceptance of pure capitalism was not an intellectual shift as was, for example, the shift from a belief that the world is round rather than flat or that the Sun rather than the Earth is the center of the solar system.

Power and the Turn to the Right

What it was, rather, was a change in thought generated in response to a shift in *power*. Over the last two decades, the corporate elite, the leaders of businesses who act as a community to defend their rights to act as individuals, has become more powerful than it was before. Though always the main power, observers did not in every instance recognize business as the strongman that it was. The reason for this failure was that the corporate elite of earlier decades found it expedient to make concessions to workers and ordinary people. It also wisely masked its power in the aura of democracy. However, in recent years, challenges to corporate profits seem to have made it necessary for corporate leaders to wield more power than they did before. Foreign competition has given urgency to the task of maximizing the ability to "compete." Other changes, such as the ability to move operations to labor-cheap nations, have made concessions that have already been granted to American labor seem unnecessary to business leaders, as Ross and Trachte argue in *Global Capitalism*. As a result, the structure of power in the United States has been clearly defined: the corporate elite is in charge. William Domhoff has documented this in his *The Power Elite and the State* with great care and thoroughness.

With this clarification it becomes possible to understand a number of changes that have taken place. People, always on the lookout for what will advance their own positions, note where power is located so that they can align with it and profit from its favors. In doing this, they are not only acknowledging the power elite but bestowing and enhancing its power. No person, group, or stratum can stand all-powerful by itself. It has to get support from a large number of others. Once the impression that someone or something is "in charge" has been created, others will rally behind it so that they too may become part of the group in control. Their siding with whatever or whoever possesses power thus makes it true that the entity has power. Power begets power; it is self-perpetuating. This explains how emperors became so great and majestic in the past.

Among those who close ranks behind the corporate elite are some whose principal function has to do with interpreting what is going on in society--journalists and scholars. Reporters and newscasters are like canaries that react to poison gas before men do. They catch on that something is "in style" and frequently go along with it. By doing so they signal to others what the style is, and these others, the readers of newspapers, and watchers of TV quickly get into line and follow along. The style also functions as a restrictive structure that limits what journalists can write and say. They cannot say good things about certain people, movements, and policies; they cannot say bad or damaging things about others. Their use of political labels changes as readily as does the length of a woman's skirt or the width of a man's tie. The position that was considered to be center twenty years ago they now call leftist or radical, while a position which people now consider in the center is one that was considered right-wing or extremist in the past. "Liberal" has become a derogatory term, though it is not easy to pinpoint what led to the label's demotion. (In Latin

America, the label neo-liberal, however, is all right, since it means the same thing as neo-classical.)

In reporting on Central America during the 1980s, the performance of American journalists can be said without exaggeration to have been truly disgraceful. Reporters dealing with Nicaragua, El Salvador, and Guatemala, especially, displayed an amazing ability to call a spade an armchair. Those who visited Nicaragua regularly ignored or downplayed atrocities committed by the CIA-supported Contras and provided no information about the humane projects carried out by the Sandinista regime, notably in the areas of health, education, and agrarian reform. The election of 1984, won by the Sandinistas, was virtually ignored, since the winning party did not enjoy the favor of the American State Department. Similar sloth and distortion characterized reporting about El Salvador. Mention of government "death squads" did appear on occasion, but was made in a way that gave the impression that the atrocities were not serious. The fact that a government which was called "democratic" because elections were held was murdering its own citizens and opponents was not allowed to enter the sphere of American public awareness. Whether reporting got worse during the 1980s or had always been that distorted is open for discussion. But there is no question that it was badly slanted during that decade.

Many scholars are singing in the same chorus as do the journalists. A large number in the economics profession are on duty for the corporate elite, providing them with the intellectual justification they need. Of course, the issues and ideas they expound are customarily arcane and scholarly. Proclamation of the view that human beings are always and by nature rational calculators rather than beings moved by sentiment and sense of obligation is not likely to be a topic on the evening news. Yet this view of human nature does provide support for an image of human beings and society which rationalizes and justifies the pure capitalist model, an implication that is not lost on the business elite. It provides ideological or theoretical support for an image of human beings and society in which people both do act and should act in their own economic self-interest. The same holds true for elaborate discussions of the logic of the market. Nor are economists the only scholars to jump on this bandwagon. Sociologists with "exchange theory," political scientists, and others have also done so. An examination of recent issues of *The Christian*

Century will reveal that erstwhile liberal ("social gospel") theologians have not been immune.

Service by intellectuals to powerful elites is not a novelty of our era. In the book of Micah in the Bible, the Prophet declares,

> Thus says the LORD concerning the prophets,
>   who lead my people astray,
> who cry "Peace" when they have something to eat,
> but declare war against him
>   who puts nothing into their mouths. (3:5)

The prophets were, properly speaking, intellectuals. They claimed to receive word from the Lord, a word which was from outside of the ordinary communications taking place among kings and noblemen. In this, it was like the data of the scientist and the logical conclusions of the philosopher. The intellectual is always an outsider. His/her message is from "elsewhere." Yet it enjoys a certain honor among kings and nobility, as is indicated by the fact that the kings seem to want prophets, sages and the like included in their courts. A modern economist who develops theories to justify unmodified capitalism is not different from the sages who served kings. He does ideological service to elites in our society, just as prophets did in another era.

The writings and speeches of these and other intellectuals interact with the speeches and actions of men of affairs, notably politicians, to produce a national atmosphere--a mood or widespread feeling that the pure capitalist model is right and good, noble and true. People believe this model is right because it seems to be accepted by people-in-general. Or, better yet, each person thinks it because he thinks that everyone else thinks it. It is "in the air" or is a national "mood." It seems from the standpoint of an individual to have an objective character, one that constrains him to go along with it. However, it could attain this character only by being thought to be an opinion held by many individuals. Such is the nature of intellectual styles or definitions of the "in." A person does not think certain things are true because of evidence or because they are logically implied by other beliefs which he holds. Rather, he holds certain opinions because of what he thinks others think. The belief that "they" believe a certain thing seems compelling to him. He feels he must hold the same view, lest he appear to be a fool or to be "out of it."

In thinking this way, he fails to realize that he is part of everybody else's "everybody else." That is, he holds the opinion because it is "in," but it is also true that it is "in" because he holds it. Once an impression is created that an opinion is fashionable, people hold it because it has the blessing of style, but in so doing they create the reality to which they seem to be merely consenting. A belief is in style because persons hold it, but persons hold it because they think it is in style. It has, for them, an objective character; it appears as a reality beyond and outside of themselves. Yet in fact, they are implicated in its general acceptance.

This feature of human thinking explains why civilizations such as ours develop certain institutional patterns, those designed to counteract the hegemony of style. It is worthwhile to note that an impulse to repress a tendency arises when the tendency itself is formidable. It is because style ("social pressure") is so strong that forces opposing it are marshalled. Among these, due process in law and academic freedom in the university are especially important. They are formed to highlight a person's right and obligation to withdraw into solitude and form opinions on the basis of evidence, logic, and basic value commitments. They make elbow room, so to speak, for the individual who wishes to make his judgments *as* an individual.

Though the group seems to have tremendous influence on its members and is able to control what they believe and what they think is right and good, there is another factor that must be taken seriously into account. This other factor is *power*. Certain persons and groups are more able than others to control what people within the group do. They determine events more than do others. As with opinions, power is always based on what people think--people think.

Some power is political. A certain individual, perhaps a king, is believed to be powerful. People do as he directs, but they do so because they believe that others do so. That is, if I think that many people will obey the king's commands, and I think that such obedience might include grabbing me and throwing me in a dungeon, I very likely will obey the King's commands too. My obedience will then, in turn, be the reason why still others obey, and so on and on. Political power is circular.

So also is economic power. Perhaps I believe that someone has the ability, as if by magic, to bestow on me an ability to induce other people to give me things or do things for me. Since I believe that, I am willing to do what that person requires me to do so that he will bestow that ability upon me. I will give him things, and I will do things for him. I will give him those things that have less value for me than the ability to claim things from others which he bestows upon me. In usual thinking, we say that such a person has money; he pays it to me and I can then spend it for what I want. This of course is circular just as is political power. People with the capacity to bestow claims--with money--can control what others will do.

If we combine the concept of "groupthink," the observation that people believe what the group constrains them to think, with that of power, we have the explanation for the turn to the right in American politics. It did not happen because evidence in favor of the belief that people-in-general prosper best under a pure capitalist system accumulated, and, in effect, forced acceptance of the belief. It was not a matter of evidence at all. Rather, power entered the scene and became determinative. Because a corporate elite in fact controls what people do more than do others, many people decided to go along with it. "If you can't beat them, join them," was the motto. Initially a few people jumped on what appeared to be an embryonic bandwagon, their doing so induced many others to follow suit, and before long the bandwagon was fully grown and functioning. The belief that the pure capitalist model was "in" was not only accepted, but took on the character of objective fact. The idea that we must operate in a "global market" appears, not as a choice that we or most people have made, but as state-of-affairs, as the way things "are." The conclusion, then, is that the renaissance of the pure capitalist model is not an intellectual change; it is not a response to accumulation of evidence or experience. It is an accommodation to power.

Virtue and Vice of the Market

Before turning to what should be done, recall certain basic propositions about the market. First, market operations do serve people to a great extent and in many ways. These operations consist of many people pursuing their own interests within a set of rules. Though selfish in motivation, they accumulate wealth by providing goods and services to others. They take care of their fellow community members accidentally, so to speak, in the course of taking care of themselves. The market also has some ability to achieve an equilibrium of actors. Labor flows away from areas of excess and towards areas of shortage. Prices rise and fall to a point which represents the value of things and the difficulty of providing them. As image, the market is truly beautiful, and it is in some degree descriptive of what happens in reality.

Second, in consequence of certain accidental factors, the market rewards some people more than others. In theory, it should not do this. If some are paid or realize profits much greater than others, the others--so goes the theory--will flock to the more rewarding jobs or businesses. And before long, the abundance of their numbers will drive the rewards down, thus reaching an equilibrium. However, it does not really work this way. There is a sluggishness inherent in the market that prevents people from making the necessary changes. The notion of equilibrium assumes a flexibility in market processes that those processes do not truly possess. People make decisions on the basis of circumstance and belief, and once they move in a certain direction, they are committed to it. A forty-year-old police officer does not readily quit the force and become a business tycoon. Nor, for that matter, can the tycoon become a policeman! What happens, actually, is that there are many jobs and business opportunities in different areas (some yielding much greater material reward than others), and people are distributed among them by the swirl of circumstances and by highly fallible understandings and beliefs.

Third, people in touch with fundamental values recognize that the vast differences in incomes in various lines of work are unfair and unjust. There are of course many jobs in which people are engaged. Some are far more crucial to the maintenance of life and health than others, but a large proportion of them are jobs that people want someone to do. As long as there is the wish that these kinds of work be done, there is an obligation to enable the worker to participate in consumption as well as production--that is, to pay him. If, for example, a wealthy owner of a mansion with many servants wants to extend his yard to include what has been a meadow, he appoints one of his servants to do the work and pays that servant on the same basis as his other servants. The job is merely something that the wealthy man would like to have done rather than something he needs. His other servants are busy at tasks that are closer to home and which are essential for life. Clearly there is a hierarchy of jobs. He does not, however, reward his servants differently depending on the importance of the job each performs. Either he rewards them equally or he bases differences on the quality of their work, not on the importance he places upon the job. Similarly, everyone wants people out there in the world to do many different things. Society wants some people to sell tickets at the local motion picture theater while others hand out hamburgers at the fast-food store. If there were a severe labor shortage (as in wartime), people might get pulled away from these less crucial jobs. But since no such emergency exists, society can indulge its wish to have people doing all sorts of things. And since these people are doing part of the work of the community, they deserve a fair share of the reward. Hence the vast differences in pay are not fair.

Nor does an abundance of workers justify low wages. Some people can charge a high price for their services because there are few who offer those services. Doctors are an example. Others must compete for jobs with many, since many or most can do their jobs. But it is not fair to impoverish workers just because they have a weak bargaining position. We must recognize, then, that the market functions well to some degree, but only to some degree. It rewards people properly to a certain extent, but only to a certain extent. We can appreciate what it is does, but we should do so without exaggerating its achievement. It is good as far as it goes, but it is not a king or a god.

Loosen the Link between Jobs and Rights

What is the right thing to do? The market serves people to a great degree, but it distributes rewards very unequally and unfairly. Rewards, or claims on goods and services, are very closely tied to employment. The job (including self-employment) yields a wage, salary, or profit in the form of money. People then use the money to obtain necessities and amenities. The *job* is a person's ticket to a place at the feeding trough. Its serving in that way seems so obvious and natural that one hardly considers that it could be otherwise. People assume that employment gives individuals the *right* to claim good things. If some receive food, shelter, or other things from people who simply give them these things, that is viewed as charity and is outside the sphere of "rights."

Actually, the correctness of intimately tying jobs to access to goods is far from obvious. People have a right to goods regardless whether they work, and they have an obligation to work quite apart from the need for goods, or even if they have no need for goods.

Understanding that access-through-jobs is just one of many ways to link individuals to the goods they need allows us to be more flexible in judging what is fair and better at discerning ways of solving problems. Some forms of access that are not dependent on money and therefore on jobs already exist. Goods that by their nature have to be shared such as public streets, public parks, and public schools, are examples. The word "public" indicates that items are available to everyone, or to everyone in certain categories. For the purposes here, "public" refers to access because of citizenship or even because of presence in an area rather than because of job-and-money. The streets are especially public, as indicated by the convention of saying that people who do not have somewhere to stay live "in the streets." Are not the streets somewhere? Of course the streets are somewhere, but not in the sense of a shelter or space to which one has access through the job-and-money (or charity) nexus. The streets are the place to which *anyone always* has access.

Public schools are a special case. They are available to all children because of a *simultaneous decision* made a long time ago. That is, every state made the same decision; it is unthinkable that any one state would have made a contrary decision. The decision was that public funds would pay for universal, compulsory elementary and secondary education. The communities decided simultaneously that education was so important a human right that it had to be given to all. As minors, children could not refuse it, and their parents could not deny it to them. The belief was that the child's rights exist independently of their parents. It is reasonable to think that inequality in American society, great as it may be, is less than it would be if education had not been available to all.

Education could have been like everything else, a good or service which parents provide for their children if they choose and are able to do so. If this had been the case, education would have been directly tied to money and therefore to the *job* just as is everything else. Noting this clarifies that it is not inevitable or natural that the job be the basis for people's claims on things. There are other bases for rights to a share of what is available. Among them, just being a person living in the community endows one with some rights of access to things. It is in the American tradition to deny sovereignty to the job as basis for the privilege of having or using the goods or facilities the community offers.

In general, the link between the job and access to goods should be less than it is now. It is not fair that people who work and earn very low incomes should be deprived of food, clothing, shelter, and TERM. They are, after all, doing a share of labor; they are doing something that people want them to do. They therefore should have a fair share of the goods which are available. If their incomes do not suffice, then goods should be made available to them on some other basis, for they too have rights. Conversely people who earn very high incomes also deserve a share of the goods. No one may mind if their share is a bit more that of others. But a sense of justice will not allow us to approve the mammoth claims which their incomes make for them. Many wealthy individuals have incomes in the hundreds of thousands and even millions. The proportion or quantity of goods to which they can lay claim with those sums is clearly inappropriate and beyond any proper notion of what is fair.

Of these two forms of monetary (or claim) injustice--unfair deprivation and unjust superfluity--the former is of more interest in this discussion. The wealthy person's huge mansion and imported caviar hurt people only if the labor required to acquire them is diverted from producing basic goods for the less affluent. And since labor in American society has been available in excess, that is unlikely to happen. People may thus grudgingly allow, or at least view with indifference, the opulence in which some live. The fundamental task at hand is to *loosen the tie between job and access to goods*. A person's right to have what he needs should not depend as much on whether, and at what, he is employed. It should be based more on his citizenship, residence, or membership in a community. He has an obligation to work; but that obligation should be tied less to his claim on goods, just as the claim on goods should be tied less to his work. Simply having money does not relieve the person of his obligation to work.

Just as a rowboat tied to the shore and then cut loose can float down the river, so rights to goods, cut loose from the job, can move in accordance with needs and fairness--rather than being forced to move according to the arbitrary motions of the market. To accomplish this loosening, government should first increase the social wage--entitlements and assistance. Social security should be sufficient to enable retired persons to live comfortably. Some complain that providing for them takes away too much from working people and gives large amounts to the increasing number of retired persons.

However, people also grumble that jobs are in short supply and that older people should retire sooner to make room for youth. We cannot have it both ways! Money, after all, is nothing; only labor is real. If the community needs the elders' labor, these people could be allowed to work as long as they can. Only true disability, not age, has to limit them. If their labor is not needed, no one should complain; the younger populace is quite capable of providing for both themselves and the retired. After all, with advances in technology, less human power can produce more goods. This discussion has already noted that *over*production is one of America's problems. Thus, providing for the retired elderly is one way of dealing with the surplus. It certainly is no worse than exporting goods when Americans--as a community--cannot benefit by importing enough to justify (pay for) the exports.

Similarly, unemployment compensation should be generous and should never be subject to exhaustion. It may be necessary to induce people to go back to work, but arbitrary terminations of benefits should not be used as an inducement. Many people do not work because jobs are not available at all, or because what jobs there are do not pay enough (cannot be said to "pay"), or the person is not trained for the kinds of jobs that happen, at a certain time, to be available. Certainly people should be willing to work, and certainly they should accept jobs that are less than ideal. But depriving those who truly cannot do so of benefits is an evil that cannot be justified by the need to push people into jobs.

The same holds for assistance. For example, single mothers with small children often take the brunt of Americans complaining that these women are a burden on the rest of society because they are supported by the government and therefore by taxpayers. Such complaints are based on an incorrect assumption about money. All people who eat, live in dwellings, and wear clothes are *always* supported by the rest of society. That is, they consume what others produce. This is true regardless whether mothers work or not. If they do not work and receive government assistance, their claim on goods derives from taxes. If they work and do not receive assistance, their claim derives from the prices people pay for goods and services which the mothers had a hand in producing. Society will pay in one way or another. The question is not how they cease to be a burden, but whether (and how) society *wants them to contribute* to the pool of goods and services. Perhaps people imagine the women selling goods in a store, while others see the mothers devoting their time fully to caring for their children. Caring for the children, it might be argued, will do more for society in the long term, and is in this sense a better use of labor resources. If the married housewife who takes care of home and children on a full-time basis is properly devoting her energies to those tasks, might not the single mother on welfare be doing the same?

Where unemployment or the lack of adequately paying jobs is a problem, the controversy over whether government should invest in infrastructure emerges. Such a government plan does have a triple benefit. It provides wages for workers, gains customers for businesses, and provides roads and bridges for the community. Beyond a doubt, it is appropriate and beneficial to the society.

Imagine an aerial view of the United States. Looking from above, it becomes evident that workers are able to provide an abundance of goods, with labor and laborers to spare. These extra hands can best serve the community by producing goods that are shared within the group as a whole rather than owned individually. Indeed, commodities to be sold in stores and claimed by people are already available in such abundance that America duplicates stores and maintains a massive advertising industry in order to dispose of the product. So further production seems superfluous; it is production of non-goods, since they really serve no purpose. In contrast, roads and bridges *are* goods, goods shared by all rather than owned by the individual. Clearly, the way to use surplus human labor is to provide these public items.

Expenditures for infrastructure cannot be considered a burden on the community. The people who work to produce food, clothing, and shelter are well able to produce the items needed by those who work on roads, parks, and bridges. This is really all that "can afford" properly means. It might be different if society needed all workers to produce basic necessities (though the community would still need roads!). But the fact that our society suffers from unemployment means that it has a surplus of laborers. In basic terms, it stands to reason that if people currently producing necessities can provide for advertisers who cancel each other off hawking different brands of products, they can take care of those who are building parks and bridges.

Basic thinking also leads to the more general notion that the close linking of a job to a claim on goods is a major obstacle in making a

good life possible for everyone. The job market is an inevitable part
of American society. This market distributes jobs among people and
assures that there will be people to do things that society likes done,
even things that are not necessary. But this market does not distribute
rewards as it does tasks. Many jobs do not pay what any objective
observer would consider fair. Indeed, the jobs cannot pay enough.
Unfairness exists in the allocation of rewards to businesses,
government bureaus, and nonprofit organizations--just as to
individuals. It seems that the market itself is not fair and cannot be
made fair. In light of this, justice seems to require pulling away from
linking jobs to claims on goods so closely. Society can set up other
ways for people to gain rights to goods and services and to reward
people more fairly so that they may live decently.

One might think that advocates of the market would embrace this
notion enthusiastically, for it provides a way in which the market can
continue to function while, at the same time, avoid its unhappy
consequences.

Chapter 8

Leadership and Knowledge

America is an unled nation. It does not have leaders, and it is without leadership. Because of this lack, the nation is unable to live and act on the basis of its fundamental values, and it is unable to act in the interest of the welfare of its people or to achieve the goals in which these people believe.

To say that America lacks leaders may seem strange. When we read newspapers, we see frequent descriptions of what people in positions of authority are doing. The president of the country, senators, governors, and others are constantly being brought to our attention. Their actions are presented in detail and with dramatic flourish. Noting this, we would most certainly think that there are leaders. And if there are leaders, we further think, there is leadership.

Moreover, many writers have asserted that in addition to the corps of highly visible authorities, there is also a behind-the-scenes cadre of leaders. This group consists of people who do not occupy official position; they have been neither elected nor duly appointed to high office. Yet their influence over the actions of those who are in office is considerable, and they therefore control in great degree what happens in the nation and beyond. In the late 1950s, maverick sociologist C. Wright Mills said in *The Power Elite* that an informal circle consisting of the top leaders in three areas, those of government, the military, and business, effectively manage the affairs of the United States. In saying this he was opposing what was then a popular thesis, one stating that impersonal trends determine events, with people, including leaders, serving only to administer what they cannot determine. In contrast to this, Mills argued, that these elites consisted of people, and that these people were able to--and did--

decide what would happen.[32] This would certainly suggest that there are leaders. More recently, Noam Chomsky[33] and William Domhoff[34] have argued much the same.

There is another reason why it might seem strange to lament an alleged lack of leadership in the nation. This is that America is supposed to be a democracy which, as such, eschews "top-down" rule. Rather than being governed by high officials, it aspires to effective decision-making by the people themselves. Officials in high position may administer the affairs of state and of the nation, but they are supposed to do so as representatives of the people. Acting through elections, the people are to determine the basic contours of policy, while the task of leaders is to implement these policies. They of necessity make decisions about details as they implement policies, and in this sense determine a great deal of what happens. But, the idea is that the fundamental policies are determined by the people as a whole and not by someone at the "top."

In thinking this way, we assume that there is such a thing as "the people," and that those who make up this body have a collective will which is properly the basis for shaping basic government policy. Assuming this to be what is intended by the concept of "the Republic," we might think that there is nothing wrong with *not* having leaders and leadership. We may think that "democracy" or rule by the people means that there are no leaders in any sense other than officials who implement policies wanted and approved by the populace. Other nations may have kings or dictators, but we do not, nor do we want them! What we want, rather, is a cadre of officials whose own agenda for governing is congruent with, and indeed an expression of, "the people" and their wishes.

The Nature of Leadership

Despite these reasons for thinking it strange to speak of America's lack of leadership, the statement is here made in all seriousness. To see what is involved, we need to consider what leaders and leadership are, and how leaders and followers relate to each other.

Leaders are important in any society, organization, or movement. They are important, for one thing, because of the need for coordination. The many people within any society are always busy doing many things. These numerous actions are determined by each person.   With so many different centers of decision-making determining so many actions, the actions are in the nature of the case random relative to one another. Unless either a person or a process causes them to go together to form some sort of coherent pattern, they will remain random.

This randomness of actions would not be good. Communities of people have a need for some process by which the actions of each person are made to "go together" with the actions of others. Without such a process, the many actions will, in effect, cancel each other out. In their struggle to live, people will try to take things away from each other or will undertake to get to things before others do. They will engage in conflict or competition with one another. And doing so will exhaust the limited energy which could have been used in the battle with nature.

Additionally, communities often have a common objective of some sort. They need to fight human enemies; they need to hunt buffalo that roam in herds; they need to construct irrigation channels or build a "Great Wall." To do these things, they need a program by which the actions of each person will combine with those of others to produce a single effect.

To achieve this or any kind of coordination, leadership is commonly necessary. Leaders are, of course, individuals, and individuals, unlike groups (committees!) can think. They can conceive plans in their minds and envision ways in which the plans can be carried out. If they then tell the individuals within the group what to do, they can determine each person's action to be one that will fit with each other person's action. In the hunt, the leader can tell one man to sneak up on the deer from the north while others are to do the same thing from the east, south, and west. In consequence, the deer cannot escape, since a hunter approaches him from four--in effect from every--direction. Without a leader to conceive that plan and give the necessary orders, four men might have attacked the deer from the same direction, leaving the animal free to run in the other direction and, taking advantage of his superior speed, get away.

Two facts, then, explain the first reason why leadership is necessary: to survive and prosper, communities need to coordinate the actions of individuals. And, only individuals can think--can conceive plans and ways of implementing them. Individuals, then, must lead others so that all can do what they want to do.

Equally important as coordination of action is the role of leaders in relation to a group's values. Every group has values. Its members live together and talk to one another, and as they do, they give rise to shared ideas about what is right and wrong, good and evil. Each person affirms these definitions as he talks to the others and as he responds to what the others say. There is a nodding of heads or other signals indicating that certain ideas about what people should do are correct, worthy, and noble.

These definitions of the good--the values--are, however, jumbled and disorganized. They do not form a coherent whole, and they do not have determinate application. There is no certainty about how they fit together. In what way, for example, did the American ideas about human equality and freedom relate to ideas about loyalty to family, ethnic group and nation? How does the belief in hard work and taking care of oneself fit in with a commitment to tender concern for the unfortunate and deprived? How does a love of science and a disinterested search for truth mesh with an approval of a robust and joyous faith and declaration that "I believe?" The list could go on. Values, like persons within a community, can exist in conflict and competition with one another, or they can fit together to form a coherent scheme.

Closely related to this is the question of how values are to be applied. We hold an idea or an ideal; so what, then, do we *do*? The answer is often unclear, for an action that is designed to implement a value is of necessity concrete. It is a specific thing done within a specific setting. It is certain to have consequences, and these are, in every case, going to be many and varied. Among them, very likely, is the objective or goal which the action was intended to fulfill. But even if the action does bring about the desired state of affairs, it may well have other consequences that were not intended. These other effects of the action may be benign, leaving the goodness of the consequence unimpaired. Or they may be harmful, possibly so harmful as to cancel the virtue of the achieved objective. The saying "the cure was worse than the disease" refers to just this state of affairs.

The application of values, then, is a problem. Values are by their nature abstract and for this reason are nothing at all unless they are applied by means of specific actions. This vacuousness of the abstract value can be seen, for example in something that occurred in the 1994 campaign for governor of California. Kathleen Brown, a candidate for governor, was accused of not taking a stand on the issues--of, as they said, "ducking" them. She responded to her accusers by saying that she had been quite clear on what she stood for. She stood for "progress" and "prosperity" and "one million new jobs." In view of this answer, it would be necessary to concede that her accusers were right. These three items are values. The first two are highly abstract, and the third ("a million jobs") is only a little less so. But none of them is anything at all apart from a program designed to achieve them. And proposing such a program is what would properly be meant by "taking a stand on the issues."

We can see then, why leadership is necessary. The community as a whole cannot act without making decisions. Decision comes first, then action. Among the decisions that must be made before anything can be done are those that pertain to values. Questions about how values go together to form a system have to be resolved. Themes through which this systematization is accomplished must be conceived and declared. "Democracy" is such a scheme. It is a set of values, such as basic equality, rule by the people, respect for minority rights, the various freedoms, and so on. These go together to form a single thing which is then referred to by a word: "democracy." The same is true of "family," "Christianity," "humanitarianism," and others.

In addition, priorities among competing values have to be established. These make it possible to determine which value applies when two or more are involved, and it is impossible to realize all of them in an action which must be taken. The concept in criminal law of the "assumption of innocence" is such a priority scheme. It is considered good to convict (punish) the guilty, and it is considered good to acquit the innocent. Where it is unclear whether a person is guilty or innocent, a decision has to be made about which is the more important. If we cannot have both, which do we prefer? Presumably, we prefer the right of the innocent to be exonerated over the obligation of the guilty to be convicted. Therefore the judge instructs the jury to vote for acquittal if they have "a doubt." Leaders are necessary for the setting of priorities. A community cannot do this by itself any more than it can plan an action by itself.

In addition to clarifying values and arranging an order of priorities, leaders are also important in applying values. If an action is to be taken, a decision about how a value is to be applied is necessarily made. Because of the belief in racial equality, for example, groups of people engaged in boycotts. They all refused to patronize certain businesses, as happened to the bus system of Montgomery, Alabama. A boycott, we may note, is not identical with racial equality. The two are not the same thing. But the one is thought to be a device for achieving the other. However, it takes a leader to conceive such a thought. It does not arise spontaneously within a community and is certainly not carried out in that way. It took a leader, specifically Martin Luther King, to formulate the plan to boycott the bus system and to lead a large group of people in implementing it. In doing so, the leader presumably takes note of other consequences of the action. Even if the action achieves racial equality in some way and to some degree, it may have other effects as well. The leader decides in his own mind whether these other consequences are bad and, if so, whether they are too much so. He asks whether they are too high a price to pay or are, on the other hand, a fair price to pay for what is accomplished. He then seeks to persuade others that the course of action is the right one. The leader applies values.

Leaders are also important in giving a people a sense of identity as a people. We could call this a feeling of peoplehood. A king, a president, or a leader bearing any other title serves as a symbol of the community as a whole. Often, he/she has an aura of sacredness which reflects that of the society itself. To serve this way, the leader must be an embodiment of the values of the community. The people see him as an incarnation of the group itself and of what the group "stands for," and as having an aura of goodness or nobility which emanates from it. The role of the Queen of England in enabling the people of that country to "feel English" is a case in point. So also is the Pope of service in giving communicants of the Roman Catholic Church a feeling of being part of a world-wide ecclesiastical body-- "the Catholic Church." The difference in sense of belonging which distinguishes the Catholic from, for example, a Baptist, can dramatize the role of the leader here, since among Baptists there is no great leader and there is little feeling of being part of a large entity or group. Also, the president of the United States serves, among other things, to make Americans feel strongly that they are Americans.

Relation of Leaders to the Community

In a proper community, there is a *dialectical relation* between leaders and followers. A dialectical relation is one in which each of two items related to each other is given its full value. Instead of a totality being divided into two parts, each of the two is the totality, but is so in tension with the other. There is an interaction between the two which produces the outcome. In the case of leadership, a leader takes charge, so to speak, but he does so in relation to followers, who also take charge. The leader and the followers then interact to produce what it is that the group is and does.

The leader makes proposals or proclamations concerning what the group's values should be. That is, he gives indications about priorities, which values take precedence over certain other values, and how in general values are to be arranged. He also argues for applying values in certain ways. Throughout, he is a symbol of the group itself and what it stands for while standing over against the group as leader. His actions as leader--that is, his proposals or directives--serve to lead and guide the group. Through them, the group takes on a consciousness of its values which is clearer and better arranged than it would be without leadership. And it stands ready to act in a way that would otherwise be impossible. Decisions are made on what actions should be taken, and both people and facilities are coordinated in the interest of doing so.

However, in performing such a function, the leader cannot go too far afield. Though his proposals come from him and are not simple copies of the group's consciousness of itself, he cannot deviate too far from that consciousness and continue to lead. Leaders, of course, know this in most cases and have an intuitive awareness of just how far they can go without evoking rebellion in the ranks. What the leader actually does is to clarify value priorities and propose applications of the values. The followers then process these proposals or directives in their own minds. Having done so they, in effect, adopt the priority arrangements and applications, either as proposed by the leader or as modified. Once they have done this, the proposals become their own, and they act on them. But when they do, they are arranging and applying values they already hold. They are not agreeing to new or alien values, nor will they. For this reason, the leader must stay within the fold; he must keep his proposals and directives within the boundaries of the group's value system. Thus, the relation between leader and followers is one of interaction.

A major difference between leader and followers is commonly one of knowledge. The leader knows more about the foundations of the group's life than do the others within the group. That is how he is able to embody group values to an exceptional degree: he knows the structure of belief and evaluation that produce those values.

For example, it is difficult to imagine the Roman Catholic Church without there being within it a corps of people who know, among other things, about the Arian controversy of the Fourth Century. These people understand the arcane distinction between "similar substance" and "same substance," a matter about which the average communicant cares even less than he knows. Without the presence within the whole body of believers of some who understand the issue, there would be a danger that the intellectual structure undergirding Catholicism would weaken and even fall. And if the layperson were to become involved in religious issues, there could always come a point when he would need to know about the quarrel between Arius and Athenasius.

Similarly, the concept of "America," complete with patriotic symbols and stirring sounds, would be unthinkable without there being people who know about the Revolutionary War, the Constitution, the Bill of Rights, due process in law, and related matters. Not everyone who is "patriotic" needs to understand these in depth.   But could the intellectual-emotional   edifice   of "Americanism" survive without there being some who do?   The follower perceives the leader as someone who embodies values in great degree, but this commonly means that the leader *knows* matters of which the follower has only a dim awareness.

The Problem of Knowledge

People, as a matter of fact, know very little about what is going on in the world and about the affairs of the nation and of other nations. Their ignorance is not due to a lack of intelligence, nor are they altogether without information. Rather, it is because of the inherent difficulty of knowing what it is that is happening in the world. The things that happen "out there" in societies around the globe are so complex and reveal their secrets so reluctantly that a person simply cannot readily know those things. This lack of knowledge is a basic feature of the social and political landscape. But it is one whose existence and nature are generally not noticed or taken seriously. The failure to note how *little* people know is a major cause of error in interpreting the relationship of ordinary citizens to the affairs of the nation.

People react to events which take place in the world in a variety of ways. Both members of Congress visiting their districts and journalists observing what people say and do note citizens' diffuse grumbling and complaining. Election outcomes and the trends in these results give indication that people are happy or unhappy about certain things that happen in government and the economy. Polling organizations do surveys in which they find out "what people are thinking" in certain areas or in the nation as a whole. Throughout this observing of people, it is assumed that citizens observe what takes place in Congress, in business, and elsewhere and respond to it with joy or anguish, and with approval or disapproval.

What is not sufficiently understood is that people do not and cannot react to what is going on in the world; they do and can react only to what they *think* is going on in the world. They respond to events as they perceive them, not to events as they actually are. This may appear to be a truism, something that is obvious, but it bears noting. It is of course true of all human behavior. We always do what we do because of how we "map" the world around us. We construct a picture of the objects that comprise our world, and we gauge our decisions to act on that picture. We do what *will* achieve certain objectives *if* the objects which comprise our world are as we picture them.

This picture or "map" of the world may be basically true, or at least sufficiently true that our actions based on it prove to be adequate for doing what we want to do. This is the case much of the time; if it were not, we would not be able to do anything, to get home from work, for example. But the picture may also be inaccurate or false. Where this is the way it is, our actions will prove futile or may even defeat our purposes.

In the matter of the larger world, people react to events as they perceive them. These perceptions also can be accurate, inaccurate, or just plain false. But the odds against them being true are much greater than is the case with one's efforts to cope with one's own personal affairs. It is a very large world "out there," with innumerable events taking place at any one time. And it is extremely difficult to discern form and pattern in these events. Consequently, it is the usual, not the unusual, case that people's response to events is not properly speaking a response to those events. Rather it is a reaction to a distorted and altogether false perception of those events.

The Difficulty of Knowing

When the question comes up about how much do people--or for that matter how much does anyone--know about what is going on in the world of society and politics, an answer suggests itself immediately and with great force. That answer is that people know very little. Ignorance is the order of the day. To say this is not to belittle people. It is simply to note that to know about the world is extremely difficult. It is, after all, a very big and complicated world. Events taking place in it exhibit a massive complexity that defies our efforts to conquer it intellectually. It could be compared to a violent snowstorm. Snowflakes in astronomical numbers are swirling in all directions. No form or pattern can be seen in their movements. At most, an occasional circle may be observed, but for the most part there is simply random movement. So it is with society and politics. Events are so numerous and move in so many directions that a person's efforts to discern form and pattern--to see "what" is happening--are bound to be frustrated.

Moreover, each person is small and occupies a tiny place in the world. From the perspective of his little space, the large swirl of events taking place in the world touches him at only a few of an extremely large number of points. He has or is able to get a certain job; he receives a certain salary or wage; with that salary he is able to buy certain things and not others; the community accords him certain recognitions, but in other ways either denigrates or ignores him; there are people who love him and others who hate him and many others who take no notice of him. In these ways, the world touches him. The events of governments, nations and economies are taking place, and because they do so in certain ways, the world touches the person as it does rather than in some other way. His wage and what he can buy with it, for example, are as they are because of national and international events. But only a very small part of those events have intruded into his life-space.

It is evident enough that this is true of the average person. Caught up as he is in the work and play of his everyday life, he has little time to study the events about which his newspapers tell him, to say nothing of the many, often significant, events which the journalists pass over in silence. But it is also true even of those same journalists who spend all of their time trying to find out what is happening in the nation and the world. They may be intelligent and energetic, but even from their standpoint, events are so large and complex that efforts to understand them make little progress. It is simply too awesome a task. This of course does not stop people from acting as though they know what is going on. But pretending to know and knowing are not the same thing. Truthfully, to ask ordinary people, or for that matter to ask journalists or scholars, to explain world events is like asking a blind man to feel an elephant's skin for one minute and on the basis of that contact to deliver a series of lectures on elephant anatomy and physiology!

Scholars and the Complexity of Reality

As further indication of how difficult it is to force the complex world of events to yield its secrets--to find out what is happening out there in the world, we may consider what certain great social scientists did when they undertook that effort. While there have been many such scholars, we will consider just a few. They are Karl Marx, Max Weber, Emile Durkheim, and Sigmund Freud.

When Marx looked at European society, he saw social classes. To him, people divided into those who get wealth from wealth (from investment), and people who get it from selling their own labor. These two classes, the bourgeoisie and the proletariat, were to him naturally opposed in their interests and so destined to engage in continual, recurrent struggles with each other. That struggle, he believed, would continue until a decisive victory is won by the proletariat and the private ownership of the means of production and distribution is cast out or terminated, thereby putting an end to the social classes themselves.

Max Weber saw classes as did Marx. But he saw the class drama taking place as being confounded by "status." That is, he saw groups of people set apart by estimates of honor and traditional lifestyles, people who, in being so set apart, obscured the class struggle. To him, there was no true historical process taking place. The only one that could be given credence was the process he called "rationalization," a process in which bureaucracies and other structures become progressively more systematic in organization and outlook.

In contrast to both Marx and Weber, Durkheim was preoccupied with the problems of order. He saw order within the community and in the individual as being correlative. That is, as people affirm the moral order of the community, they also tame and order themselves.

He held that such order is essential to happiness--only a person who has an internal ordering corresponding to that of society, that is one who has moral sentiments, can be happy. These sentiments legitimate a set of limits on what the individual expects to be and to have and so relieve him of the need to accumulate ever more. Without such a relief and limitation, desire rises sky high and leaves the person miserable.

Freud believed that what happens in society derives from a drama which takes place within the individual. He asserted that humans are basically irrational. The seeming rationality which they exhibit in speech is really a thin veneer covering an internal jungle in which desires (sexual desires being the model) struggle with equally powerful feelings of guilt. Out of that struggle comes the person, and out of the person comes civilization with all that it contains.

As oversimplified as these capsules of various scholars' ideas may be, they show that the reality which people call European civilization is multiform and bewildering; it does not readily yield its secrets. The talented men just cited devoted their full time and energy to grappling with the evidences available to them and to discerning form and pattern in a recalcitrant reality. As one Psalm in the Bible states it, they wanted to "make visible the channels of the sea and lay bare the foundations of the world" (Psalm 18:5). Yet in the effort to do this, each came up with very different pictures of civilization. It was the same reality, but each perceived that reality differently.

Involved in the differences were contrasts in the concerns and worries of each scholar. Marx was moved primarily by the injustices he saw that people who worked were suffering. He felt these laborers were cheated in their wages, oppressed by horrible working conditions and long work days, and denied the charm that work brings to those who exercise skill and ingenuity in performing tasks from beginning to end. Rather than experiencing this "work satisfaction," workers were someone's employees who carried out mundane tasks entirely as directed. Durkheim, on the other hand, was impressed that people who succeeded in getting what they wanted could be even more miserable than they were before. Their unhappiness increased because with their improvement in circumstances, mainly financial, came an even greater rise in their aspirations. This left them with a larger gap between aspiration and reality than was in force earlier when their aspirations were lower. Comparing Marx's soot-covered, underpaid, overworked, and over-regimented laborer with Durkheim's unhappy business tycoon reveals that something within each scholar made him perceive reality differently. Thus, when today one tries to answer the question "What is going on?" one not only struggles with a bewildering mass of facts that defy understanding but also carries the struggle forward with his own inner concerns affecting his world view. Consequently, it is very likely that a business executive making a half a million dollars a year and a factory operator struggling on a fifteen-thousand-dollar annual income see things very differently when they look at the same world. William Domhoff's book *The Power Elite and the State* sharply focuses on individual humans' perceptions of reality. The typical reader is likely to be puzzled by this writer's seeming to feel that he must refute other scholars who hold opinions different from his. Why, such a reader might ask, does he not just tell us how it is rather than dragging us through discussions of what he thinks is *not* true about how it is?

There is, however, reason why Domhoff does as he does. The reason is that we can see pattern in the bewildering swirl of events only by "trying out" various interpretations of those events to see which ones fit better than which other ones. Serious scholars, he notes, have held four different ideas about what goes on in the world with specific reference to how America is governed. There is, first, the pluralist view that there are many competing groups exercising various degrees of power struggling against one another to determine how society will be governed. The result is that no one controls the national community; events are determined in the negotiation between the contrasting groups. Second, there is the "government autonomy" view that sees government as originating power within itself. It decides what to do and then does it, with other sectors of society having to come to terms with those actions. Third, there is the structural Marxist view that governmental officials are constrained by the economic structure of society to act mainly in the interest of an elite class, though without that class being actively involved. And, fourth, there is Domhoff's own view that a corporate elite controls government from behind the scenes, and in controlling government, determines what happens in society.[35]

What we see here is that events within the nation are complex enough so that it is not simply obvious that one of these (or some other) world views is true while the others are false. Rather, it is necessary to look at the complex reality and to hold up these models next to it like transparent paper with an outline drawn on it, to see how the model fits the reality. Certain areas of fact, such as data on campaign contributions, then need to be brought into view in order to see which, if any, of the four models is correct or most adequate. The need to do this should highlight for us the difficulty of knowing our world.

The Problem of Bias

Sheer complexity seems troubling enough, but in addition, there is also the problem of *bias*. People are confronted with a complex array of facts and are assigned the task of interpreting those facts. Quite naturally their interpretations will be different. Individual or accidental factors will cause them to handle the data differently. What they notice and what they ignore will be different, and they will see any given reality from different angles. But, in addition, one person may *want* the facts to favor a certain interpretation of events, while someone else will just as earnestly *want* the facts to refute that way of explaining what takes place. A certain person, for example, wants measures designed to maintain high wages and therefore wants "demand" to be a policy which serves to keep an economy going and its people prosperous and happy. Another has an equally strong desire for such a "statist" policy to fail. This second person wants tax reductions for the wealthy to have the effect of shoring up investment, which in turn moves the economy into high gear, to the benefit of everyone. In the meantime, the first person wants *that* policy to fail. What we wish would happen may determine what we think does happen.

This is not to deny that people take the facts seriously. A person getting ready to cross the street takes the data about cars on the street very seriously indeed. No wish about the facts distorts his perceptions of what those facts--those cars--are. More generally, we human beings have a considerable ability to note the true facts of a case. The wish only influences our perception of facts; it does not altogether determine what the perception is. If this is true of what we think about cars on the street, it can also be true of our perceptions of political and social realities.

Still, wish and fact do interact, for wish has a power like a magnetic or gravitational pull. A person can contemplate bodies of fact and reason logically. But a wish pulls on his line of reasoning and makes it bend away from its natural direction. Just how far it bends depends on the wish's strength and on the person's self-discipline. Some persons are more determined and more inclined than others to repress wishes in order to remain faithful to fact and reason. Others more readily allow their desires about the world to shape their beliefs about it. There are occasions where wish is so strong and so augmented by a note of legitimacy or goodness that it distorts thinking and pulls it from the course to which evidence and logic would push it. There are other times when the need for objectivity or the moral commitment to it is so powerful that it overcomes mighty biases and keeps observations within the intellectual "straight and narrow." We presume that scientists, scholars, and jurors in court all have such a commitment.

Examples of such interplay between fact and wish abound. People who work in the tobacco industry find the arguments which link smoking to cancer and other diseases to be *un*convincing more frequently than do others. The facts, in their view, just do not point in that direction. Similarly, people who owned slaves in the United States prior to 1860 found it easy to believe that Negro people had a basic slave nature and were for that reason happier in the slave condition than in any other. In general, people who profit from something are easily convinced that the profitable thing is right and just. If facts are involved, they quickly find facts that are consistent with their position. This can usually be accomplished by a judicious selection of facts from among the mountain of data available. Even in cases where the facts seem clear and certain conclusions seem unavoidable, human ingenuity is equal to the task of picking and choosing so that a desired vision begins to look like a true one.

Partisans of socialism or a strong welfare state can, for example, cite certain facts. They can note that statistics on infant mortality and life expectancy are far better in China than in India. Since China has been communist or socialist, while its neighbor to the south has been capitalist, this fact would seem to support their assertion that socialism performs better for people than does capitalism. Additional confirmation is derived from setting communist Cuba and social welfarist Costa Rica alongside most of the rest of Latin America. By contrast, those devoted to capitalism, such as Peter Berger, cite the cases of the four Asian "dragons," South Korea, Taiwan, Hong Kong, and Singapore, who seem to fare so well as capitalist performers in the world market.[36]

Marxian thought holds that a person's entire view of reality is shaped by his position in society. Members of the bourgeoisie have a vision of economic and social reality that justifies their privileged position within the social order. They do not see a pure capitalist system as being good only for them; they see it, rather, as best for all people of all occupations and economic levels. To them, it has power to generate approved macroeconomic conditions such as economic growth or increased productivity, and these conditions, they believe, will produce more of what is good for everybody, notably for the poor. Indeed, Peter Berger, a sociologist and leading advocate of pure capitalism, accepts the view that economic systems should be evaluated on the basis of how well they provide for the poorest sectors of society, and he argues that capitalism does the best job of providing for those sectors. Additionally, members of the capital-owning class commonly have views about the nature of human beings, about society, and about God that favor the capitalist system.[37]

So strong is this association of privilege, according to Marxian thought, that only a few can be expected to escape it. Just a minority in the capitalist class, those gifted with uncommon vision and a sense of justice, can rise above their own class position to see things as they really are. Apart from them, people in the working class, being free of capitalist entanglement, can see things more clearly. The role of wish in determining thoughts and beliefs is, however, not just a matter of identification with certain sectors of society. When people believe in any cause, they typically seek out others who share their enthusiasm and then organize a group to take some sort of action. They interact with these others over periods of time, and eventually the like-minded group becomes important for its own sake. A person wants to belong and to gain rank and recognition within the group. Being as important as they are, the groups then give shape to people's image of reality. If the group is the Ku Klux Klan, the participants will see reality not only in a way shaped by their identification with the white community, nor will it be simply the racial prejudice that inclined them towards the Klan in the first place. Rather, for them reality will take on a shape which is specifically KKK and which justifies and exalts the Klan's existence and actions.

Similarly, when feminists organize to promote women's interests and equality among the sexes, the group is not simply pro-women or committed to equal rights for women and men. More than that, the members of feminist organizations hold an image of reality which is nurtured by the social circle in which they are intensely involved, by the feminist organization. This construction of reality occurs because the partisans of the group spend a great deal of time together, and in their conversation, they generate images of the world and of the true and the good. And it occurs because the group is important to each member for her--or his--sense of self.

In both cases, that of the KKK and the feminist organizations, the images of reality will be different from those held by people who share the group's initial value commitments. The views of the KKK will differ from those of people who share their views about white people, black people, and the relations between these two racial groups, but who have no identification with the Klan as a group. People who believe in greater justice for women in many spheres of life will also see things differently from the way things are viewed by those who not only hold that belief but who also participate in feminist organizations or informal social circles. When people come together to support a cause, the group they form takes on a life apart from the cause and produces its own images of reality.

This world view may feature, for example, proposed changes in living patterns that have no hope of being realized. Racists on both sides of the black-white divide have, for example, suggested that there should be a total segregation, one in which the two races would occupy different parts of the country. Some black leaders speak of having a world apart without explaining what the economic base of that world would be. Some feminists have advocated a solidarity within a "sisterhood" for which the majority of women, especially those of heterosexual orientation, see no need. What makes these fanciful imageries viable as group cultures is that they are material or intellectual "charters" for the group's solidarity or feeling of itself rather than serious proposals for action within society.

Social reality is complex and multiform, and it touches the observer only at a few points. Therefore, it is very sluggish and of uncertain step in displaying intelligible pattern. Bias also complicates matters further by bending images of reality to conform to a person's specific wishes. There is a special kind of bias that appears in groups which exist to support a cause but which take on their own nature and construct realities to fit that contrived nature.

Journalism and Knowledge

If the swirl of events touches an individual himself/herself at only a few points, much more reveals itself to him through the mass media of communication. Both broadcast and print media serve as a major go-between which brings the great, wide world of events close to people so that they can know about those events. These forms of "news," as we call them, make it possible for people to know much more about what is happening than they would be able to find out from their personal experience. Even so, there are tremendous limits. At best, the media also make contact with only a tiny piece of what is taking place in government and society.

Much more is wrong with the media, however, that just their finitude and inherent limits. In addition, there are features of newspaper and television news which assure that the versions of reality which they present will be distorted. Foremost among these confounding aspects is the fact that the media are themselves business enterprises, and the people who determine the shape of their operations are identified with business. This identification is economic, professional, and also ideological. There is a point of view which is taken for granted among the owners and editors of the broadcast and print media which determines what events will be regarded as "news" and how the news about those events will be presented.

In the past, journalism was a profession. Newspapers were businesses of course, but in addition they cherished an ethic and a sense of honor of the professional. The journalist was not just selling something; he was also a central figure in the drama of Democracy. He was a guardian and hero of rule "of, by and for the people." A people could comprise a democracy only if it was an informed people, and the journalist's office and task was to inform the people. In everything he did, he exerted his best efforts to enlighten the citizens of the republic about matters of importance to them. He gathered the news and he reported it with as much accuracy and objectivity as he could muster. Further, his work was important from the "First Amendment" standpoint. He was exercising freedom of the press and making its benefits available to the public at large, whether the government (or anyone else) liked it or not. His communications were an integral part of the democratic way of life.

Nowadays, this professional character of journalism, if not totally eclipsed, is at least seriously compromised. In the present era, newspapers have become substantially dependent on advertisers for their revenues. Advertisers are businesspeople; they do all they can to encourage people to use (buy) their products, and they take a dim view of anyone or any action that threatens to stand in the way of that project. If the newspapers in which they advertise are publishing material which is unfavorable to their sales efforts, they take steps to stop it. No belief in the importance of free and objective reporting is going to stand in their way.

Also, there has been a trend in recent decades towards merger and consolidation of media enterprises. With the enlargement of the corporations that present the news has come an increased identification with corporate elites and a strengthened determination to bring the troops (the reporters), into line. Views about the professional character of journalism and the importance of reporters' freedom do not thrive in this kind of environment. Several reporters who sought to write the truth about what was going on in El Salvador and Nicaragua, for example, found their work being questioned or rejected. Even a simple presentation of facts was labelled "advocacy journalism" and ruled out on that account.

Alongside the biasing factors associated with identification of journalism with elite circles have been certain features of the journalism as a profession. Like many other workers, journalists operate under a great deal of pressure. In order to keep their jobs and hopefully to advance, they have to perform well in accordance with the criteria by which their work is to be evaluated. The wish to acquit themselves well in their professional activity, moves them, over time, to shape their entire activity to conform to the bases actually used in judging them. Whatever way of performing a task elicits a "job well done" from superiors is carried out with gusto, and whatever has no bearing on the boss's response tends to be ignored. It is easy to imagine that after several years of working in the environment of the modern newspaper or television channel, reporters come to think and feel in very standardized ways.

Further, there is an understandable tendency for journalists to identify with an American nationalist world view. The central feature of this view is that America is good and right. If the nation is engaged in an activity outside its borders, that activity must be good and must be in support of what is good--that is, of democracy.

Americans, we may note, talk to each other all the time, and as they converse, they generate definitions of the good and noble. These definitions inevitably make the group which Americans together comprise appear to be good and sacred. With people in general sharing this view, the reporter will usually take his place among them. He will do so because he *is* one of them, and he will do so because he understands well that his writing must reflect this nationalist point of view if he is to fare well in his career.

What we have here, then, is a *culture of journalism*. This is an image of reality in which certain events in the world are "news" while others are not and in which it is good, noble, and dignified to speak of these events in certain ways. The journalist who chooses the events properly and presents them in the approved ways feels assured that he is a member-in-good-standing in the journalist fraternity. So strongly does he covet that good standing that he will ignore alien ideas that might haunt him in moments of solitude.

Among the approved ways of doing journalist work is to put emphasis on those events that take place within eminent social circles in American society. The president of the nation, members of Congress, and others talk about things that happen and about issues. They also make decisions. This talking and deciding are themselves events. Those who do the talking are of course speaking about something. Their comments refer to things that happen "out there" in the world. Perhaps the president, some senators, and other dignitaries are discoursing about a famine in Africa, a strike in Nebraska, or a sudden rise or fall in the stock market or the unemployment rate. But what is important for journalism is not the famine, strike, or change in rate. Rather, it is that elected officials are talking about these matters. The crucial thing is not the objective event; it is instead the discussion or the giving of speeches *about* that event.

Inevitably, the reader or listener who wants to know about the world will be frustrated. Little scraps of information will of course be given to him. But these are the crumbs that fall from the table of a report in which verbal exchanges among dignitaries are the vital subject-matter being reported. Even the details of congressional activity fall victim to this selectivity. The fact that two senators, or a senator and the president, are arguing about a plan to solve one or another problem, perhaps a health plan, is more important than the plan itself.

In addition to frustrating the person whose gaze reaches beyond Washington, journalism of this type also gives the news a superficiality it does not have to have. Whenever a thing happens, eminent people of course react to it. They talk, they make gestures of approval and disapproval, and they do things. An observer might like to see these responses as well as the event itself. But he does not want to see them *instead* of the events. They are not supposed to take the place of observations of the happenings to which these people reacted. Just this, however, is currently what happens when the news is reported. The reader or listener hears about what happens right now or today and about what the important people are saying to each other, but he is left without knowledge of processes which take place behind these visible and dramatic events.

Throughout, the journalist is of course asking about the audience which hears or sees his reports. He wants to know just what will seem interesting to the people and what will not. More precisely, he wants to know what will hold their attention so that they will continue to buy his paper or tune in to his channel. For if they do, his employers will then regard him as valuable and will reward him accordingly. In thinking about the audience, he has certain ideas about them which he learned early in his career. One of these ideas is that the people who hear or read what he says have little patience and must be informed very quickly. So, what he presents must have a "flash" character; it must say something that can be understood immediately and without much explanation. Certainly any explanation that is made must not be elaborate or go through a series of steps. Thus, there is the rule in television broadcasting that "talking heads" are not to be on longer than ten seconds. The listener, after all, can change the channel so easily, and he is likely to do so unless there is a vibrancy in the presentation that he finds gripping.

This belief that the audience is impatient is only partly something that is discovered--or thought to be discovered--by journalists. The other part is that it is *created* by newspaper writers and by broadcasters. In thinking that it is so, they make it so. That is, they treat the audience like a person who has to be entertained by "flash" reports of events, and as a result the people who hear the news come to expect it. Journalists have created the reality and have not just discovered it. Reports by foreign journalists will often seem dull to the American listener, since these reporters from other countries have not learned the "flash" or "soundbite" style of newscasting and are in the habit of explaining things in steps. In their case, calling their reports "boring" should be taken as compliment; good reports that truly inform will seem dull to people accustomed to reports that strain for vibrancy more than they struggle to convey knowledge.

Reports of the fighting in El Salvador during the 1980s provide illustration. These reports mentioned that there were "death squad" killings going on in that country, with agents of the government being the perpetrators. But, as noted in Chapter Seven, these reports somehow managed to convey information in a way that made it seem unimportant. The listener did not catch on that the government of the United States was providing military support to a government that was killing its own people. And George Bush, then the president of the country, could speak about El Salvador as a "democracy" without being asked how that title could be given to a government that murders its own citizens. In this example, we see both the fact of bias in American news reporting and the superficiality inflicted on the American public by those who purport to be giving the people information about the world.

As if the problem of knowing about reality were not awesome in itself, the fact that the United States has such poor news reporting certainly adds to our perplexity. How can people *know* what is happening in the world when it is complex to begin with and when the media give them so little help?

Knowing and Wanting

Considering all of the above, we should be very cautious about saying what it is that the people of the United States *want* government policies to be. Reporters and commentators speak constantly of just that. They say that the nation's people want one or another measure to be taken, or are in a certain degree conservative, liberal, or "centrist." Politicians speak frequently of going "to the people" to find out what they want.

What we should say by contrast is that the people *do not know what they want government policy to be.* They certainly have wants, and they certainly know something about the way they want their lives to be, but this does not mean that they know what they want government to do or what policies it should carry out. Another way to say this is to assert that they do not know how to *line up* the wants or desires that are inside them, that are in their minds and hearts, with the options of policy that are "out there" in the world of society and politics. We can think of those policies as items on a menu, and people are going to choose from the menu. Just as the diner in a restaurant seeks to assess what on the menu will please his taste and satisfy his hunger, so the citizen looks for a match between available options and the lacks or wishes that he has. To do so, he of course must know something about the options. He must, indeed, know a great deal about them. And he must also know about what it is that he wants. He must, that is, have some clarity about his own desires.

The knowledge of options is what Americans are lacking. They do not know enough about the proposals that are before Congress or about the decisions which that body is making. They do not and cannot know enough because the matters involved are terribly complex. Even experts, or supposed experts, do not know enough. Economists, after all, do not have a good record of understanding the effects of policy options. In addition to being overwhelmed by the complexity of the reality which they study and by its reluctance to yield its secrets, these scholars are also affected by the factor of bias, their own and those of others. Thus we cannot expect economists, or for that matter scholars ("experts") in general to provide the necessary knowledge.

Additionally, expressions of opinion are often made for the emotional satisfaction they afford rather than because they are serious assessments of what the effects of government policies will be. When a person expresses himself in certain ways, he "feels better" than he did before. He is angry, though he may not know what or who the proper object of his anger is. But by locating a person or group who appears to be that proper object, and expressing hostility against him or against it, he feels that he has "gotten it out of his system" and is no longer so frustrated. Thus, people do not know enough in the first place, and when they express themselves, that expression may serve functions other than the serious effort to find out what it is in the world that is causing their troubles and problems.

Further, people do not know how to "line up" their inner wishes with broad policy categories. Could they get what they want from a "liberal," a "centrist," or a "conservative" policy? Assuming that these terms can take on determinate meaning, people do not know which degree or kind of any one of these will give them want they want. Nor can they judge among a related set of categories, such things as "socialism," "capitalism," and "the welfare state." Here also, the news media and politicians are not helpful. They do not describe or consider in a serious way what the options are.

In the 1984 presidential election, the Democratic candidate, Walter Mondale, said in a speech that he had inquired of the American people during the last four years about what it was that they wanted. He carried out that investigation as a response to the defeat of the Democratic candidates in the previous election, that of 1980. He seemed to be saying that this was an effort to recover from that loss and prepare for a victory in a subsequent contest. Presumably, the previous Carter administration had erred on that point. It had failed to give the people what would satisfy them, and that is why they elected Ronald Reagan in 1980.

The contention here is that Mondale was fundamentally in error. It is not the task of leaders to find out what the people want and then do it. The people do not know what they want, and it is part of leadership to help them find out. His job should have been to figure out what it was that was making people unhappy and to then propose to the people ways of solving their problems.

What are People's Wishes?

It would seem obvious enough that people want to be in better shape economically. They would like their incomes to be greater, their expenses less, and their taxes lower, and they would like all of these to be more secure in the present and in the future. Noting this takes us some distance towards understanding what it is that bothers people. There are, however, other wishes that move people. For example, members of certain ethnic groups who make their livings in occupations of little prestige feel left out in American society, and are resentful of fair-haired "college-boy types" who seem to outrank them and possibly to denigrate them.   Much of what appears to be excessive patriotism or religious or moral fundamentalism is really an effort to prove that "I am as good as you are." This being viewed as being "as good as" can take a number of different forms, and the wish for it explains many of people's actions and attitudes.

Similarly, for some people, being "as good as" others is no problem, but it is also not sufficient. They want to be *better* than others and they feel entitled to that status. Perhaps a reason why corporate elites have so little interest in the "demand" side of the economic equation is that it does not seem to allow them a sufficient exaltation. As leaders of business and industry, they feel they should be in charge and that others should submit. What they seek from economic measures is, for this reason, not only that the economy should function well, but also that their authority should be respected. Unemployment, for this reason, is not so terrible--to them. It weakens the working man's position and thereby increases the power of the owners and managers of industry. This wish for authority is different from a simple desire to be rich.

To systematize this, we can suggest that there is a vertical and a horizontal dimension to people's wants or wishes. In the vertical dimension, we can see a contrast between a person's wanting to be "as good as" others and the wish to be above them. In the horizontal dimension, we can note that people want (1) to be regarded or evaluated by others in a certain way, (2) to be accepted as having a certain relation to others within the community and, (3) to be able to determine what happens. The two dimensions are combined in the following scheme:

Rank	Evaluation	Acceptance	Control
Above others	Prestige	Fame	Power
Equal to others	Dignity	Belonging	Autonomy

In distinguishing one kind of wish from another, we frequently begin with the economic wish, the wish for good income and low expense, and we then set it apart from wishes that seem to be more of a social-emotional or psychological character. From the standpoint of the desire for economic well-being, the latter is something of a residue; it is what is left when the economic motive is taken away. It is people's *other* kind of motivation.

The above scheme is a presentation of the residue, of the social-emotional wishes that people have and that often have a bearing on their voting and other kinds of political behavior. We note first that some people want to be above others. These want *prestige*; they want to be admired and accorded high rank, or regarded as being better than common or ordinary people. If a person does not aspire to being above others, his wish is one that is similar, but in his case it may be called a desire for *dignity*. It is a desire to be respected as being on a level with and "just as good" as others. Second, the person with the higher aspiration wants to be *famous*. It is important, to him, that people in many places would know who he is and a great deal about him. He wants to be a celebrity whose name is recognized, so that everywhere he goes, people say to each other, "do you know who *that* is?" To live in obscurity is what the person most wants to avoid. By contrast, the person who wishes only to be on a level with others wants to *belong*; he wants others within a group to accept him as one of them. His wish is to be regarded as a "good American" who is a member of the national community. Or he may want to be a member of a subgroup, to be an Italian, a Mason, a Presbyterian, a scientist, or an AIDS activist.

Third, the individual who aspires to high position would like to have *power*. To him, it is satisfying that he tells others what to do, and they do it. He wants to be like the Roman centurion described in the Bible who says to one "go" and he goes, and to anther "come" and he comes, and to his slave "do this" and he does it (Luke 7:8). That is, he wants to control the behavior of others and to direct what happens within the community regardless what the content of this control or of this direction may be. Very different from him is the person who has no wish to be over others but who does want to manage himself. To him, the important thing is *autonomy*. He wants to have some control over his circumstances and over what he will do. He wants to escape the fate of the puppet whose every action carries out a directive from elsewhere--or from above. The feeling of being controlled is what he wants to avoid. He likes, for example, to plan just how he will do his daily work and then to carry out that plan. When workers at any job are closely controlled, they often exhibit signs of anger and resentment, even when other features of the job are good.

Unlike the economic wish, about which people are quite open, most people are unclear about these other wishes. American culture encourages people to be assertive when it comes to the desire for income or low expenses, but it does not provide much support for people who are lacking in dignity, belonging, or autonomy, and is even less approving of the wishes for prestige, fame, or power. Therefore, it is not easy to assess the role these wishes play in people's political responses and actions.

Yet we should be clear that they are involved in what people think and do in the realm of politics. A person may not say that he voted in a certain way because that candidate held out more promise of dignity for ordinary people--or for him--than did his rival. He is likely to say that the rival seems conceited or proud, and that the favored candidate is "just plain folks" or "more like one of us." Behind these comments, however, there may well be a smoldering anger over the loss, or threatened loss, of dignity, belonging, or autonomy. Further, it may not be the policies of the candidate for whom one votes that seem to promise help on filling these desires. It may instead be something about the person, such as the social group to which he seems to belong or which he seems to favor.

And we may be reminded at this point that what seem to be economic desires are not purely economic most of the time. People do not want money just for what it can buy, certainly not for just what it will buy that will provide comfort or pleasure. Rather they want money--always more money--because it is good in itself or as abstracted value. The wish for it, that is, is social-emotional or "psychological" in nature and not simply practical.

Knowledge, Wishes, Values and Leadership

People engage in many political acts. Among them are voting, commenting to friends and neighbors about candidates and issues, and participating in organized efforts to persuade officials to use their powers in certain ways or to induce voters to vote for certain candidates. Some of these acts are instrumental. That is, they are intended to achieve an objective. A person may vote with an intent to increase the probability, if ever so slightly, that a candidate will win. He discusses politics with others because he hopes to thereby influence their vote. Others of his political acts may, however, be expressive. In performing the act, that is, he is "getting it off of his chest"; he is getting an emotional satisfaction from the act quite apart from whether he achieves anything by it. A political action, like any action, is a concrete act, and it may have any number of motives or objectives.

Involved in any political act are some things that are interior to the individual. These include his knowledge or beliefs about the world around him and his wants and desires. These have just been discussed. Also interior are the values which he holds, discussed earlier in this chapter.

In performing an act, the person seeks to "line up" the elements that are interior to him with those that are exterior, to the objective world beyond him. He does so with the belief that the objective world will cooperate. If his beliefs about that world are true, his action will of course be based on the world as-it-is, and for this reason he will enjoy a far greater likelihood of achieving his objective. That is, the world of fact is in more cases going to cooperate and grant success to the persons's effort to control it. It will yield what he wants and bring about the condition of which he approves.

For example, if he thinks that a certain government policy, perhaps reduced taxes for ordinary people (to encourage demand) or for the wealthy (to encourage investment), will overcome a recession, he may or may not be right. If he is right and if the policy he favors is carried out, then the recession will be overcome and people--including him--will be able to find jobs. His action was based on a belief about reality. That the belief was congruent with reality is true, and the action based on it worked. The same thing holds in the case in which a person has a commitment to a value or an idea of what is "good." Perhaps a white person believes in equality for Afro-Americans. He also believes that demonstrations and other overt acts will help in overcoming tendencies towards discrimination and in hastening the achievement of racial equality. If he is right, he will get what he wants. But since he is, in this case, unselfish and wants something for others rather than for himself, we say he gets that which he approves rather than that which he wants. Whether it is a wanting or an approving, the desired state of affairs will be achieved if and only if the value is coupled with a correct assessment of the factual order, or how things work in the world.

There is, then, the problem of the "fit" between what people believe and what is really "out there" in the world. That is, there is the question whether what people believe is *true*. Do the interior elements and objective reality go together? There is also a question about the contents of the interior life itself. How well do a person's wishes and desires match up with his beliefs, and to what extent do his values fit logically with one another and form a system?

This is where leadership comes in. People have beliefs about economic and related matters. They do not know whether these beliefs are correct, much as they might think that they are. It is the leader's job to help them find out. As leader, he is always also a teacher. He makes a more intense study of the realities, perhaps the economy, than do others, and on the basis of that study, he can help people find out whether they are right. Of course, he can be wrong too. Scholars and journalists as well as politicians commonly hold opposing views, and when they do, no more than one of them can be right. Leaders cannot, therefore, tell people for certain what the truth is. But they can bring about a more serious kind of inquiry than people engage in on their own.

Also, just as the leader does not take a conception of people's beliefs as data or solid "givens" which will serve as the basis for his efforts to convince them that he is the best candidate for office, so he also does not take their wants and their value judgments as simply given. People, we may note, believe many things and hold many values. Among these beliefs and values, many are inconsistent with one another. As said early in this chapter, the values are not well organized or ordered in terms of priority, and they do not automatically apply themselves. People constantly arrange their values and apply them. It is the task of leaders to help them with this undertaking. If people, for example, believe in "equality of opportunity," leaders should help them to assign that value a place in their larger scheme of values. That place may be as top priority or in some other place, but it should have a place. And leaders should be busy suggesting how the value is to be applied.

We could say that the governmental measures which were called "affirmative action" illustrated such leadership in action. The belief in equality of opportunity was assigned a place in a value scheme and then applied. Here as elsewhere, the place assigned to the value cannot be at the very top. One cannot simply support equality with total abandon or in any and all circumstances. It has to have a place alongside of and often in competition with other values. It could, for example, be more important than order and peace within communities, or it could be less so. Or it could be the one under certain circumstances and the other in other circumstances. Whatever is of value has to be honored to a proper degree, but so do other things that are of value, and decisions about what-is-more-important-than-what have to be made. There have to be priorities. They do not have to be rigid and unchanging, but they have to be.

Along with this clarification of values, there is also the question of application, of achieving the desired state of affairs. The affirmative action programs may achieve the desired goals or may fail to do so. This is a question of application, not of the value itself. The fact that one favors equality does not of necessity mean that he favors affirmative action or any specific program. Such a program may fail to bring about a realization of the value, in which case it could be wrong even if one embraces the value. Or it could achieve it but have too much in the way of "side effects" that are not desired. Possibly it sets black poor people against white poor people with the result that the poor-as-such are divided and therefore weaker as they confront the wealthy adversary. On the other hand, even if it does not achieve its stated objective, it may have results that are good and of value so that the program merits support. Perhaps affirmative action has not brought about economic equality between African-American and their white fellow-citizens. But it may have resulted in white people becoming accustomed to black people and in black people being found in all positions, being randomly distributed among the roles that people play, so to speak, and that may be good as far as it goes. Because there are questions about value priorities and application, there is a need for leadership. Establishing priorities and applying values are by their nature tasks that groups as such cannot carry out. They can be carried out only when leaders interact with a group to bring about the necessary inquiries and clarifications.

The thesis of this chapter is that America lacks leadership and leaders. The nation seems, in one way, to exalt rank-and-file citizens to the point where there is no need for leadership. The politician needs only to find out what people "want" and then give it to them. As a candidate for office, he thinks his job is to convince the voters that he can deliver what they want better than can his rivals. It would seem that he wishes to respect the people of the nation so much that he is afraid to suggest that they might need leadership. What is wrong is that by so doing, he accepts what Ortega y Gasset called "the revolt of the masses" in his book bearing that title.[38]

In another way, however, we do the opposite. Both people who influence what office-holders do and the office-holders themselves conceive what it is that all of them want to do, and they set out to do it. In acting this way, the office-holders feel that they are equipped with the best possible counsel. A group of experts, perhaps corporate leaders, have suggested what should be done, and their suggestions appear to be unassailable. It is therefore followed without question. The people--that is, the large mass of voters--are viewed as a problem. It is necessary to induce them to go along, and for this reason policies have to be marketed or presented by experts on public relations. There is no notion of give-and-take with the public. The only problem is how to obtain the public's compliance, as Barry Sussman notes in his *What Americans Really Think and Why Our Politicians Pay No Attention.*[39]

In contrast to both, this discussion proposes the concept of leadership. Leaders lead. That is, they do not begin with where followers are and go on from there. Rather, they make proposals to which followers will respond. In doing so, they help them learn what the truth is about relevant sectors of reality, and they help them clarify and apply values. In other words, leadership seeks to help people *line up* their wishes and their values with the social, economic, and political options that are before them. A further analysis of leadership will be taken up in the next chapter.

Chapter 9

Types of Leadership

The last chapter asserted that America is a nation without leadership. In support of this statement, the chapter considered what people know about the world of affairs, and suggested that they in fact know very little. It also discussed values, and noted that people have a system of values that is only partly consistent and that the application of values is problematic.

In Chapter Eight, it was suggested that people do not have the knowledge necessary for lining up their wishes with the set of policy options available to them. They are not able, for this reason, to choose among the proposals that are being processed by their governments and cited in campaign speeches by candidates for office. Nor are they able to make choices among broad categories of policy, such as liberal or conservative or such as socialist or capitalist. Political parties and their rhetoric remain equally mysterious relative to what it is that people want. The sheer complexity of the world "out there" in combination with the distorting effects of the "wish" make it all but impossible for people to know which of the political options available to them is best.

On the matter of values, Chapter Eight noted that the community's value system is an uncodified collection of partly consistent, partly inconsistent principles or proverbs. These define what is considered good and what is viewed as bad. But they cannot develop into a value *system*, properly so called, unless some work is done. The work that is necessary is that of systematizing the values and of applying them. This is work that by its nature cannot be done by a community acting simply as a community. It is necessary, instead, to have leaders who will do the work on their own and then invite the people, in effect, to join them in the process. Leaders and community do the work in interaction with each other.

If this work is not done, people are left with a jumbled mass of values and with tribal-like loyalties. That is, the preservation of the group itself becomes the one and only value; others are at best subordinated to it, and at worst, ignored. In America, if the work is not done, patriotism emerges as the prime, and perhaps only, value. The constellation of values denoted by the phrases "the American way" and "democratic freedoms" lives on, but only, so to speak, at the pleasure of patriotism. The values are always in danger of being washed ashore by the waves of tribal enthusiasm.

Power and Authority

This chapter now moves on from the above issues, covered in Chapter Eight, to discuss *leadership and leaders*. A leader is someone who exercises power. What he wishes would occur within the community is more likely to actually take place than are the wishes of others. Or, in Max Weber's words, a person has power when "he is able to influence the course of a communal action, regardless of the content of that action."[40] A person's power derives from several different bases, but all have in common that a person or small group can by wanting others to do certain things and by making that wish known in certain ways, cause people to act in the desired ways.

As was noted in Chapter Eight, power has a circular character. Certain people have power because everyone else thinks that they have it. Each person thinks that each other person sees a certain individual as having power; he therefore sees himself as outnumbered by all those others, so to speak, and for that reason acts on the assumption that the individual has power. And in acting that way, he makes it true. The thinking is self-validating; it is true because believing it causes it to be true.

There are several types of power. One type is governmental or *political* power. Here the leader has what Weber calls a "staff," a tightly-organized group that follows the leader's orders precisely. This small group enforces the leader's decisions within a much larger, less closely-knit, group of people. When people do not act as the leader wishes, the staff punishes those malefactors in one way or another. When people follow the leader's lead, the staff rewards them. They give people very good practical reason, we could say, for conducting themselves in ways that please the head or chief. Additionally, because each person thinks that each other person will do the chief's bidding, he thinks that he should do so as well. If he does not, others, acting at the behest of the man at the top, will do bad things to him--or so he thinks.

In other cases, the power base is *economic*. In this case, a person has a claim on goods and services (money) that others within a group will honor. They honor it because each person thinks that every other person will honor that claim. People give someone things because when they do, some of the claim will then transfer to them. Interested in gaining a claim to goods, then, many people do the bidding of the person who is able to bestow that claim upon them (give them money). In still other cases, the basis of power is *priestly or sacerdotal*. The person can control what others do because he stirs in them feelings of obligation. With his priestly power, he can make people think that they should do certain things. They then do them because they think that others think that one should do as the priest says. Each of these others, in turn, thinks that way because he thinks that others do, and so on. The leader's messages about obligation come clothed in rich metaphors and symbolic systems--he expounds upon God or the gods; he preaches the threats of hell and the promises of heaven; and he discusses the location of the soul in the next life. Still, his symbolic exhortations all imply that people *should* act in certain ways.

In addition to these power bases, the leader also obtains his power from the legitimacy that those whom he influences grant him. He has, as Weber said, *authority* as well as power. His directives affect what is in people's minds and not just their behavior. Of course, people who exercise power do not always have authority. Sometimes they have only power. The word "tyrant" refers to a ruler who has and uses power over people, but does so without legitimacy; for this reason his control of people may be called raw power and is not authority. Such a person is not properly speaking a leader. People may do as he says, but they do so because they recognize that he can affect their lives in many and quite specific ways. He can, for example, impoverish or even kill them. Or he can reward them with wealth or high position. People follow his orders because of what they calculate may happen to them, for good or ill, and not because of the leader himself. There is no sense of obligation to take and follow the orders. There is only a calculation that it would be smart to do so.

A leader, then, is someone who is able to control, in some degree, what others do, and he exercises that control legitimately. Max Weber has distinguished three types of leaders. The traditional leader, such as a king or bishop, has authority grounded in a sacred order inherited from the past. Rational-legal leaders, such as corporate officers and administrators, get their authority from an organization or a structure that has a specific purpose and which is maintained by force of law. The charismatic leader contrasts sharply with the other two types, for he holds no office. His authority, rather, arises from his interaction with the group he leads. It seems, to those in the group, that his leadership ability is intrinsic, resident in the leader's unique presence or in his personality.[41]

In this discussion, distinguishing between these three types is not crucial. Instead, leaders will be divided into three types on the basis of the relation of leaders to those who follow. A contrast will be made between three items--the leader, the followers, and the knowledge-and-values systems of the community. In the first of these, the absolute leader, the leader is expected to shape the system himself; in the second, the non-leader, the community does the shaping; in the third, the counselor leader, the knowledge-and-value system is shaped by the leader and the followers in interaction with each other.

The Absolute Leader

The absolute leader has *authority* that can be political, economic, or priestly. He can be traditional, legal, or charismatic. What sets him apart from other leaders is that his authority is absolute. He has the right, according to the community, to tell people what to do, what to think, or both. If he tells people to do something, the fact that he has issued such a directive is in itself reason enough why they should do it. They do not have to understand the purposes of their actions, nor do they have to agree in their conscience that it is right, moral, or just; they need only to act in certain ways because the leader has so ordered. That is sufficient. Obedience is the prime virtue. An act is good merely because the leader has ordered it. For this reason, any person who performs the act is doing exactly as he should.

In *The Varieties of Religious Experience*, William James cited documents from certain religious orders that explicitly state that God would approve actions on the part of members of the orders which were in obedience to superiors even if the actions themselves were wrong or immoral.[42] Whether they were good or evil acts was not the proper concern of the lowly members. Only the superiors who issue commands needed to worry about that, for only they will have to account for their decisions in the Final Judgment. The monk or nun at the bottom of the hierarchical ladder does right simply by following superiors' orders. Since the call to obedience is open-ended (that is, it can take on any content), such obedience is a virtue that is prime or primary. It is, in other words, one that includes or swallows up all others.

Some absolute leaders, such as military commanders and ship captains, command--and wish to command--only overt actions. In their cases, people recognize that there is reason for the absoluteness of their authority. The humblest soldier or seaman knows that a great deal depends upon the coordination of the actions of many people. His very survival requires it. What one person does must combine with what others do to produce a single effect or carry out a single task. The only way such coordination can be achieved is for everyone in the group to obey a certain person. That individual can, indeed should, confer with others and should receive information from them, but he has the authority to make the final decision. A coordinated action carries out a plan, and a plan can be conceived in its entirety only in the mind of a single individual. Committees can discuss and weigh many plans, but only an individual can conceive one. There is an intimate relation between the very idea of a coordinated action and the reflections of one individual's mind.

There is always the possibility that something may be wrong with the leader. He may not be the best person in the group to give the orders. Others may be more intelligent, knowledgeable, or capable of functioning well under stress. In the past, when men were being drafted into an army, there was fear that the new recruits would be under the authority of non-commissioned officers who were less intelligent than they. The reason for this fear was that the selective service system was drawing men out of college and career, while the men already in the service were career soldiers who were not selected for intellectual capability. The fear was that men of inferior intelligence would be in command in combat situations in which higher ability was necessary for directing actions in ways that would maximize the chances for survival. In other cases, there was concern that commanders might be insane or in the grip of an obsession. Military codes commonly make provisions for extreme cases where leaders are seriously disturbed or suffer diminished capacity. They provide ways for immediate subordinates to replace them. Despite this, it is recognized that the increase in chances of getting out of difficult military situations alive and with objectives achieved are improved so much by everyone obeying a single commander, that such obedience is right even if the commander is inferior to some of the people he commands. Certainly a cost is incurred because a company is commanded by one of its less intelligent members, but even so, the advantage of all obeying a single person is so great that it yields a net profit in effectiveness of action. The cost is, so to speak, a fair price to pay for the advantage of the coordination which obedience makes possible.

Absolute leadership is to be expected where there is, by general agreement, a highly specific objective. For instance, soldiers in combat have two very definite things they wish to achieve: they want to win the battle, and they want to survive doing so. Similarly, men aboard a ship want to weather the storms and reach port safely. People's subjective lives are not, at this point, of concern. What they think in their minds or feel in their hearts is of little importance compared to the supreme urgency of the goal. Overt behavior, physical activity, is the only thing that matters. There is no need to love the commander or admire his character; the only need is to obey him. He may be someone with whom no one would want to have dinner, but as long as his plans and orders can get people through a crisis, people will obey him.

In contrast to legal authority is the authority of a religious leader who claims he has a right to tell people what to believe and do. The members of the hierarchy in the Roman Catholic Church are the best examples. Children educated in Catholic schools and in other religious education programs are traditionally taught to regard the priest as God's representative on Earth. He is not considered to be God, but has full credentials as God's emissary to his parishioners. The bishop is in a similar position relative to the priest, as is the pope to the bishop, and, indeed, to the entire body of believers. In the latter case, there is still confusion embedded in Catholic history; the relative authority of Pope and the Council of Bishops has been a bone of contention for many centuries, and is a question that has never been fully resolved. The concern here is with those leaders who claim authority to tell people--not just advise them--what they should think as well as what they should do.

In the case of the pope, this is accomplished by a special verbal device. It is said that the pope speaks "for the Church" or even that he "is the Church." This way of speaking requires closer examination. In saying that the pope is the Church--in the sense of speaking for it--there is no intention of saying that "pope" and "Church" are synonyms. Rather, the statement that the pope is the Church is intended to make a substantive assertion. The Church is more than just the pope, for it is more than any single individual. It includes all communicants, more than a billion people. Yet it is not just they, either, for "Church" cannot be equated with a mass of people any more than with one person. Instead, it is that mass as a *led* people. It is all the faithful and leaders in interaction with each other. When, therefore, it is asserted that the pope speaks for the Church, it is being asserted that he "is" the entity called by that name. So definitely "is" he this entity, that he can even speak out counter to the opinions of collections of bishops (such as the American bishops) on certain "Church" teachings. "Church" teaching means the *pope's* teaching, since he is the Church when issues of belief are to be delineated. The linking verb "is" becomes a mischievous device for making it appear that two things are equal to each other, when they are not so in fact. The subliminal effects of using words in such a manner, as in the case of the pope and the Church, enlarges the leader's (here, the pope's) authority. It adds emphasis to the assertion that people should believe and do as the leader (as Pope, bishops, and the Magesterium) directs.

In asserting that this sacerdotal kind of authority is different from the rational-legal (military) type, one should note that it pertains first to what people believe, a matter to which the military commander is totally indifferent. Second, where matters of behavior are involved, the authority pertains to zones of conduct in which the intrinsic rightness and wrongness of acts, and not just their results, is at issue. Most Church teaching that is expected to have absolute authority concerns family and sexual issues. The obligation to follow Vatican directives in these matters is far greater than it is in others, since these are actions whose goodness or badness is resident in them.

In other zones, there are exercises of authority that resemble the absolute type, yet which do not really have that character. This is the case when the basis of authority is a person's knowledge. People do certain things because someone who knows a great deal tells them to do so. When a person visits a friend in a faraway city, he follows his friend's instructions on how to find the friend's house. He does not obey with such docility because of an august majesty possessed by the friend. Rather, he assumes that the friend knows the city's layout much better than he. Should the friend one day visit him in his hometown, the friend will in turn follow the first person's instructions. Following the "doctor's orders" is a prime example of such authority. Many people obey the doctor as though he were God. They know full well that he/she does not have a divine nature, but obey him because they assume that he knows a great deal. His knowledge is enough greater than theirs, they think, to make following his orders the best course to follow. The physician is not different from them in his basic nature. They could have joined him in medical school and learned all that he learned. But they did not, and so they treat him as one with authority. The doctor's authority is not fundamentally different from that of the friend who knows his city. Such authority-by-knowledge is not true absolute authority.

To say that a person has absolute authority, then, is to assert that the person's right to give orders and people's obligation to obey those orders is intrinsic. If he tells people what to believe, they should believe it because--and only because--he has told them. They should do as he says because--and only because--he has told them to do it.

The extent to which people actually obey absolute authorities varies greatly. Following orders in military organizations and submission to charismatic cult leaders are probably the closest human beings can come to perfect obedience. On the other hand, communicants of the Roman Catholic Church have shown little inclination to follow the directives of the pope and bishops when those officials stated their opposition to "artificial" contraception, as they have done consistently. According to Charles Westoff and Norman Ryder, American Catholics know about Vatican opposition, but are little different from Protestants in their contraceptive practices, while in many poor countries, Catholics make decisions on the basis of folk culture and do not expect Church officials to define right and wrong for them.[43] Also according to the *World Population Data Sheet*,[44] published by the Population Reference Bureau, European

Catholics use modern means of contraception less than do their Protestant neighbors, but they use other methods with equal effect; their birth rates, on average, are actually a bit lower. So, the fact that authority is of the absolute type does not mean that the people actually obey the orders of an official. It means only that there is an opinion to the effect that they are supposed to do so.

The Non-Leader

The second kind of leader is the *non-leader*. The term is, of course, paradoxical. The non-leader is a leader who is not a leader, or, more specifically, does not lead. While he appears to merit the title, he actually follows a group or a community too much to be called a leader. In some cases he does so explicitly. The candidate for political office who says that he consults the people and attempts to give them what they want (to be "in touch" with them) is clearly following rather than leading the group. In other cases, the leader presents himself as representing a set of values and markets them as the values of the people he proposes to lead. But he does not offer the people anything they do not have already, other than himself as leader. Many religious leaders are good examples, notably certain fundamentalist or evangelical Protestant preachers. Among them, the "televangelists" are probably the purist examples. Conservative (their own term) or right-wing politicians also fit into this category. Indeed, virtually all United States political figures of any stature are the non-leader type. The practice of politics in the nation makes this virtually inevitable. It is very difficult for people who are true leaders to become candidates for office and to win elections.

Characteristic of the non-leader is that his authority does not derive from being in a position within a large-scale organization, such as the Roman Catholic Church or just about any army. He has not risen through the ranks by superior performance. Nor does it come from being the representative of a scheme of values that has to be sold to people, as with the heads of civil rights organizations or promoters of environmental, peace, or any one of many other causes. Rather, it comes from direct appeal to the populace as a whole--to the people. He may act as though he has a message to sell or get across to people who live on Main Street, U.S.A.; however, his message is really what those people already think. And it is the fact that the people already think it that gives him authority. He takes the wellspring of sentiment rising from the people and rises with it. He does not try to change those sentiments. Indeed, he glories in the fact that he takes them just as they are. He is like a glider rising in an updraft coming from the people; he has no upward propulsion of his own, but depends entirely on the community he purports to lead. His position as leader is based entirely on his being a follower. The televangelist is an especially pure example of the non-leader type. Sometimes called an "entrepreneur," this mass media preacher has not risen through the ranks of an organization that existed before he arrived on the scene. He is not elected by the members of a denomination or communion; he is not appointed by a high-ranking official, church, or convention. Instead, he commonly establishes his own church congregation or uses one to which he has been called as pastor. It then serves as the base of his operations. Through it, he takes in enough funds to begin his television ministry. Once on the air, he appeals to viewers for funds. If he is successful, he buys more television time; and so it goes until he has a national audience and source of funds.

Unlike the pastor of a church or official of a denomination, he does not need to appeal to a large portion of a potential constituency. If one percent of television viewers tune in to his program, he has one or two million listeners. If half of them send money and a few send quite a bit, he may get several million dollars to support his endeavors--such as missions abroad and schools at home. Together these projects comprise an empire which is entirely his. He is a new kind of religious leader, indeed a new phenomenon on the religious scene. Though prefigured by the founders of orders in the Catholic Church and the wandering Protestant revivalists (such as the fictional Elmer Gantry), television has given him a technological launching pad with which to rise above those who have gone before.

The political non-leader has a longer pedigree. He often appears as a demagogue; he evokes enthusiasm in a crowd, and may move it to action, but he does so on the basis of passions already smoldering. He does not direct the feelings and actions of the group by appeal to abstract values which enjoy priority in the group's sense of its own identity. Instead, he follows the crowd's enthusiasm. He is submissive to the crowd in the act of leading it. It is noteworthy, however, that in doing so, he makes the group more formidable and even fiercer than it would be without him. He does so by serving the group as its mouthpiece and organizer. He amplifies its cry and energizes its actions. He attends to the crowd in every way except one: He does not lead.

Whether religious, political, ethnic, racial, or other, the leader addresses people in terms of what is in their minds--their values and their knowledge. He speaks specifically to their values and knowledge in their *raw form*. That is, he takes them as is, without doing any work with them. He does not endeavor to find general, abstract principles and use them to systematize the values. Nor does he apply truly abstract or high-level principles to concrete situations. When it comes to beliefs about reality, he goes to no pains to consider the evidence, and he does not worry about logical consistency. He does not do the work that is necessary to lift up values and make them effective in community life. Thus, there is a strange paradox--there is a robust emphasis on goodness, yet no concept of the good stands out; people do what they want and no ethical values move the group to veer from the paths they would otherwise follow. The 1980s are an example of a decade in which people were seemingly both more religious and more devoted to selfishness than they were in the preceding decades. This is not as strange as it seems. It is what happens when values are exalted or emphasized, but emphasized in their raw form, without the work of systematizing or applying them being done.

When that work has not in fact been done, it is not values in the sense of beliefs that certain things are good or bad. It is not, that is, certain *contents* lifted up and approved that energize and sanctify what people undertake. Instead, the group itself does that. A heady feeling of belonging takes over and, it is this value that actually guides courses of action. Religious beliefs, ethical principles, and political ideals become simply supportive symbols for group enthusiasm. It is to this jingoistic "we" feeling that the leader makes appeal, with himself added as one of the symbols of group sentiment. Thus, Jerry Falwell, a leading television preacher, regards it as naturally expressive of his religious devotion that he holds "I love America" rallies alongside his specifically religious or "preaching" services. He equates his Christianity and his Americanism; to him they are two expressions of the same thing. "God and country" is his motto. No such thing as a Christian ethic or value stands over against the country and serves as a basis for criticizing it. Christianity is seen as being a religion that, by its nature, supports and exalts the country.

There is an epistemology, a form of *knowing*, implicit in all of this. It is that people *know* intuitively and immediately about their world and about right and wrong. There is no need to reason or seek evidence. Indeed, to do so is to blunt the edge of the moral convictions. Just as a joke ceases to be funny if it has to be explained, so an idea about what is moral or immoral retains its force only if accepted spontaneously and not as the endpoint in a process of reasoning. Current debates about homosexuality illustrate this point. Frequently, people assert that the Bible "clearly" condemns homosexual behavior. In fact, it does no such thing. It has very little to say on the subject. The sayings in Leviticus (18:22 and 20:13) are part of a code that no one, least of all Protestant fundamentalists, intends to follow. Those in I Corinthians (6:9-10) and I Timothy (1:9-10) are unclear. Even Romans (1:27), cited most frequently, is far from clear and certainly a slender thread on which to hang the condemnation. The truth of the matter is that supporters of the condemnation ground their belief in a feeling, not in a written document. They feel that certain things are wrong, and they then assume that the Bible must say the same thing because the Bible condemns all things that are wrong. The feeling comes first. The Scriptures are then, in effect, recruited in support of the feeling. Finding support for hostility towards homosexuality and homosexuals in the Bible is a good example of "culture" religion in which the code of a particular society is attributed to the scriptures when it cannot, in fact, be found in those documents. Nor, for that matter does the code include what *is* found in them, as with the rigorous commandments to not resist evil and to love the enemy given in the Sermon on the Mount of Matthew 5-7. Scriptural literalism is a point of view *about* the Bible, not *of* the Bible.

Extending the idea of knowing immediately, there are two methods by which the truth of an assertion is established within a community: these are *taking-for-granted* and *shocked response*. In the method of taking-for-granted, there is no need to argue about a specific belief. Everyone just assumes that the truth is obvious. A listener, perhaps one who is not certain about the belief, catches on that the belief is being taken for granted. Because he sees that it is assumed and not argued, he thinks that it must be right. It is what "everybody knows"--or at least what every good person knows. He feels that if there is no need to argue, then logically the belief must be in no need of defense; it is simply obvious to those who see things rightly. And if the listener does not himself see the correctness of the belief, it must be because he alone fails to perceive what is clear to everyone else. His lack of perception is something he then determines to hide. In this, he is like the man who laughs at a joke which he does not "get" because he assumes it must be funny, since others seem to think so, and who thinks he would see its humor if he had clearer vision or more time to think about it. He also wants to avoid having others know that he does not understand it. A person represses doubt, usually without a great deal of effort, for the process of taking for granted is like swimming in a stream of water that pulls one in a certain direction. It thus inclines him to think that the belief must be right. Furthermore, assuming a belief and not arguing it gives a listener the feeling that he must accept the belief if he is to be part of the group. His wish to belong, or his feeling that he does belong, also sweeps him into an accepting attitude towards the belief. Holding the belief means that he is part of the great "we" and not an outsider.

For example, in the mid 1970s there was controversy about the Panama Canal Treaty. Plans were being made to eventually turn the Canal and the Canal Zone over to the government of Panama. Both Democrats and Republicans favored the plan, including Gerald Ford, who was president at the time. Opponents, however, spoke vehemently against "giving our Canal away." Some expressed amazement that anyone, especially a Christian, could be so unpatriotic as to favor the plan. The issue was genuinely controversial. Objectively, a person could support the plan to return the Zone to control by a Latin American government, or he could argue that it would be best for the United States to retain its position in the area via the Canal. People could have given sensible reasons for each position. But in using phraseology such as "giving away our canal" and making references to being patriotic and Christian, speakers gave the debate a different character. The reasons for taking either of the positions on the issue were dissolved into a question about loyalty to God and country. Such lingo might have caused a person to feel pressured to oppose the return of the Canal, lest he be viewed as disloyal. That it would be indeed wrong to return the Canal was taken for granted, and that was what gave force to the argument. There is no tentativeness present in such utterances. The air of certainty which is conveyed excludes it along with all doubt.

Closely related to taking for granted is shocked response. An event takes place or someone says something, and a person responds in shock. His tone of voice, facial expression, and bodily movements all suggest that he is stunned by what he has seen or by what someone has said to him. The event which occasions this response may well be one which allows differences of opinion, as in the case of the Panama Canal Treaty or in revelations about someone's sexual orientation. But the response does not acknowledge any honest differences in point of view. Instead the person reacts to these matters of opinion with sheer shock, much as he would to revelations that the treasurer of the local United Fund had been embezzling funds or had been caught in bed with the wrong woman. Because he does so, all possibility of seeing the event in different ways evaporates. Being in favor of the Treaty or being homosexual is viewed as if it were on the same moral level as embezzling or committing adultery. Here also, the listener feels constrained to accept the views implied by the shocked response lest he appear to be a bad person himself or as an outsider to the group.

There are variations of these methods. The television commentator speaks with great dignity and suavely conveys the notion that anyone who is wise and discerning will see things the way he does. Some use humor in a way that invites the listener to join in the laughter-- and thus in the opinions. Some write prose that makes such imaginative use of metaphor that the cleverness of the language dominates the message and gives the reader the feeling that anyone who is knowledgeable would hold the views that either have been expressed or have simply been taken for granted. All of these tactics support certain opinions, expressed or assumed, and they all replace reasoning. Common to these devices, then, is an absence of thinking-things-through and of the tentativity that such a process necessarily involves. Taking for granted, shocked response, the suave voice, the witty writing--all make assertions that seem believable even--or especially--in the absence of any valid bases for believing them. To disagree, or even to insist on reasoning, is to be the odd man out, the "wet blanket," or worse.

There is reason why television preachers seem to be right-wing in their political and religious views. Jerry Falwell, Pat Robertson, and Jimmy Swaggart are all preachers; but all are also outspoken advocates of rightist politics. All equate piety or "godliness" with their social and political views. Interestingly enough, it would be difficult to imagine the reverse happening. To envisage leftist or liberal-progressive versions of these leading preachers is all but impossible. For instance, it is impossible to conceive of Jesse Jackson and Martin Luther King Jr. as televangelists. At least the possibility that they could have achieved that status is more than imagination can hold in view.

To elicit the enthusiasm from television listeners that yields tens of millions of dollars, it is necessary to appeal to people's wishes to see themselves as good and on the right side. This feeling needs to be immediate and intuitive; it must be of the kind that is evoked by the methods of taking for granted and shocked response. It must involve a certainty about being in the right which depends upon these features. Its force and source of power must therefore be *the group.* The televangelist's listener as member of the group must feel that he is an American--and is so right now, absolutely and for sure. One cannot question whether he is an American anymore than one can, to use Jean Paul Sartre's expression, penetrate a stone.[45] And feeling this way about his nationalism is coextensive with his feeling that he is a Christian. He believes in God, and he believes in the Bible. In holding steadfastly to these and all related beliefs (such as special creation or the Virgin birth of Jesus) he therefore confirms his Americanism. Or, more accurately, he confirms that he is totally a member of the Group. A central feature of his sense of belonging and his enthusiasm is the *absence* of reasoning processes. There is no thinking it through or moving step by step from premise to conclusion, for any of this would dampen enthusiasm. If someone says, "three cheers for the Red, White, and Blue," and someone else says, "now let us sit down and talk this over,"a case of trying to mix oil and water would exist. In other words, the leftist or the moderate cannot be a successful televangelist, for both invite people to reason with them, and reasoning does not market well in the mass media.

The non-leader is not averse to using science and technology. He is usually quite an expert in using the electronic media for his purposes. And he uses science and its methodology in supporting his beliefs. Often he makes appeal to archaeological findings which he says prove that the stories in the Bible are true in their literal sense. For example, a quite elaborate presentation was made recently on television concerning the story in the book of Daniel of the three men who were thrown into the fiery furnace because of their refusal to worship the idol which the emperor had set up. The program, sparing no effort, undertook to show that the survival of three young men in the furnace could truly have happened. The explanation did not make appeal to the notion of miracle, which was what the author of the story intended. Rather, it developed the idea that ancient furnaces had cool spots in them and that the three men were inadvertently cast into that spot and so survived. The implication drawn from this was that the Bible is true after all, and we, having seen that this seemingly incredible story could have occurred as described, may believe everything else in the Scriptures. The people who put on that program, along with many others making similar presentations, are clearly identified with the scientific view of reality enough to want to make appeal to it. But when all is said and done, they wish to use it to promote a static world-view. They do not accept the suspension of judgment which is of the essence of science. Rather, their conclusions are all determined at the start.

Virtually all politicians in the United States are non-leaders. In the American political climate, a true leader has very little chance of succeeding in the political game. In those instances where candidates for office do offer reasoned statements of a position in their campaign speeches in the place of the yells and cheers to which the voters are accustomed, they get severely trounced in elections. Indeed, news reports about candidates and campaigns treat them as contests between people. They discuss whether a candidate "scored" in a speech or in a debate. Whether he strikes the blow he needed to get his campaign going is their prime interest. In talking this way, reporters feel they are speaking for the vast audience of voters. To score or make a hit is to say something that will impress people, and will do so right now. Conceivably, this could be viewed as an insult to the people of the nation. To speak of politicians' "scoring" with their arguments is to imply that people do not know the difference between the "wow" effect of an assertion and the truth that emerges from careful thought and examination of evidence. Actually, it is not that each individual within the group lacks the intelligence necessary for seeing difference. It is, rather, that the people as a group can know it only by interacting with a true leader, and this is what is lacking. Indeed, the reporters who describe the contest between political debaters make what they say to be true in the act of reporting it. They are, in effect, informing the voters how they--the voters--feel about things. In this kind of political circus, it is difficult for proper leaders to emerge.

While the non-leader appeals to the crowd with its raw system of knowledge and values, the people do not determine what actually happens in domestic and foreign policy. Not even aggregate effects-- the things that happen when people react without an effort to coordinate their actions--determine it. Rather, groups within society that are able to use the political process for their own purposes commonly determine what happens. Just because the values are raw, groups or social circles in society that are more organized can recruit the larger public to serve its--rather than the public's--purposes.

Certain groups have much more power than others. They are more able than their fellow citizens to determine what will happen within the community. This power is partly political and partly economic, as was noted at the beginning of this chapter. But an additional observation on the reasons for their power is that they are able to use the non-leader and the mass of people whom he mobilizes. There are several ways in which this is done. Appeal is made to people's perceptions of their immediate, selfish interests. These include low taxes and things thought to pertain to taxation, such as welfare expenditures. By appealing to these values or concerns of the people, special groups are able to induce the people to favor policies that, as a matter of fact, favor the special groups. The people have not pulled back from their immediate interest to attain a broader view in which they could see cases in which other policies are favorable for them in the long term. Lacking true leaders, there is no way they can. In consequence, the non-leader, often an agent of corporate groups, is able to use people's perceptions of their interests as a vehicle for obtaining their cooperation with interests that are quite alien to theirs.

Another way in which this is done is through appeal to patriotism. Love of country has always had considerable resonance in the United States. And love of country, whether called patriotism or chauvinism, is usually a motive to endorse the existing prestige and power structures of the country. If a person is patriotic, so the thinking goes, he accepts the way his country is set up. Or, put negatively, anyone who favors restructuring the life of his community (as in the Civil Rights Movement) must be unpatriotic. At the very least, his patriotism is suspect. The fact, then, that Americans wish to be patriotic and want to feel that they belong is used to make them accept without question the patterns of power and prestige found in the country.

The Counsellor Leader

The counsellor leader is more of a leader than is the non-leader and less of a commander than is the absolute leader. He makes it his business to systematize the community's system of values, and he undertakes the task of seeing how the values may properly be applied. He invites others to join in both of these tasks. Inevitably, intellectual activity is the mark of this kind of leader. He/she reasons, and develops perceptions of the world which would not have been possible for him if he had not engaged in the necessary mental labor. If he grew up in a community that was racially segregated, he sees segregation as "open for discussion" and might decide that it is wrong. He takes time to think about what is good and right, and arranges his values in order. Since the belief in human equality has a prime place among these values, he rejects specific instances of inequality, no matter how honored by tradition they may be, and no matter how up-to-date, fashionable or "in" they may have become. Perhaps he also believes in a free and fair market. Moving from principle to application, he may therefore affirm that it is good to encourage labor unions so that negotiations between worker and manager can be proper market transactions. It does not matter to him that others have not moved from "free market" to "favor labor unions"; what does matter is that it seems to him that the one follows *logically* from the other. He reasons and then comes to conclusions, and he urges others--without asking them to blindly accept his views-- to use their reasoning skills so that they too might arrive at conclusions. He of course thinks that if they reason well, they will join him in his conclusions, but he retains a mind open to the possibility that they may arrive elsewhere.

Of course, when divers people reason, they come to various conclusions. The counselor leader accepts this as part of the game, that is, the game of observing and reasoning. In that sense, disagreements comprise a portion of the cost of the free inquiry which he treasures. Of course he believes in his conclusions, and he may have a passionate wish to see them applied as he thinks they ought. But he realizes that he is indebted to the process of reasoning for his conclusions and must, for that reason, affirm the process itself. And, affirming it, he must allow the possibility that others who engage in reasoning may come, precisely through it, to hold views different from his. Much as he may wonder how anyone could possibly reason differently from the way he does, his zeal for reasoning itself and his belief in its dignity require him to maintain an open mind towards those who disagree with him and towards their points of view. He assumes that if he is right, free and robust reasoning, combined with humane values, must in due course bring anyone to the same opinions. He also assumes that if he is wrong--reasoning being the fallible process which it is--the thinking of others will in the future rescue him from his error.

The counselor leader is not opposed to enthusiasm. But the enthusiasm he displays and which he seeks to evoke in others is different from that of the non-leader. The counselor leader's emotional intensity arises as a *sequel* to a process of reasoning. It comes after the reasoning is completed, and is supported by it. Careful thinking clears the way for excitement and commitment, and give them their due place and nature. Enthusiasm that appears after reasoning has a character very different from that which arises from raw values, that is without reasoning. The fact that it is poised on top of an edifice of rationality gives it a freedom and flexibility which are not to be found in the enthusiasm that replaces reasoning.

There is explanation for this difference. When the work of systematizing is done, values take on content. They assume their character as values that are not just emblems for a group, but instead are approval of images of possible forms of human life. "Freedom," for example, in the hands of a non-leader simply means--America. It is an emblem of the nation. When "freedom" becomes a value with a content, however, it refers to people's ability to make determinations that pertain to their fulfillment. It refers, that is, to something about how people will live and how they will relate to each other. Here, then, is the difference: when enthusiasm appears as a sequel to the process of reasoning, it is directed towards a content. It promotes a value properly so called and does not serve just as a symbol for something else, as loyalty to a certain group. It is a commitment that involves emotion, but it is emotion *for* something, for a way of life, a mode of human relations and the rights of persons. On the negative side, it is not just an affirmation of a "we" group together with the hatred of outsiders that such affirmations commonly includes. To put it simply, it is an affirmation of humane values.

Martin Luther King, Jr.'s "I Have a Dream" speech of 1963 is a very good example of counselor leadership in action. In that speech, King spoke with great gusto, in the best tradition of Negro preaching.

But his enthusiasm did not, as such, stand alone. The listener readily perceived that there was thought and not just "taking for granted" behind it. The speaker cherished certain basic principles. He thought them through and noticed their implications, and *then* spoke with emotional intensity. His main concern was racial equality, but this did not stand alone. The listener perceived that racial equality was a value, but one that derived from other values that were more fundamental, those of peace and equality among human beings. While racial equality was the immediate concern, indeed King's passion, much more was involved. Since it was an expression of more basic values, one could be certain that other expressions would be generated as well. And for that reason, to be loyal to what Martin Luther King was urging, a person could not and would not get stalled on racial equality. He had to affirm the other expressions along with it. His declaration of support for racial equality could not be the declaration which it was unless he joined it with other implications of the belief in equality and solidarity among people. He would, for example, have to favor equality for all peoples everywhere and not just for black people in the United States and to favor peace and peaceful resolutions of conflicts, and he would have to oppose vindictive attitudes towards opponents. It was after--and only after-- thinking things through that the speaker could give emotional intensity to his views. The enthusiasm was a sequel to thinking, not a substitute for it.

When the Old Testament prophets condemned the worship of "foreign gods," they were referring to an adoration of the group itself. Their concept of the Word of God, on the other hand, referred to an affirmation of values that had content--that pertained to relations among people and to human community. The prophets were leaders of the counsellor type. They made no claim that people should believe what they said just because they said it. Rather, they assumed that anyone who wished could, by thought and attention, discern the rightness of what they said, especially as compared to the pure group-affirmation of the false prophets. Jeremiah 7:5-7 and the whole of Isaiah 58 are among the many passages that illustrate this.

Central to counselor leadership is the belief that the leader has a *right to be heard*. He does not have a right to be believed and obeyed, nor does he claim any such right. Only the absolute leader asserts that people are under obligation to believe what he says and should do as directs. The counselor leader, in contrast, claims only that people should hear and consider the things which he has to say. He grants that once they have heard him and have taken notice of his reasons and evidence, they can make up their own minds. They are the final court of appeal.

This kind of leader demands no more of people than that they listen to him and give him a chance to convince them. He requires people to hear and seriously consider what he has to say. They are not free to simply ignore the leader's comments or to pass the comments through their minds without actual consideration. The leader has the right to be heard, and the people have an obligation to listen. They do not have to be convinced that he is right, but they do have to expose themselves to the possibility of being convinced.

In the history of obligations, this requirement to hear and consider is peculiar. Laws, both political and religious, have usually pertained to overt behavior. Visible actions are either prohibited or required. A person can know for certain whether he is obeying or violating a law or ordinance, and others who observe him can also see that he acts in conformity with law or against it. By contrast, hearing and considering are covert actions which take place within the privacy of a person's mind. The individual himself--and only the person himself--has access to his own thoughts, together with some ability to know whether he fulfills obligations to which those thoughts pertain. Yet he cannot know for certain whether he fulfills the obligation, since hearing and considering are not visible and determinate but invisible and vague. Only by a stern act of conscience can a person judge rightly whether he has fulfilled his obligation to use his thinking skills. If that person himself has trouble judging his own actions, those around him will have even more, for they cannot see into his mind. They do have some overt actions which they can see; they can note whether a person appears to be listening. However, these are merely vague indicators of invisible actions.

Thus, the conscience plays a major role in the person's obligation to hear and consider. No threat of imprisonment or fines can induce anyone to act in certain approved ways. No condemnations or ridiculing can force him to fulfill such an obligation. People will either do as they should because they think they should, or they will not do it at all. Counsellor leadership can therefore be active only among people for whom conscience as such plays a large role in determining what they do. Only by its prompting will they meet the fundamental obligations, which are subjective in nature. They pertain to what one does in the privacy of his mind, to the actions of listening and considering.

Once individuals have listened to the leader and taken notice of the values he espouses, the evidence he presents, and the reasoning in which he engages, they must then draw their own conclusions. In so doing they fulfill their obligation to the leader. If, having heard and considered, they then decide that the leader's opinions are wrong, they have not failed to give him his due. They have done what he has a right to expect of them. They are, after all, supposed to decide for themselves. It is the hearing and considering that is essential, not the subsequent agreeing.

Comments by officials of the Roman Catholic Church on social issues illustrate counselor leadership well. For over a century, popes have been issuing encyclicals on issues pertaining to economies, social structures, and relations among nations. In these statements, the leaders of the Church expressed opinions and presented them *as* opinions. They have not claimed the kind of authority for these utterances which they assert in the case of their statements about family and sexual matters. Rather, they offer them as ideas which the faithful should consider, since they are offered by the popes, but they are offered without any stipulation that people are obligated to agree. Church officials do this in part because of a wish to affirm democracy, in part because they do not think that there is a determinate Church position on the issues involved, and in part because they wish to reach non-Catholics as well as Catholics. Donal Dorr discusses such Church teaching in *Option for the Poor: A Hundred Years of Vatican Social Teaching.*[46]

Pastoral letters issued by the National Council of Catholic Bishops in the United States serve similar purposes. They have issued two such letters, one on peace and one on the economy. The bishops assumed that these matters pertained to specific situations in the United States. In the case of the "pastoral" on the economy, a great deal was done to bring the bishops' comments to the attention of all Americans. The various dioceses held meetings to ensure that all Catholics were made aware of the pastoral and encouraged members to become familiar with its contents. The bishops distributed large numbers of copies. In fact, it was this activity that led to the development of the idea of counselor leadership discussed in this chapter. The bishops claimed that the people had an obligation to pay attention to the writing on economic issues. However, they did not wish to imply that the people would be doing wrong if they disagreed. Respecting American democracy, the bishops left the final decisions with the people. It is this combination of obligation to hear and consider with the privilege of making one's own decisions that is the essence of counselor leadership.

There are other examples of counselor leadership in the Roman Catholic Church. The most important of these, apart from the hierarchy, is the utterance of theologians and other intellectuals. The Church, like all organizations, has two kinds of leaders: the administrator on the one hand, and the expert or scholar on the other. Leadership in knowledge has always been important in the Church. It arose first in the monastic orders and then later in the universities. Today, there is a large cadre of Catholic theologians who write books and who try, often unsuccessfully, to avoid conflict with the Church hierarchy, especially the Vatican. Many Catholics all over the world look to these theologians for leadership, yet it is beyond question that their leadership is of the counselor type. The people who read the works of Hans Kung, among others, never doubt that the point in doing so is to expose themselves to ideas, not to hear authoritative dicta. They expect the ideas to commend themselves on the basis of their inherent correctness and adequacy as expositions of Christian Truth. There is no notion that one should believe the ideas simply because of who stated them. In addition to theologians, at various points in the history of the Church certain people have been granted the special status of "Doctor of the Church." These people teach the Church in a special way, just as the saint manifests the power of God in a special way. According to the *Catholic Encyclopedia*, these doctors include both men and women. All of them are clearly counselor leaders.

Counsellor Leadership and Democracy

Again, America is a nation without leadership. Based on the analysis given in this chapter, it is clear that the leadership in the United States should (ideally) be of the counselor type. Americans have little problem rejecting absolute leadership, for it is altogether inappropriate in a democracy. It is inconsistent with the culture or "mood" of American society which places value on individualism and people's right to think for themselves. But non-leader leadership is similarly out of place in a democracy or a republic. If the only leaders available are of the non-leader type, democracy does not exist any more than if the leaders were absolute. People may be given what they seemingly want, but as we have seen, they do not truthfully know what they want. They do not know, that is, what possible political programs or policies hold out promise of making it possible for them to live as they wish. Therefore, they are not in point of fact being given what they want. And worse, organized groups or circles can manipulate elections and assume control of government and society. Clearly, neither absolute leaders nor non-leader leaders can serve in a democracy.

In contrast to both of these, the counselor leader is the kind which is appropriate. He/she does the work of systematizing and applying values. He does not take values to be, in effect, his property, as when a religious official claims divine revelation as the source of his proclamations, or when a charismatic chief presents them as emanating from himself as a person. He does not, that is, demand obedience, as does the absolute leader. Nor does he view values as taken for granted within a community, as does the non-leader. The counselor leader invokes basic principles as the bases for constructing a consistent system, and he appeals to the values affirmed in that process for decisions about how to act in concrete situations. That is, he systematizes and applies values.

He also seeks the truth about what is going on in the world. He refuses to accept the interpretations of events that are put forth as being popular with important people or with people-in-general. He insists on testing by observation, and on checking them against the facts to see if they fit. He tries out various interpretations in the hope of discovering one that is consistent enough with the facts to be accepted provisionally as true. Regarding both values and interpretations of the factual order, then, the counselor leader performs the intellectual *labor* necessary for achieving the most satisfactory view of the world possible.

Most importantly, the counselor leader seeks to discover the arrangement of values that seems right and proper to him. And he asks himself what model for understanding the events that take place best fits the facts of those events. And he arrives at his own idea about the good and true. On the negative side, he takes little interest in the polls and their indications of what is fashionable or up-to-date. When he asks what is true and good, he wants to know what is-- permanently--true and good.

If he is a candidate for political office, he campaigns without striving to give people what they want. Instead, he uses what he himself thinks about values and about what is going on in the world as the basis for his platform. He constructs in his mind a program for state or nation. This program, as he sees it, is one that has maximum promise of making the economy work, and work fairly and work fairly for all the people. Having conceived a program, he then tries to convince people that his view of things and of what should be done to solve problems is an idea that they should adopt as their own. He does not try to sell himself to the voters. He tries, rather, to convince them of his ideas. Like any candidate for office, he would like to win an election. But serving the community, not beating or winning over an opponent, is the most important business to him. Winning simply means that he can serve the community through exercising the powers of his office, whatever those may be. If he loses, he serves the public in another way. By his campaign speeches and other communications, he educates them about his and their understandings of what is going on in the world, how well these understandings fit the facts, and whether there is another vision that would do so better. Since he has tried to convince the people of a set of ideas rather than trying to get them to think that he represents ideas they already hold, his campaigning cannot help but leave a legacy. The community is better educated because of it.

As a losing candidate, he may also prepare the way for his ideas to win in the future. Perhaps there are grave economic problems in the society (when have there not been?), and he has a plan or strategy for dealing with those problems. Perhaps his ideas are right, though that is something a person could not know for certain unless he occupies a position beyond history. Even so, he may still lose the election. Perhaps he loses because his opponents waged a public relations, rather than educational, campaign. Perhaps the other side won because its plan appeared at the time to be better. Whatever the reason for the counselor leader's loss, as events take shape in the years to come, it may become evident that he was right. An alternative plan that looked so good at the time of the election loses its luster in the years that follow and under the impact of the events that take place during that period. When it becomes time for another election, the candidate may run again and win, or another candidate who espouses the same ideas may win. It does not matter who the specific winner is, since service to the community and not being elected to office is this leader's objective. After all, most people will never be president, governor, or senator. Yet it is important that those who are elected be the right people--those who have good and effective plans for dealing with problems. Such is the appropriate approach to candidacy for office in a democracy.

A candidate who promotes his own ideas may of course be wrong, yet even he makes an educational contribution. He, just as much as the one who is right, presents a model for understanding what is going on and a plan for dealing with the problems. His model, like any other, can be checked against reality to see how it fits, and its failure to do so, if that is what happens, helps in the process of clarifying what the truth is. By putting what is wrong on display, he helps the community to see what is right. That is, presenting his own ideas is every candidates' obligation. It is the right way to participate in democracy.

Thus, Walter Mondale was in fundamental error in 1984 when he said that he had made great effort to discover what the American people wanted. That is *never* what a candidate should do. His question, rather, should be: what exercises of the powers of government would serve best to obtain for the people what they want? What among the things that government can do holds out the most promise of enabling people to have a good material existence and a robust and humane lifestyle? He should ask what is good for them, not what they think is good for them, for it is his task and calling to help them figure that out. He has, that is, to do own thinking; he cannot be just echoing the voters. Once he has formed a clear opinion, his job is to present it as lucidly as possible. The people, then, can decide whether they find his arguments convincing and his plans for dealing with problems appealing. When he has stated his views and the people have decided, he has done his part and they have done theirs. He does not have to worry about whether he is "in touch" with the people as he formulates ideas. He need only worry about the adequacy of the plans and proposals themselves. He is not being paternalistic, nor is he acting in conceit as one who thinks he "knows better" than everyone else. He is, rather, doing his part in the process. The people will then decide whether his ideas fit in with what they want more than do those of another candidate.

In this sense, candidates for office are like prosecuting and defending attorneys who speaks to a jury. They both do their best to convince the jurors of a certain point of view about a person accused of a crime. They do not have to decide whether the person is guilty. That is what the jury is to do. They need only make certain that the jury has all the arguments before it. Similarly, a candidate for office should present his own views as well as he can and then should allow the voters to make their decision.

Sadly, in American politics today, differing points of view are not presented to people. Candidates for office are too anxious to win. In their anxiety, they try too hard to convince the voters that they are what the voters want, while in fact the voters' desires are a confused mass in which no determinate lining up of wish with available options is possible. Additionally, people's ideas about what they want are only partly their own. The other part is the content of the mass media. People "want" what the newspapers and television have told them they want. Behind the expressions of opinion which may be heard on all sides is a mixture of anxiety, frustration, anger, hope, greed, and some other things as well--all interpreted in terms of whatever concepts are available. Candidates try to follow when there is nothing to follow and when they should lead.

To present different points of view would be to consider the complex swirl of events, to interpret it as well as possible, and to conceive plans for dealing with problems. Given the complexity of economic and political systems, it is certain that people of rational and humane dispositions who think about problems will develop divers plans, schemes, and strategies for dealing with the problems. It is part of the nature of any strategy that it is altogether different from alternative strategies which are available. By definition, strategies exclude one another. The various individual plans differ, not just in detail, but in the processes upon which they stake their hopes. One hopes for a burst of entrepreneurial activity (supply side economics) while another sees salvation in an augmented consumer demand (Keynesian fiscal policy). Both are schemes that rational human beings conceive and recommend.

Much of the difficulty derives from the fact that people who run for office in American politics put all of their eggs in the basket of "winning." That goal would of course be entirely appropriate if what they are in politics for is glory and power. These are motives that always move men and women to act in certain ways, though they do not always yield the pleasure which people expect from them. But if we could take politicians at their word, that they wish to serve the public and to pave the way for a better life for people, then victory in

an election should *never* be the goal. The goal, rather, should be to
have made a lucid statement of one's own opinions, arrived at in
solitude, and so to carry forward the process by which truth is
discovered and policies that are both humane and effective are
adopted. In a democracy, these strategies (called "game plans" in the
Nixon era), should be well developed as systems of ideas that can be
presented to the public for consideration. Obviously, candidates for
office should present plans as capably as they can. So also, however,
should journalists and everyone who communicates with the public.
They all should articulate and explain each of several different plans.
Some of these plans will fit neatly into a specific scheme. Others will
not fit into preconceived schemes but will be contrasted to others
along different dimensions. The concept of economic communities
developed earlier in this book is an example. It is not different from
other ideas in being more capitalist or more socialist. It is a different
difference, so to speak. Regardless of how plans are to be
distinguished from each other, they should be presented. They should
be presented in newspapers, on television, on radio, and in every form
and kind of communication.

Of special importance in this process is dropping inhibitions about
"left" and "right." Plans and strategies should be viewed and
evaluated on the basis of what they are concretely. They should not
be viewed as tending towards socialism, capitalism, or any other
specific ideology or system. If someone has a plan, that plan should
be seen as a collection of details that fit together in certain ways.
People should note the processes on which it stakes its hopes and then
assess it on the basis of facts, on how likely those processes are to
take place as projected. They should, to put it more simply, *think*
about the plan and arrive at an opinion of it. Throughout, all
tendencies to scruple about its pointing too much in one direction or
another should be ruled out as a matter of principle. Yes, there are
actions in this world that sometimes seem innocent enough in
themselves but initiate a process that leads people to further
elaborations of tendencies that are not innocent--such as the young
woman who allows her date a kiss and then ends up pregnant. But
being perceived as a trend toward capitalism or socialism is not the
same thing. It is just as likely that a measure that seems socialistic
would solve a problem and thereby relieve pressures toward moving
further in that direction. It should be a rule in a democracy that plans

should be considered as plans and not as being too much "like" one or another thing that they are not, as matter of fact, like.

As ideas are presented, people should practice and become practiced in *non-ideological thinking*. Thinking should insist that things are purely and simply--what they are. Adopting a certain policy is not getting on a sled that is inevitably going to slide to somewhere else, unless it can be shown that it will indeed do so. If someone suggests, for example, that a certain welfare program should be initiated, that program should be seen as a specific, concrete, and therefore limited change in the economic and social landscape and not as leading to a massive welfare state, to socialism, or, for that matter, to any "ism." The people should then decide whether they want that change, viewed as the change it is and not as something else.

This is not to say that all should be moderate or centrist. The point of being nonideological is to focus on the specific, not to be located in a middle between extremes. On occasion, there may be a need for radical proposals. And these too, should be given a hearing. Americans, as a matter of fact, are rarely treated to any genuine consideration of what the alternative strategies for dealing with problems are. So bereft are they of that kind of presentation that one could well imagine that really workable plans will never go into effect simply because people never have a chance to consider them. Newspapers and television should make it their business to offer a full menu, so to speak, of plans for dealing with our recurrent crises that *could* be adopted. Do we not believe in the marketplace of ideas?

America should have leaders for a democratic society, and America is not a democratic society unless it has leadership. The people are the final court of appeal, but they should have leaders who help them interpret the bewildering swirl of events and who help them to systematize and apply their values. Properly speaking, the expression "the people" means all citizens in relationship with leaders.

Chapter 10

Affordability and Debt

Previous chapters have developed ideas that can be used to understand the nation's problems and to suggest ways of coping with them. Counselor leadership should exert itself vigorously, though without compromising its counselor nature. Leaders should think about what is best for the nation (and world) and should seek to persuade people to join them in that process of thinking. The leader's presence should be an invitation, so to speak, to engage in a process of putting two and two together to get four as regards political and economic issues. In this process, the leader does his own reflecting on events, but he then undertakes to induce others to join him both in the reasoning and in the conclusions at which he arrives. Simply stated, he tries to persuade them through a step by step process of thinking.

Further, the course for politicians, journalists, clergymen and others to follow is to induce people to join them in deliberating and making decisions, but decisions of a certain kind: community decisions. Under their influence, that is, people should see themselves as part of a community and should make their decisions as such, and not just as individuals. In doing so, they will hopefully solve the individual-group problems which beset the nation. They will, that is, decide in favor of those courses of action which serve everyone best when taken by all individuals within the community. In so doing, they realize freedom in a way that is impossible when each person and organization acts only in its own interest and is thus defenseless against undesired aggregate effects.

Counselor leadership presiding over community decision-making should be especially directed towards the economy. The task at hand is to so organize the community that everyone participates in the work that must be done and everyone receives a share of the goods and services which the work produces. This share must be fair, which means, first of all, that it must be adequate for maintaining a decent level of living as that level is imaged within the community. This fair share should be provided for everyone, regardless of whether he works, what work he does, or how well he does it. Then, whatever surplus remains after everyone has received a share, could be used to reward people who work especially hard, long, efficiently, or artfully or who have to know a great deal to do their work. These rewards will presumably serve as incentives for people to work better than they would otherwise.

Human foibles being what they are, such special rewards for the few may be necessary. But there are ways in which rewards can be granted without subtracting from what is available to others. This can be done by taking the pool of goods available and arbitrarily designating certain objects within it as "more" than others. Words such as "designer" or "authentic" are now used as prefixes for the names of objects, giving the objects a luster that their utility or beauty alone do not give them; others are called special names such as "jewels" with the same result; or, an item's marginal differences in utility or pleasure can be exaggerated, as is done with wines, television sets, and automobiles. This augmenting of the value of things makes it possible to give certain people extra doses of prestige while maintaining the level of provisions available to others.

To achieve this, the community decisions should do something important: they should *sever, or at least weaken, the tie between jobs and access to goods and services.* With people no longer dependent upon the market to give them the things they need to live, the market could proceed on its own terms without causing the brutal effects it has had in the past and which it has in the present. The social wage should be enlarged beyond its present scope and should include many items, notably health. No one, especially the person who is willing to work, should fear that it will be impossible for him to live in fundamental decency. With people depending less on their jobs for the things necessary for living, the pressures on the community to make changes in the pattern of economic activities would be eased. Decisions could be made to reduce military production and to shift labor and resources to such alternatives as repairing infrastructure, or converting from petroleum to solar and other sustainable forms of energy. As things are now, any suggestion of such change evokes understandable anxiety, but if transitions could be made without threats to the individual's home, mortgage, diet, or material welfare in general, resistance might be less. A greater social wage would help in smoothing things.

Also, the peoples of the world should live in more or less self-sufficient economic communities. Goods should be traded within exchange circles. If a person gives or sells something to someone, he should receive goods in exchange, if not from the same person, then from another, one who also trades with that person. They should comprise a community. Exports and imports--exchanges with buyers and sellers outside the exchange circle--should be kept to a minimum and should consist of those goods that a community cannot produce for itself, perhaps because of climate or similar reasons, as when the United States has to import coffee. The more self-sufficient a community is, the more the exchanges which take place within it will be trade in its proper sense, rather than financial machinations in which claims to goods are made on a gaming basis rather than on the basis of production and exchange of things people want.

The Meaning of Can or Cannot "Afford"

In a society in which claims on goods are based less on the job and in which there is a somewhat self-sufficient economic community, certain issues will appear in a different light. One of these is affordability, a matter about which people speak constantly. They discuss what a person or an organization can afford, and they ask what the community, what "we," can afford.

As generally used, "affordability" suggests two things. It suggests that a person has enough money in hand (or in a bank account) to pay for something. And it suggests that his funds continue to be sufficient for that purpose even when other demands on his resources are taken into account. There is no question that a person cannot afford something if its cost is beyond the reach of his supply of money. This would be the case if the average individual thought about buying a jet airplane capable of carrying three hundred people. But he also cannot afford something he wants if he wants or needs other things more, and the charges for these other items do not leave him with enough to buy the thing. A man may want a motorcycle, and he may have enough money to pay for it. But after he pays the house note, the grocery bill, and his child's dentist, his funds may be diminished to the point at which the motorcycle can no longer be considered to be within reach. So "affordability" has reference both to funds-in-hand and to a person's or a group's system of priorities.

Ability to Afford and Basic Thinking

Basic thinking sees affordability differently from the way in which usual thinking views it. In usual thinking, when someone asks whether "we," as a community, can afford something, he asks, "Can we pay for it?" The question is whether "we" have enough money, or have enough after making other payments. Actually, the issue is whether the government has enough, since government acts on behalf of "us." And this question, in turn, rests on what is available in tax revenues and what other demands on these revenues are in effect. Central to all of it is the simple question, "Can 'we' pay for it?"

Basic thinking views the matter differently. To ask whether "we" can afford something is to ask whether the community can spare the labor necessary for providing it. If the community needs all working people to devote all their labor to producing things that are fundamental and indispensable, then it cannot afford something. If, on the other hand, only part of the total numbers of workers is needed produce food, clothing, shelter, and TERM for themselves and the others, the thing is affordable. There are person-hours left over when the necessary market-basket of goods has been produced, and these extra hours can be devoted to things that are "merely" desirable. They can be used, in fact, for whatever people or the community want or view with approval.

Actually, there is little question that American society has enough person hours to afford whatever it wants. The country has, in fact, workers to spare. It has them now and has had them for a long time. And with every advance in technology, it has even more. It is well able to provide a good material existence for all its people and to go on to provide many things that are good, edifying, simply interesting, or "uplifting." This ability was demonstrated in World War II, when the United States provided (if "provided" is the right word) a massive military apparatus and allocation of human labor to military purposes that dwarfs anything that has even been dreamed of since. And it did so with a less developed technology than is available today.

So what is the problem? The problem is that the question "can we pay for it?" does not disappear just because we Americans see that we have the labor power to fill our fundamental needs and also to take care of things that we want or that we believe in. If workers are to get busy and take care of these tasks, specific arrangements have to be worked out which enable them to do that work and still to have a claim on the pool of fundamental goods. People pay varying amounts in taxes, which are determined by such things as their income, their purchases, or their property. These taxes are then the income of a unit within society, the government. That unit contracts with organizations or employs people to do the work. Unfortunately, resistances to these processes appear. People do not wish to pay taxes. No matter what the amount, they always think it is too high. It affects what they easily see is their economic standing. They receive wages, salaries, or profits; some of those funds are paid as taxes, and what is left is less than it would be without the tax. Therefore, everyone wants lower rather than higher taxes, regardless of what the current level is.

Admitting this brings one back down to Earth after flying in the basic thinking stratosphere. One way to state the matter is that talk about what we Americans can or cannot afford is cast in terms of the battle with nature. The talk is, that is, framed in a way which suggests that our problem is whether we can do the work required to wrest from nature the things that we want. In fact, however, it is not that kind of battle. Americans have little problem struggling with nature. The people of the United States can provide for all of their number well. But we have a struggle-with-society problem that is altogether different. The fight is with society and not with nature. Yet it is still very real, for society is real, just as is nature. It is an uphill battle to break down the patterns by which we are related to each other and to rebuild them in ways that yield the things that people want and need.

Still, there is a point to stating things in basic terms. These terms consider the boundaries that are set upon our activity by nature. They also reveal that those boundaries are far wider and less limiting than one might have thought. It is well within America's ability, as far as the battle with nature is concerned, to provide for everyone within the nation's borders. Actually, it is within the ability of the human race to adequately feed everyone who now inhabits the world.[47] Humanity could do it if everyone made the requisite community decisions to accomplish these feats. It is the failure to make those decisions, not nature or lack of productivity, that prevents people from doing so. Thinking in basic terms shows what is within the reach of community decision-making.

The issue of affordability frequently arises in connection with the government. People wonder what "we"--that is, the government--can afford. And it seems that governments at all levels are now able to afford much less than they once were. In the 1960s, the United States experienced a mood of expansiveness. Government was supporting all sorts of projects and programs and doing so at increasingly generous levels. Education, health services, public assistance, and other causes benefitted by this readiness to foot the bill. A partnership between government on the one hand and business-and-people on the other was building a bigger and better nation for everyone.

Since then, however, things have gone into reverse. Not only is it no longer possible to continue the expansion, but it is also not even possible to maintain a current level. The mood seems to be that government cannot support what it supported before, and so will have to cut back, retrench, spend less, and in general do and provide less. Like a family that has just suffered reverses--either a loss of income or a drastic increase in charges against its income (outgo) and so needs to cut down and cut out expenditures, the government, it is thought, needs to reduce spending here, there, and everywhere. Little in the way of explanation is offered for this. None, really, is considered to be necessary.

Adding force to the belief is the idea that government expenditures by their nature are bad. This is an idea that has been in the background of the discussion in this book all along but which now comes to the foreground and commands attention. What was before a vague disapproval by people who were of right-wing persuasion now takes on the urgency of the "cannot." Government, people say, cannot afford what it was able to afford in the past.

Implicit in this statement is the belief in the primacy of goods that are offered for sale in the market and are owned individually. Quite apart from what the goods are, the fact that they are sold for money and used or consumed by persons or families gives them a higher place on the totem pole than goods or services provided by public agencies and used by the community as a whole. A firm ordering of priorities occurs in which the condition of being owned privately confers a blessing on goods and makes them superior to anything in the public domain. On the basis of this ordering, it seems reasonable to suggest that the government should spend less and therefore tax less and that people should spend more. This inevitably means that the corpus of goods produced will include fewer of the kinds of goods that government provides and more of those which industry produces for private consumption. The priority system, that is, determines not only the proportions of goods that are private and public, but also what those goods will be.

The public goods destined for reduced emphasis include many items. Education at all levels suffers successive cutbacks. Parks are not easy to support. Research on AIDS and other diseases is certainly funded, but not as well as it could be. Roads and other infrastructure require repairs which are not forthcoming. Only the military enjoys special immunity, and even its funding is no longer certain. In contrast, privately owned goods flourish. New high-definition television sets head the list,[48] along with many other goods. These household and automobile items enjoy a special place, not because they do more than do public goods to make life good, but because they are produced by private enterprise and are sold to individuals who then own them individually. The cynic who does not concur in this sanctification calls the goods "nonbiodegradable junk."

Distinctive about this array of privately owned or market goods is that their continued movement (being sold) depends upon a massive advertising industry. Left to their own devices, people do not feel a great need for more consumer goods. The thought that life would be more worth living if they had a television set with a slightly sharper picture has not occurred to them; thus, communications which convince them that they want what they have hitherto not wanted are essential. The sheer massiveness of advertising is evidence that our society produces goods in abundance and that productivity, as such, is not our problem. The fact that so much productive prowess can be devoted to the project of persuading people to avail themselves of the largesse available in retail establishments is indication that the nation has productive power to spare, that need not be used to provide what people need. Clearly, if people were not stimulated to want more goods, the merchandise available would not appear desirable and people would not buy it. Goods would exist in excess of what people are aware of wanting or needing. Indeed, a major part of what is meant by the expression "information society" has to do with advertising. A major use of high-tech communications is getting into people's living rooms to persuade them to keep buying.

As noted earlier in this book, such a state of affairs has priorities upside down, A careful assessment of what people have and of what more they could use to make life good would reveal that public goods would be very prominent among these additional items. Much as people hunger for VCR's and tape decks in their automobiles, those that have money and can therefore demand goods reach saturation points quickly, and they want more or will want more only under the influence of aggressive advertising. In contrast, life can be truly improved by more vigorously attempting to control pollution, beautifying the environment, building parks, providing more and better education, researching illnesses and treatments, and providing other public goods. The problem is that in order to shift the spotlight to what people can use and away from what they cannot, it would be necessary to make community decisions. And this, in turn, would require counselor leadership, a resource which America lacks. Once more, people are not free, but are bound by aggregate effects. To become free would require the leadership which the nation presently does not have.

In reference to affordability, the awesome productive prowess of our industrial society is equal to the task of giving us whatever public goods we want. Do we need more research on AIDS? Do we need more treatment for people who have that illness and for those who have others? Do we need to beautify our environment, or to educate our young people and our not-so-young people? Whatever it is, we can have it. We can have it all.

How Many Workers Can a Society Afford?

Cutting back on work forces has been a regular item in the news for the last decade or two. It occurs with the same regularity as do automobile accidents, storms, and political revolutions. What does not seem to happen, even irregularly, is the opposite, the hiring of a large number of workers. One looks in vain in the newspapers for instances of plants opening and seeking a few hundred or a thousand workers. In the few cases that occur, hiring is usually just a recall of workers "laid off" a few months before. Moreover, the cutbacks take place in all kinds of organizations. Governments, at all levels, dismiss workers to cut costs; so also do entities associated with them such as schools and universities. Religious and nonprofit organizations see their incomes go down and decide to get along with fewer employees. Reduction in manufacturing industry work forces is a continuous process; some plants are closed entirely, while those that remain employ smaller numbers. Organizations of all kinds that hire workers seem to be hiring fewer of them. "Downsizing" is high fashion in every kind of organization.

In many cases, the employers explain that the cutbacks are a necessity. Tax revenues are down, or contributions to religious and nonprofit organizations fail to reach their previous levels. In business, customer demand and profit levels go up and down constantly, and many companies are forced to dismiss workers in order to survive. Some, of course, do not survive. Necessity is not, however, always the reason for cutbacks. Sometimes the reason is possibility. Technological advances give employers the ability to get by with fewer helpers. That is actually the whole point of these advances; a worker can do more work in any given time, and any specific volume of work can be dispatched in fewer hours and therefore by fewer workers. The manager who has word processors does not need as many stenographers as he did when his equipment was more primitive. The apparatus replaces some of the workers and ultimately some of the cost. While it takes money to acquire the new equipment, doing so saves in the long term--and equipment does not ask for raises or benefits, complain about working conditions or demand a pension when it is no longer useful! Another way in which possibility is the reason for reductions in work forces is the transfer of operations to sites where labor is available at lower wages. These sites may be in other parts of the country or in other countries. Cutbacks are sometimes due to necessity and sometimes to possibility, but they mean losses of jobs in every case.

For present purposes, attention focuses on government. What happens when governments, here or abroad, reduce the size of their work forces? A problem with affordability is typically the reason given for the dismissals. Revenues are down; there are debts to pay, or taxes to be reduced. Put simply, the government--any government--says it cannot afford to continue with the current number of employees. Clearly, however, the matter could be reversed. The question does not have to be whether the government, or the nation, state, province, or city it governs could afford to have the workers. It could, instead, be whether it can afford to be without them. There is good reason to consider the matter this way as well as the other.

Actually, there are three affordability questions which are

significant here. The first has to do with the workers themselves. If
it is true that the government cannot afford to retain them, it may also
be true that *they* cannot afford to be dismissed. What happens to
them is just as serious--to them--as what happens to government when
its outlays exceed its revenues. And they, being people, are what
ultimately matters. A person's expenses are certain to exceed his
income if he has no income, and they are likely to do so if he has
reduced income. Groceries, housing, clothing, and all the rest of what
one has to have to live continue to cost money. Stores do not stop
demanding payment just because the customer has ceased to receive
any himself. Certainly, noting this does not solve the government's
problem. If it does not have the money to pay people, it does not
have it. Most likely, however, it could arrange income and outgo
differently and so have enough. It did in the past when hiring those
workers, and probably could again. Moreover, government workers
are people, and people, we may recall, are what "it is all about."

For the purposes of understanding, it is important to register the
two-way character of the question of affordability. The worker cannot
afford to lose his job any more than the employer can afford to retain
him. Moreover, morally, when people make their living in certain
endeavors, they acquire rights to continue doing so. This right is
really the most fundamental and abstract of all. Property rights, by
contrast, are more concrete, specific, and therefore derivative. That
is, they arise from something more basic than themselves, which
might be called "squatters'rights." This is the right to use what one
has already used in gaining the goods he needs to live.

Throughout most of human history, squatters' rights referred to
land. People made their livings from land, and their right to continue
making a living was their right to the land. A piece of the Earth's
territory was therefore defined as "property of" a certain person or
family (usually a family lineage). But the linkage of land to person
was, before it was anything else, a right granted the person to
continue winning his daily bread from the land. The land was the
source of his living. Accordingly, whenever a person labors to gain
his living from something, he acquires a right to that thing, and for
that purpose. The person who has a job has a right to it. If justice
is to be done, he cannot be dismissed by an employer simply as an
exercise by the employer of his property rights. He cannot be
dismissed, that is, just because the employer wishes to dismiss him.
Certainly an employer as property-owner has rights, but so does the

employee; no one can simply exercise "his" rights without taking into account someone's else's rights as well.

To see this, we may note that historically, farmers who farm land become owners of that land. This is implied in the "homestead" actions of the American government in the previous century, and in a widespread feeling that there is something morally suspect about the absentee ownership of farm land. Certainly the homestead policies of the American government were a way of dealing with a large mass of land suddenly bestowed on a people whose earlier European homeland had provided no such offering. But it was also a policy with moral implication. It recognized that rights to land were primarily "use" rights. A person owned land because he had used it and was using it. This right is more fundamental than the abstract or total property rights which people take for granted today, since it pertains to the right to live. What we may then see is that for people who live in an industrial society, the "job" *is* their land. And, speaking morally and from the standpoint of justice, this right is more basic than others. Stated negatively, justice is denied whenever workers employed by a company are treated as simply "factors of production." This is an observation about morality, and as such may seem strange in a no-nonsense market system. But then, all community life is morally structured. Or, better stated, a group comprises a community only when morality is taken seriously.

The second affordability problem pertains to the services which government workers perform. Workers presumably do not just draw salaries, but do something for people or the community. A surprising thing about discussions of this topic is that this is rarely considered to be a serious matter. One would think that cutbacks in government work forces are cost-saving devices and nothing else. There is, it would seem, no valuable service performed by these workers which the community must now forgo. Actually, it is possible in certain cases that this could be true. The work done by employees could be make-work that attends only to frills; it could, that is, be activity that does not accomplish anything of value for the people within the community or for the community as a whole. It could be mere paper shuffling that serves no purpose or, in line with "Parkinson's Law," it could be a finding of things to do when nothing needs to be done. But if this is possible, it is far from certain. It may well be that workers were employed because there was a job that needed to be done. People or the community needed to be served in certain ways.

For example, when Nicaragua cut back on its health services, the sick were not being seen by doctors or nurses. In health services and in many other ways government employees do things for people. If dismissed, they cease to do those things and people are left in the lurch. Whenever the reduction in government work forces is discussed, people should always ask what are the services that will *not* be performed because of it. They should ask whether they can *afford* to do without those services. The third problem concerning affordability has to do with the employee's status as a customer. If he works, is paid, and then spends his money, he buys things from people. Those sellers are thus able to make sales--dispose of their excess, receive money for it, and exchange that money for what they need. From their standpoint, the customer is essential. Only if they can sell to him/her can they receive money and so buy from others in turn. Only so, that is, can they participate in the exchange circle and so keep it going. The government employee is part of that circle. If he is taken away--or deprived of income--he ceases to participate, and the circle breaks down. Viewed from the standpoint of society as a whole, there is a danger of *depression*. Productive processes continue, but there has been a slashing of demand as some government employees lose their incomes. Goods therefore do not sell and so serve no purpose; they retire to the status of non-goods. The people who have produced things but cannot sell them are also deprived of income, and so cannot buy things from other vendors, and the multiplier continues. The money that would have been paid the government workers is, in effect, lost--uncirculated, and so the exchange circle breaks down.

In Latin American countries, inflation has often been the problem. Rather than a lack of money, they had a great excess of it. Goods, on the other hand, were scarce, at least relative to the cash available to pay for them. It is in that kind of setting that the dismissal of government workers took place. This dismissal was viewed as, among other things, a way of doing battle with inflation. Considered that way, it was one of several ways of dealing with shortages. A decision is made, in effect, that certain people can do without things altogether while others continue to consume at their accustomed level.

Reducing the size of a government work force may be a virtue or a vice, depending on what those workers were doing. Assuming that they were performing genuine services, there are these three evils which flow from paring down the size of the force: the workers themselves are deprived, which is unfair; the community is deprived of their services; and their withdrawal from the exchange circle damages the economic system.

The question remains as to whether similar reductions of the work force by private industry are the same or different from that of the government. To a great extent, they are the same. The only real difference is that employees of private firms serve the public first by serving their firms. There is, for this reason, a question about just who the beneficiary of their labor is--their employers or the community. The community could profit from a full retention of the work force: the product they buy may be better or its use better understood; unhurried employees of firms may be better able to advise customers on the use of products; features of products that are important, such as their safety, can be attended to, and so on. When the work force is reduced, these amenities may be missing. The community will be deprived of the services that would otherwise be provided. There is, therefore, question whether the community can forgo the services and so afford the dismissals.

Apart from that, there is not much difference between the loss of public and private workers. Employees of firms can no more afford to lose their jobs than can people who work for governments. These workers also acquire a moral right to their positions, evidenced in the employers' feelings of obligation toward long-term employees. They may not always honor that obligation in practice, but it remains in their consciences. And of course, the loss of income among dismissed private employees affects the rest of the community exactly as does that of government workers who lose their jobs.

Dismissal of employees as an economy measure is harmful both from the standpoint of the community and in regard to what is just and fair. It takes place, when it does, as a resolution of problems of units within the community, not the community itself. A particular commercial firm assures its survival or prosperity by reducing the number of its workers. And when government cuts down its force, it acts as a unit within the community, though it is not truly such a unit, since it represents the entire community, and has both responsibilities and powers that other units do not have. Here an individual-group problem exists. A unit within the community fares well by firing employees. But all of the units might do better if all of them kept their full cadre of workers. The maintenance of services would benefit the community as a whole, and what is equally important, the exchange circle would be maintained--a condition upon which everyone depends.

The Concept of the "Market Friendly Economy"

The explanation given for reductions in government work forces in Latin America and elsewhere is that doing so enacts what Amy Sherman called a "market friendly" policy[49]. By cutting down on workers, the government needs to tax less, and private business is thereby enabled to function free of tax (and regulatory) burdens. Its executives for this reason have incentives to work hard and well, and investors have maximum reason to invest.

This explanation is basically incorrect. If an executive's motivation is determined by material reward, it is not necessarily a function of the reward's absolute dollar amount. Rather, it is determined by that amount in comparison to the incomes of colleagues and others in the community. The person sees himself as doing poorly or well depending upon how he ranks within a group. To see himself as doing well, he needs only to gain more than others. How much more is not critically important. To be doing all right, he needs only to be more or less equal to others. If income tax takes a big bite out of the amount added to his earnings, he knows that other successful money-makers suffer the same fate, and that his ranking relative to them is unchanged. The size of his personal income cannot be taken as the measure of his motivation to work hard and produce.

Nor can we be certain that prospects of high income are crucial to the motivation to work well in any case. There are, we may note, large numbers of workers who have no prospects of experiencing a rapid upward movement in their incomes. Hordes of small businessmen and businesswomen, police officers, teachers, and others work hard and well even though their incomes are quite modest and their hopes for increases even more so. The belief that the basic motor of economic improvement is generous incentives for business leaders is one that will not fare well under an examination of actual human behavior.

The intellectual eggs of the "market-friendly" idea are pretty much all in the incentive basket. The belief that people who work for government have no need to worry about what the customers want and therefore no reason to work well is of course not altogether wrong. Nor is the correlative idea that those who must fret about what buyers will freely buy have motive to work hard and well altogether mistaken. But if these beliefs have some truth, they by no means have all of it. The empirical record does not bear them out. Peoples have not in fact fared better under "pure" capitalist regimes than under others. For the most part, they have fared worse.

As is commonly the case when explanations are given more credence than logic will allow, a truer but less appealing reason hides in the background. According to this not-so-lovely accounting, a genuinely free market was never the idea. The condition hoped for, rather, was one in which groups or social classes now in power (or aspiring to power) would continue to have the upper hand. Power was the issue, not freedom of any kind. Yet the advocates of the free market could not announce that power is what they are striving for, since that would not appeal to the masses of people and certainly not to voters. It needs, for this reason, to be covered by an explanation which cites the idea of "freedom," a concept which is at the very center of American self-consciousness.

Corporate executives do not actually want total freedom from government interference in the economy. They are quick to clamor for subsidies and utilize government powers whenever it is to their advantage to do so. But by presenting themselves as favoring a free market, they look much better. Further, since government has served to protect the lower classes against the wealthy on occasion in the past, it is from the power of government specifically that the affluent wish to be independent. Only so can they dominate the rest of society without hindrance. It must be emphasized, then, that the free market idea is precisely an *idea* (or emblem). It is not intended to be a program of action.

The free market is an idea that sometimes appeals to people of lower classes, despite the fact that it is "freedom" primarily for the wealthy. The reason for this appeal to the nonwealthy has to do with the resentments which they feel. They are angry, but they do not know what the object of their ill-feeling is, for it is not readily identified. They know only that they feel powerless before "bigness" of some kind. Being unable to pin it down, they readily agree with the upper class that the culprit is government. Represented as it is by tax agents, offices that grant driver's licenses, and the like, government is a handy stand-in for giants in general, even when it is not the one that is hurting people. Hence they are ready to join with the upper class battling with "big government." Ironically, they are pitting their cheering and their voting powers against the very agency that (sometimes) protects them from the people in corporations and the upper class who are their actual oppressors. This is the sort of thing that happens when social groups make deft use of imagery and ideology in pressing their case. If there is a policy that is painful in the short term but beneficial to the community over a longer period, it is that of corporations and government retaining their employees as much as they possibly can. Assuming that what the employees do is a service and not pure make-work, it is affordable.

The National Debt

Among problems confronting the United States today, few get more attention than the *national debt*. In his campaign for the presidency in 1992, Ross Perot gave it first place. His program, to the extent that he had one, featured efforts to reduce the debt. An organization called "Lead or Leave" claims to represent the needs and views of the "twentysomething" generation (people born between 1963 and 1973). Its leaders see the debt as one of two major threats to its constituency, the other being excessive social security taxes and payments. Neither Perot nor Lead or Leave represents the electorate as a whole, and it is far from certain that most young people born within five years of 1968 see things as does that organization. But it is likely that large numbers of Americans will be inclined to nod their heads at its ideas about the national debt.

Actually, the debt is an esoteric issue. That is, it does not touch people or affect then in any direct way. It is off in the distance as something about which Americans merely read. In this sense, it is very different from issues such as unemployment, inflation, and pollution which have closer relations to people's actual experiences. To have ideas about the national debt, people have to read about it in the newspapers or hear about it on television. It is for them a news item and nothing else. It does not otherwise touch them or affect their experiences. And to form judgments about it, they have to have previously established concepts of the dynamics of the economy. They have to have an elaborate idea of what-causes-what in the economic arena. The validity of their judgments, for this reason, can be no greater than the adequacy of their economic theories.

Probably the major feature of the American people's view of the national debt is that it is *debt* in the same sense in which a debt exists when one individual owes money to another individual or to a bank. That is, it is a negative holding on wealth. A person must earn a quantity of wealth in order to pay off the debt and so pull himself *up* to the point of having nothing. He previously had less than nothing. In comparison, therefore, to someone who has nothing and so must work hard in order to have something, he has to work harder still. He has to work first to fill up a hole, so to speak, and then work more to build up a pile. If he wants to have ten thousand dollars, but instead has a ten-thousand-dollar debt, he would have to earn twenty thousand in order to have ten.   Only after he has paid his debt can he accumulate for himself.   This need to pay the debt exists as an obligation.   In many instances it is a legal obligation, and may be enforced by agencies of the law.   It is also, sometimes or instead, a moral obligation.   Even where no legal debt exists (as following a bankruptcy judgment) a person's conscience may require him to make good on the debt.

Thinking in this way, people see the national debt as a burden that will have to be carried by the American people in either the near or a distant future.   In borrowing money, the idea is, the people (the government) now have more than they earn. They enjoy a benefit to which they are not entitled. And they will have to make up for it in the future by earning more than they will have. It is as if a man were to borrow money, spend it on a nice vacation, and then live at a level below that of his income so that he can belatedly buy the vacation. There is a tradition of thrift in America which takes a dim view of this way of doing things.   To enjoy now and pay later is seen as a lack of virtue and not merely as a decision that a person might decide against making because he does not want to suffer in the future for pleasures of the present.   It appears immoral and not just as an undesirable agenda. A good person, it is thought, defers gratification; he forgoes fun now in order to have more of it later. He does not go into debt if he can avoid doing so. Similarly, the nation is seen as having acted carelessly and as having put future generations under a heavy burden. Economists have not all agreed with this assessment. Some of them asserted that it is fundamentally different from personal debt.   The difference is that the national debt is money which Americans owe to Americans rather than which someone owes to someone else.   They have also preferred to deal with specific consequences of specific actions pertaining to the debt. If the government borrows more than it takes in, certain things happen. If it pays back what was borrowed before, other things happen. These consequences may include much more than just earning or having. Deficit spending may, for example, stimulate the economy so that more is produced, more is paid in taxes, and therefore more is available with which to repay the debt.

The purpose here, however, is to consider the debt in terms of basic thinking. Approaching it this way, it is necessary to recall the definition of money. Money is a claim on the existing pool of goods and services. When someone loans money to the government (buys bonds), he transfers claim temporarily from himself to the government. While he previously held cash in his hand--which is the claim--he now holds documents. These are pieces of paper which are called "IOU's." They are indications that government has an obligation to transfer claim back to the person.

The first thing to notice about this occurrence is that there is less difference between its taking place and its not taking place than one might have thought. If the person loans the money to the government, the government is in debt to the person; it incurs an obligation to transfer claim on goods to that person in the future. And since government is the agency of people, it is the people--or the taxpayers--who have that obligation. They are required, morally and/or legally, to honor that person's claims. That is, they will have to divert more of the pool of goods and services to his use or control than they would have had there been no debt. As the government repays and the person spends, the pool will flow towards him, so to speak. Just as the moon pulls the oceans and creates a high tide on one side of the body of water, so goods will pile up at the pleasure of the person who has been repaid.

However, if the person does not loan money to the government, the situation is not basically different. Instead of holding IOU's, he now holds cash. But cash also is a claim on goods and services. The community is already in debt to the person. It is obligated to push goods in his direction, just as it was in the other case. The obligation is not moral; it is based on the fact that whoever honors a claim by giving its holder something will then possess that claim himself. Also, the claim is different in that cash is liquid. That is, the person can lay claim to goods immediately rather than having to wait for the process of repayment to be completed. What is important to notice is that the *debt* exists in either case. Whether the person loans money to the government or does not do so, the community is in debt to that person. It must divert more of the product of its labor to projects which he enjoys or of which he approves than would otherwise be the case. There is no fundamental difference between IOU's and cash.

The more specific consequences of borrowing depend upon conditions. In times of depression, the effect of government borrowing may be to increase the amount of money in circulation. In the absence of such borrowing, a person who has money may choose not to spend it since he feels he has enough goods already. And he may not invest it because opportunities for investment are lacking. His money is, in effect, unemployed, just as people are. Thus the person simply holds his money rather than spending or investing it, and consequently, that quantity of money is effectively withdrawn from that which circulates within the economy. When a person does loan to the government, the buyer of bonds puts money back into circulation (and to work for himself). The exchange circle gets moving again, and people in general become more prosperous. Since people are working and producing goods, the pool of goods and services is enlarged. Labor will not be wasted as it is when people are unemployed, and goods will not revert to being non-goods, as happens when they are not sold and used. In this sense, a debt does not exist. There is no negative holding to be repaid by future generations. Because there are more goods now, there are more to divert to people who have money or IOU's and so to pay debt. Of course, loaning to the government is just one artifice by which money can be put into circulation.

Matters are different when the person who could loan to the government chooses to keep it and spend it instead. He has a choice to buy government bonds or to purchase goods, perhaps another summer home or automobile for his family. The fact that he buys the home or car does not make much difference, for either of his options affects the economy similarly. There may of course be a difference in the uses to which labor is put. If the person does not loan to the government and buys the house and car, labor is either called out of nonuse (unemployment) or diverted from other purposes to provide those items. If, on the other hand, he does buy government bonds, and the government uses the money to build public housing for the poor or fund research on AIDS and other illnesses, labor will be mobilized or diverted for these purposes. One may then evaluate government borrowing by reflecting on the comparative value of these expenditures and uses of labor.

Under the conditions of full employment and inflation, borrowing from someone who would not spend the money would worsen the inflation. This is unlikely however, since people usually wish to change money into goods under that condition. If they do not want consumer goods, they wish to invest, since money, like people, is thus fully employed and producing. Should he, despite this, loan to the government, the outcome depends upon what happens in a race between two factors--the elevation of interest rates (money being employed), and the decline in the value of money. If interests are high enough, the buyer of bonds will come out ahead. But if they are not, the money as repaid by the government will be less than when it was loaned. The money lender will come out behind. However, while inflation is certainly possible, full employment in industrial societies seems now to be a thing of the past, making these events unlikely.

But what happens in the future? Certainly people who loan to the government will be repaid, but new loans will be made, and for this reason the debt as such will not actually be retired. There will just be a change in the identity of holders of IOU's. At the moment, this seems what is most likely to take place.

However, it is at least possible that a day will dawn when government must, or chooses to, reduce the debt. If this happens, the reverse of the events just described could take place. The holders of bonds, once paid in full, could elect to hold the money, in which case there is less in circulation. The effects of action on the economy will depend on conditions. It will be good if there is too much money floating around, but bad if there is too little. The reduction in the quantity of money in circulation could worsen a depression. Yet even in that case, other artifices could be employed to get money and the exchange circle moving. The economy certainly will be affected, but a government which is determined to keep an economy going has other levers it can pull to accomplish that task. The reduction of the debt is just one of many factors which determine how well the economy--and the people--will fare.

In addition to effects on the economy, the repayment of debt also affects the distribution of goods and services. The person who once held IOU's now has cash. He has wealth, in liquid form, which he can hold, invest, or spend. If he spends it, a larger share of pool of goods and services will flow toward him than was the case before. The community as a whole was always under debt to him. He always had the ability to pull a larger share of goods towards himself. But he did not previously choose to do so. What he did instead was transfer the claim on goods to the government, and the government pulled on the supply of goods. It also enlarged the pool itself through the multiplier effects of its spending. And it used some of its claims for purposes that were good for people, as with scientific research, public parks, education, public housing, and other items. But now the claim transfers back to the buyer of bonds, and he stakes claims on the existing pool that he could have made before but did not. He always had the claim, but he uses it later rather than earlier.

Another factor, interest, pushes more of the pool of goods towards the repaid holder of government bonds. If there had been abundant investment opportunities before, this would not be a large factor. The person could invest in government or in something else. In either case, his money would "work for him." The claim on goods transferred back to him would be greater than that transferred from him. This would happen regardless whether he bought government bonds or invested in a shoe factory. In both cases, his claim on goods was used for purposes that are (supposedly) of benefit to the community, and in both cases the person experiences an increase in his claim on goods as a result.

One can judge all of this bunching up of the pool at the feet of the money-lender as being fair or unfair, or one can view it with indifference. As noted earlier, the person who invests uses claim on goods to make tools available. Tools, in turn, enhance the efficiency of labor. More is produced with any given amount of work. To invest, in this sense, is the same as to work. It is an act that adds to the pool of goods. Having put more in, then, people regard it as fair that a person take more out. He has contributed to the community, and may be rewarded for doing so. It could also, however, be viewed as unfair. Because his investment is a permanent claim on goods-producing implements, it yields him a claim on the pool of goods which goes on indefinitely and therefore beyond the contribution he made in producing it. And since the point in rewarding him so handsomely is lost unless the reward is *less* than his contribution, the reward may be seen as unfair.

On the side of viewing the high-tide of goods at the bond-buyer's feet with indifference, it may be recalled that *too much* production has long been a problem in America and in industrial societies in general. Marketing is a field of study in the university because finding customers who want the goods available is a job, while finding goods for the customers is all too easy. If goods were scarce and customers many, perhaps a course on "shopping" would be part of the higher learning! But with productive prowess exceeding the needs which it seeks to meet, what is wrong with delivering a few extra goods to people who have extra claim? It may help keep people working and the exchange circle functioning. And it certainly is no worse than other ways of disposing of excess. Much of exporting goods, as noted earlier, simply gets rid of things. It cannot add to what the community has (though it may enrich the corporation that exports), since America often does not need what the other country has to give. Military goods, unless seen as necessary for protection (an unlikely status for them) are also the fruits of labor that serve no purpose and are in that sense lost. The same is true of most advertising. In view of all of this, the opulence of the wealthy can, up to a point, be tolerated as harmless. All citizens could be given beautiful stones with which to adorn themselves. Most of these hard pieces could be called fake diamonds while a few are labeled genuine diamonds. The people who have the latter could then feel superior, even though the stones all look and behave the same. A similar thing could be done with ladies' dresses and men's suits.

All things considered, equality is not an appropriate goal. The wish for glory is so great in most people that some are going to find it in one way or another. They may as well be allowed to work hard and to acquire an excess, as compared to others. The community can tolerate their debutante balls and other signs of opulence and upper-class status. What should be a goal for the community as a whole is having an adequate level of living for everyone. Just what that level is or consists of is open for discussion, and decisions will have to be made on the matter. But once adequacy has been achieved, then if a few want to sport a wealthy style of life, they may be allowed to do so--again, up to a point. Saying this does not confirm the differences in wealth found now in the United States. These are far in excess of what is defensible. It is only to say that some special rewards for a few people do not stand in the way of a good life for people in general.

Third-World Debt

Of great moral urgency in the world today is another kind of debt. This is what might be termed "third world debt." It is the money owed by the poor countries of Latin America and elsewhere to wealthy nations or agencies within those nations. As with any debt, it is an obligation. It is an obligation to deliver goods to wealthy nations. These goods must have value which exceeds that of imports from those nations. This is called "paying" the debt. The obligation is backed up in certain ways, one of which is military force. There is a threat of intervention by force against nations that do not conduct themselves in accordance with the wishes of the United States and other industrial nations. Another way is through economic threat. Third world nations today are not able to mobilize to "develop" without trucks, electrical generators, and FAX machines, or in general without a large collection of apparatus that comes only from countries well endowed with heavy industry. They cannot repeat the performance of the Mormons on the American frontier, a performance in which each part of an economy capitalizes other parts to produce overall growth in the ability to provide goods. They are for this reason dependent on the industrial nations for machinery which only those nations can provide, and so are under their power. Also, there is the act of preempting. The government of the United States (and some others) takes over, in effect, the politically powerful circles and military organizations within the weaker countries. By recruiting them as allies, the United States gains control over these groups and therefore over the countries which they govern. And since America favors taking the debt seriously, so do the governments and armies of these poor nations.

Third world debt came into existence during the 1970s, when banks in industrial nations loaned large sums of money to poor nations, presumably for development. The idea was that the money would be used to purchase apparatus needed for production and to fund the construction of infrastructure, including roads, bridges, and storage facilities.

Such development would enable the nations to develop economically--that is, in such a way that their people could produce more with their labor, just as do the people of industrial nations. Whatever the lenders themselves thought, people-in-general assumed that the purpose was to help the countries, or, more specifically, the people of the countries. Their citizens were to produce more and therefore to have more and to be able to live at a level closer to that of industrial peoples. In fact, nothing remotely resembling that happened. Rather, the peoples of those nations are now poorer than ever. But to make their lives better was the idea in the beginning, at least as understood by the public. And the debt itself accumulates more and more, with no prospect of ever paying it in sight. Even when nations such as Brazil export more than they import and so presumably "pay" their debt, the debt does not cease to *grow* as interest builds up. The concept of debt in this case requires examination. When the money was loaned, the poor countries traded with the wealthy ones in accordance with the pattern of the last couple of centuries. This is the pattern in which agrarian countries send the products of farms and mines to industrial nations, while the latter send them machines and other manufactured goods in return. Latin American nations exported certain items which the temperate countries could not produce at all (such as bananas and coffee), and others which the rich nations wanted in greater quantity (such as citrus fruits, vegetables, cotton, sugar, and, more recently, beef). In taking out a loan and accepting a debt, the nations were implicitly agreeing to export a greater value in bananas, coffee, and the like than they would import in tractors and cars. They would thus repay the debt. Money, of course, was the explicit item to be sent, but money equals goods in exchanges between nations, so the incurring of a debt is necessarily an agreement to ship agricultural and mining materials in determinate quantities. To simplify, it was a "you give us trucks; we give you coffee" agreement.

But as is always the case with exchanges of goods, there is an abstracting of value from goods that is used to establish equivalencies among them. Bananas in a certain quantity are worth a certain amount of money. So also are trucks. But as in an algebraic equation, the money variable drops out, and a certain number of bananas become equal to a certain number of trucks. There is, of course, a great deal of arbitrariness in this. There is no divine mandate to establish what-equals-what. And if this is true of bananas and trucks, how much more true is it when there are masses of heterogeneous goods flowing in two directions? On just what basis are huge cargoes of products going from Central America to New York determined to be "more" or "less" than the cargo of other ships going in the other direction? Clearly, there is no true or dependable determination of such a matter.

The fiction is maintained, however, that there is. People all over the world assume that all of these items have determinate *prices*. These prices adhere to the products to which they apply just as certainly as they do in any department store. An object has a price, and that is that. No question of fairness exists or can exist, since the price belongs to the object just as does its name. It is different from the name only in that it can change from day to day. But in each day in which it applies, the price of an object has the character of established fact.

Though definite and seemingly factual, the price has a source. The source is the Market. It is a market existing in the world as a whole and between nations rather than within them. Thus, when the Soviet Union bought sugar from Cuba at a price higher than that which other industrial nations paid for sugar from other producers, people said that the Soviet Union was paying "more" than the world market price for the sugar and was thereby giving Cuba a subsidy. The excess of what was paid over that market price was interpreted as a gift. People assume, then, that there is a market, that this market sets the price, that this price may therefore be viewed as natural and not arbitrary, and that buyers and sellers are dealing fairly with one another when they use these prices as the basis for trading. Or, to put it another way, when they sell and buy at these prices, no one is giving anyone anything; each is trading with the other.

Missing from this view of things is the awareness that a *market*, properly so called, exists only when there is a certain equality between the partners. Each must have an ability to "take his business elsewhere" which is close to equal that of the others, and each must cope with the danger of the other's seeking someone else with whom to trade just as much as the other must contend with the danger that he will do so. If this equality does not exist, neither does the market. This is obvious enough when we consider extreme cases, as when a man is doomed to die unless he takes medicine that can be obtained in time from just one person. That person could demand a high price indeed, but no one would call it a market price. Indeed, when gasoline was in short supply in the United States in the mid 1970s, sellers who drastically raised their prices were said to be engaging in the illegal practice of price "gouging." In view of this observation about the moral judgments people make, it is by no means obvious that the prices which are called "world market prices" truly merit the term "market." Prices, they are. But are they market prices, and are they fair?

Prices could be truly market prices and could be fair only if there were at least a rough equality among the parties involved. People who sell bananas would have to be able to threaten to sell their bananas to others if those with whom they negotiate will not give them the right number of trucks for a certain quantity of their bananas. They would also have to be able to threaten to buy their trucks elsewhere. However, this does not seem to be the case. Industrial nations are far better able to set prices, both for what they buy and for what they sell, than are the agricultural nations with whom they trade. The "terms of trade," as the prices on both sides of the buy-sell equation are called, are determined by one side much more than they are by the other. And prices have deteriorated for the poorer nations in the last decade or two. These countries pay more for what they buy and receive less for what they sell than they did before. Naturally, they cannot produce enough bananas and coffee to exceed the value of their imports enough to actually retire their debt. And even if they could, the rich nations are almost certainly not able to eat that many bananas or drink that much coffee. Repayment of the debt is impossible now and in any foreseeable future.

When the debt was incurred, one could have "imagined away" the money which was involved. He could have seen it as receiving a certain amount of machinery, purchased with the borrowed funds, and promising a certain quantity of bananas, coffee, tin, and other items. Since that time, however, the price of these items has changed, and for that reason it takes more bananas, coffee, and tin to pay than it did before. Had the obligation been stated in terms of commodities, no such change would have occurred, but because it was expressed as amounts of money, it could. If a question of fairness were raised, one would have to ask whether the creditor nations truly and fairly have a right to decide on their own that poor peoples owe them more bananas than they did before.

If equity is not determined by the market, since there is no true market, there arises the question of from just where it does derive. One could imagine that the creditor owns a house and will employ a man to mow his lawn and to do other labor around the house. The hired man is desperate; he has hungry children to feed. There is no one else who will hire him, and there is no charity available. This is a condition that exists in many poor countries and is not as strange in the United States as many Americans would like to think. The employer, on the other hand, may not care a great deal whether the work is done, and/or he may be able to hire others to do it. So he can force the man to work for a pittance. He can push the wage down to a point at which the man's children will stay hungry anyway, and so there is no point to the man's deciding to work.

Imagine that the householder has a robust wish to be fair. He is blessed or cursed, as one may choose to view it, with a healthy conscience. Thus, he does not wish to push the worker as far as he can. On the other hand, he wants only to be fair, not to be generous. He is not going to give gifts disguised as wages; he is simply going to pay what is fair and proper. So what does he do? There is clearly no definite answer to this, but there may be one that is at least approximate. The employer may have an idea of fair wages based on other times when worker and employer were more equal. He may simply intuit a wage that is enough above what he has to pay to be fair, but low enough to avoid being generous.

Despite the lack of definiteness of what is fair when no true market exists, Americans can undertake the task of determining fair prices for bananas and other items. Americans could ask themselves to what amount of money a robust wish to be fair would lead them. They could suggest, for example, that *campesinos* who work on banana plantations in Costa Rica be paid a minimum of six dollars an hour, assuming that the work is regular. If it is not regular, the figure should be higher. They could then see how this would affect the price of the item in the local supermarket, complain about that, think about the worker, and decide on an amount that is fair to both banana pickers and banana eaters. There is no way to say what this amount should be, short of receiving word from the Lord. But certainly, whatever it may be, it will be well above the world market price. This is not only the right thing to do for its own sake, but also because it might cast a different light on the debt. Indeed, if prices of the goods America currently sells are lowered while those it buys are similarly raised, the debt might disappear immediately, or its end might at least be visible.

There are other reasons for doubting the debt. If there is a debt, there must be an assumption that the debtor has benefitted by the money loaned to him. It would seem reasonable to think that the countries which borrowed money used those funds to buy equipment of all kinds and are for that reason able to produce far more than they were before. It would also be reasonable to think that the people are better off because of their greater productivity. The debt should be matched by functioning production facilities and by higher wages and services available. With these facilities and wages in place, the people would then be in a position to repay the debt while looking forward to a time when the debt would be retired and they could enjoy the full fruits of their increased production. However, none of this has taken place. The poor of Latin America are as poor as ever. In fact, they are poorer than they were before. Whatever it was that was done with the borrowed funds, it has not been of benefit to most of the people. And since they have not profited, it does not seem right that they should be expected to pay.

Further, since democracy holds so high a place in the American value-scheme, the question should be asked whether the ordinary people of Central and South America consented to the loans and the debt, and whether they approved of the purposes for which the funds would be used and handled. The answer to all these queries is no. They did not consent; they were not even consulted. This being the case, how can they be expected to repay? The debt exists in negotiation between American bank officials and Latin American government officials. It is an affair between these two parties; to demand that masses of *campesinos* and workers live in extreme poverty in order to make the payments involved is clearly unjust. These workers have neither consented nor benefitted. It was not their loan.

Behind the idea of debt is the *social contract* view of the individual and society. This perspective holds that the individual is selfish, and that he participates in society only because he finds doing so convenient. His selfishness has to do with possession of goods. He owns things, and they are property in a real and factual sense. He has dealings with other people, but he has them because the dealings serve his selfish interests. He has too much of something, so he exchanges it for something which another person has in excess. He and that other person then have the same total value in goods as they did before, but each obtains goods which are more appropriate to his needs and tastes. The exchange is social in the sense that people relate to each other. But they relate because relating advances their respective self interests. Loaning and borrowing are among the exchanges in which people engage. One person loans another person goods or the means for obtaining them (money). He gives the other the goods with the expectation that they be returned with interest. The interest is compensation for the lender's pain in being without the goods for a time. The borrower may enter the relationship because he must to survive, or in order to obtain capital goods which can then be used to increase his total holdings (his estate). Everyone is selfish, and everyone exchanges with others because exchanging serves the selfish interests of all parties.

This social contract view of individuals as discrete atoms with rights is only true up to a point. When that point is reached, other definitions of individual and society and of a person's rights come into play. The traditions surrounding bankruptcy is an example of an occasion when the point is reached. The community recognizes that a person whose holdings are reduced to a level of extreme privation has a right to survive and a right to have an opportunity to go to work and recover his living. This right is seen as taking precedence over the property rights of his creditors, and his debt to them is therefore canceled. As noted in earlier chapters, the existence of this legal artifice is evidence of features of the value-scheme of our civilization. It is evidence that the social contract view of people and society is a surface view. It is intended to govern relations between people most of the time and under normal conditions. It is not fundamental or undergirding. When special times arrive and conditions are not normal, values from a deeper and more fundamental level are activated. The rights of any person to survival and to have a chance to improve his circumstances are core values at this deeper level.

If this is true in relations between individuals within a community, it is even more true in those which exist between nations. An example of this occurred in World War I, when the United States gave loans to European countries. School children in America now learn that their country loaned large sums to their allies across the Atlantic during that conflict and that when the war was over, all the debtor nations except Finland renounced the debt and never made any effort to repay the United States. Certainly, the American government could have pressed its former allies to repay, insisting that the United States was entitled to receive all sorts of largesse from the rebuilt factories of Europe. However, the major reason it did not do so was that it did not make moral sense to make such a demand. The war was, after all, a joint venture. Asking some countries to repay a debt would be a bit like expecting a soldier to pay for the rifle he uses in combat.

More importantly, why would nations devastated and impoverished by war pay one that was not? A fundamental sense of justice suggests that there is no such requirement. As with bankruptcy, a point has been reached in which social contract obligations no longer apply and a deeper level of valuation is activated. At this deeper level, the right of nations recovering from wartime destruction to rebuild their productive facilities and their communities is primary. There is no reason why they should be obligated to deliver volumes of goods to another country without receiving anything in return while doing that rebuilding. The fact that after the war the United States had no need for such goods adds emphasis to this but does not determine it. Third-world debt today would seem to be fundamentally the same. These nations are very poor. Large numbers of their people are in desperate straits. Many just barely survive, and some do not survive. Everywhere, conditions have worsened in the last several years. Most regions are little developed. Few of the capital goods needed to make labor productive are available. And when they are, they benefit most people very little. The contrasts between rich and poor are extreme. Repression is the order of the day from Mexico to Argentina. All things considered, the situation is bleak. Why, with this being the reality, industrial nations consider these struggling nations to have "debts" is mystifying. It is hard to find any justification for it. It would seem that the point at which social contract definitions cease to apply has been reached and passed. And in addition, there is little selfish reason for the wealthy nations to insist on debt repayment. It could only mean that these nations want poor countries to deliver bananas, coffee, and other items without receiving anything in return; to the wealthy countries, that is the how the poor countries repay. But, as mentioned earlier, the wealthy nations *want* markets. There is, thus, not even a self-serving reason to maintain the notion of debt. Why is it not simply written off?

The most likely reason has to do with power. First, the industrial nations have power, both military power and power derived from their ability to deliver machinery. Thus, they are able to dictate that the debt continue in a way that was not possible for the United States after the first world war. But secondly, the debt enables the wealthy nations, especially the United States, to retain power. Or, better stated, it is a structure in terms of which power is maintained. Noam Chomsky, Walden Bello, and others have argued that the major theme behind American foreign policy decisions is the desire to stay in control.[50] Negatively, it is to prevent poor nations from asserting independence. Such assertion on their part threatens to deprive the United States of what it wants from poor countries, which is cheap sources of resources and labor, cheap goods, and markets. Any effort to become self-sufficient must be dealt fatal blows. The countries must be and remain "export-oriented." Having the nations in debt helps maintain power over them. America could of course just threaten them, decreeing that if they do wrong, the United States will withdraw shipments of machinery, invade them, or the like. But it sounds better to talk instead about restructuring the debt, making loans with which to repay--or pay the interest on--other loans, and the like. So this is the way it is done. Power is maintained.

One could ask whether a powerful nation like the United States would repay Peru and Brazil if it were the nation that had a debt. Here is a nation having power, but burdened with debt. Will it pay? The answer would almost certainly be no. And, as a matter of fact, the United States *is* in debt to one Latin American country, Nicaragua. In June of 1986, the World Court handed down a decision in a case against the United States brought by this Central American country. The decision was that the United States should cease aggressive actions against Nicaragua, and should pay indemnity for damage done by the Contra forces which the United States supported. No amount was given, but estimates of what it should be are in many billions of dollars. So the United States has a debt, one that is confirmed by an international body. That body, the World Court, is the closest thing to an impartial judge relative to relations among nations that exists. Yet the United States has not paid what it owes. It in no way acknowledges that it owes anything, nor indicates that it will pay or will even negotiate the matter. What is apparent here is that *when a nation has power, it does not have debt.* In international affairs, debt is money owed by weak nations to strong ones.

This chapter has considered three matters: affordability, the national debt, and third world debt. What emerges from all of these is a picture of the world community and of communities within the world. In this picture, there is production of capital goods. There is exchange of goods for goods, and there is exchange of capital goods for the promise of delivery in the future. There are assessments of what is fair, just, and right. There are ideas about how it could be all brought together to make a decent and humane world. Throughout, the rhetoric features talk about money, limitations on money relative to certain purposes, and debts in which people are obligated to deliver money--ultimately goods--to other people. The rhetoric and conceptual schemes are quite irrelevant. They must either be abandoned or reinterpreted so that people can speak properly about their problems. Clarity of thought and speech does not itself make a better world, but it is hard to make the world better without it.

Chapter 11

Patriotism and Humanity

In this final chapter, attention turns to questions of morality and of the relation of individual to community. If people are to make community decisions under counselor leadership in the effort to establish societies which are humane and in which a decent life is possible for all, certain things are necessary. One necessity is that each person must fully accept membership in the community. He has to relate to the larger group as a social being who intends to cooperate with others in making decisions and in building a common life.

The Primacy of Morality

To do this, the individual has to be moral. He has to take seriously his sense of obligation and act upon it. Certainly, it is true that much of his cooperation with others would seem to be exchange, and in that sense selfish. A person gives things to people and does things for them, but he does so as exchange, that is, because of what he gets from them in return. Those other people, in the meantime, are doing the same. He and they have a contract with each other according to which they do things for one another, yet with each acting entirely for his own benefit. It is also true that there are many instances in which an individual sees that if he and others cooperate in certain ways, they will all fare better than they would if each sought only to do the best he could for himself.

Despite these cases where it appears that people serve their selfish interests and cooperate with others at the same time, the appearance is never quite correct. The person who makes a contract with another always has a moment in which it profits him to renege on his part of a bargain. And in the case where all people benefit from all acting in a certain way, any lone person would do better by not acting that way. Either others are acting cooperatively, in which case he will gain a special advantage, as when the barber opens his shop on Monday, or they are not, and he avoids suffering a special disadvantage. No matter how evident it is that all fare best when all do the right thing, any one of them serves his selfish interests most by doing the wrong thing.

Thus, as stated in earlier chapters, morality comes to the rescue. People will act in ways that are good for all of them only if they feel that they should. This "should" cannot, when all is said and done, be avoided.   It may be dressed up much of the time with selfish advantage. One may do what is right because it avoids problems with the law, because customers are more likely to patronize his business, because people will trust him, because potential romantic partners will view him/her favorably, and for other reasons. But there will come a point when all of this clothing will be stripped away, and all that is left will be a naked "should." That is, there will be an awareness of obligation that is nothing but obligation. There is something that a person should do, and there is no reason to do it other than that he should. Such is the essence of morality. An action is truly moral when and only when its being so is the only reason to engage in it. The "Adversary" in the book of Job recognizes this when he challenges God to see if Job will remain faithful and good when all selfish advantage is taken from him.

Basic thinking is by its nature concerned with the moral. It is thinking about the problems of community and about what is just and fair in a group in which people both work and receive the fruits of labor, both their own and that of others. As such, it is a digression from the selfish path, the one in which a concern for "Number One" would lead a person's actions and thoughts. To devote one's attention to what is good for him *and others*, one has to identify with the group as a whole. One has to have a moral motivation.

Orientation to Particular Community

Communities are of necessity *particular*. A person certainly can be social in the sense that he cares about others and is prepared to cooperate with them. But any vigorous concern for one's fellow human beings of necessity comes from an identification with a concrete group that has a name and characteristics which set it apart from others. Such a group will have an identity that is peculiar to it. It will have its own history, tendencies, moods, and symbols. The person who embraces it as his community inevitably embraces these characteristics as well, regardless whether they are ones that he would choose as an individual.

A member of society is in this sense like a married person. A man cannot have an abstract or generalized wife. Of necessity, the woman he embraces is particular and has her own special features of body and mind, along with her own neuroses and irrationalities. She has her own "rough edges," that is, her own characteristics that do not belong to the idea of a wife which the man had in his mind before he chose her, yet which are essential in the sense that she could not be the person she is, or, for that matter, any real person, without them. She could not otherwise be someone whose presence is comforting on a cold winter night or when one is lonely. The same would apply, of course, to husbands, and to sons and daughters. People are particular and have rough edges. So also are communities.

For this reason, this chapter treats patriotism. It is a word with many connotations, but all imply that the person who cherishes his membership in community necessarily embraces a particular community. Usually, the word has, for the speaker, a good meaning. If a speaker does not intend the meaning to be good, he uses a different word. If he means to imply a negative connotation, he speaks of chauvinism or jingoism. If he wishes to imply a neutral connotations, he talks about nationalism. Whether good, bad, or indifferent, being part of a community is being loyal, and being loyal has to do with something particular.

Americans see themselves as patriotic, a self-understanding which they manifest in their displaying of the flag, saying the Pledge of Allegiance, and the singing of national songs. In thinking this, however, people are mistaken. Americans are, for the most part, not in any great degree patriotic. Evidence of this is the fact that it takes wars and activities pertaining to war to evoke national feeling. There has to be a fight going on against an evil enemy, or there has to be a memory of such a fight, to elicit the spirit of "Americanism" in someone who is a citizen of this country. Indeed, if asked what patriotism is, many would answer that it is a willingness or readiness to fight and defend one's country. Patriotism is very much bound up in people's minds with military matters, with uniforms, guns, ships, and all the rest. It would be difficult to imagine patriotism without the military services, their activities, and their symbols. In view of this limited scope of sentiments pertaining to the country and the extraordinary nature of the circumstances that evoke those sentiments, one cannot affirm that Americans are patriotic.

Further evidence for this is the grumbling about taxes that is endemic within the populace. Television commentator Bill Moyers noted once that when he was young, he and his friends took pride in paying taxes. They viewed it as confirmation that they were indeed citizens of the nation. Paying taxes expressed citizenship. It is worthwhile to note that people once felt this way, for now it is rare for anyone to say that he takes such a view of paying taxes. Not only do people grumble about taxes, but they regard displaying such a negative attitude as quite respectable. It hardly occurs to anyone that such complaining might call his patriotism into question, though many would be quick to cite their records of military service to counter any such challenge. Much of the complaining asserts that taxes are too high, and it is of course possible to question taxation from that standpoint. But this must be done with care, since any tax always seems to people to be too high; indeed rarely does a person who complains have a definition of a right amount of taxation relative to which the current level appears to be excessive. A person might legitimately complain about the taxes that he in particular is required to pay. His taxes might be higher than they should, while those of someone else might be unduly low. But again, complainers do not often have an idea of fair tax structure to use as a measuring stick. While certain complaints are admissible and worthy of consideration, the generally negative attitude of Americans towards supporting the organ of community decision-making and action suggests a low level of patriotism.

Considering both the limited scope of the patriotic sentiment and reluctance about paying taxes as a form of participation in community life, it seems evident that Americans consider patriotism to be a good thing, but they do not view it as part of vital life. That is, it does not pertain to the issues that matter to them and that confront them daily.

In any positive assessment of patriotism, the love of one's country should be seen as being like his loyalty to his family. It is a commitment, that is, to a collective entity that is particular and therefore partial and limited. Being finite as they are, human beings cannot relate to all people or to people-in-general. Instead, they have to relate to particular persons or collections of persons. There is an inevitable exclusiveness in this. A person cannot relate to someone as friend or family member without relating to that person rather than to some other person. He does not necessarily have a negative attitude towards the other to whom he does not relate. He simply cannot relate to one without relating to that one alone and therefore not to others. The man who refuses to regard all women except one as his wife has no wish to regard other women negatively. His wish, rather, is to accept the one as wife; the exclusion of the others is just a corollary of that acceptance. And so it is with all personal relationships.

Implicitly, the person who relates to certain individuals as family member or friend to the exclusion of others does not thereby affirm that those to whom he relates are better persons. He affirms only that they are *his* relatives or friends. The new father who tells his two-week-old daughter that she is the "cutest little girl in town" is not informing the infant that she would win a beauty contest of girls of her age before an impartial panel of judges. He is, more than anything else, telling her that she is *his* little girl. The same is true in general when people assert that their spouses, their parents, and their sons and daughters are "the best." The superlatives are used to indicate that certain persons are the specific objects of affection, while others of equal merit or attractiveness are not. Those others are, it is supposed, someone *else's* object of affection.

So it is with patriotism and the nation. Americans often say that theirs is the "greatest country on earth," but no one is disturbed that the comment is made without any proper standard of comparison. In essence, the comment is not a comparison; rather, it is an affirmation of the country as being one's own. Presumably, everyone in the world has a country which is his, and every country has people for whom it is "theirs." The nation is really the same thing as a family, only much larger.

In view of this, three things can be said about patriotism. First, someone who is patriotic takes a great deal of interest in the expressive or artistic life of his country. Second, the patriot wishes to repress his selfish tendencies in order to participate in community decisions and actions. Third, the patriot wants his country to do what is right.

Patriotism and the Expressive Life

To be patriotic is to take an interest in the life of the community and therefore in its expressive life. It is to desire an awareness of the community as having a collective life and a memory of life in the past. By its nature, life has continuity; it exists through time. One who wishes to discern that life will therefore view it as a memory of a past that leads into a present and which anticipates a future. Awareness of community is, in this sense, awareness of *story*, of an accounting of how what exists now came to be and from what kind of past it issued. To be conscious of being an American is to be aware of old country origins, of the colonial period, of the birth of the nation, of the nineteenth century, punctuated as it was by the Civil War, and of the present century with the two world wars and other trauma. The person identified with the community sees the story of America as *his* story. Of necessity, this awareness takes on objective form in various monuments--the Liberty Bell, the Washington Monument, and others. Americans also objectify their patriotism in painting and sculpture, folk songs and other music, and in literary works including short stories and poems. In all forms of expression, people celebrate the life of the community. While the community exists in people's minds (a shared mind), it also takes form externally in physical objects, in written and remembered songs, and in writings. The memory and awareness that are within, and the forms to be found without, interact. Objects have their meaning as expressions of the community. The community achieves self-consciousness by way of objects. Americans become Americans in singing certain songs and telling certain stories.

The story begins in the Old Country, notably in England and Scotland, though for many it may originate in Ireland, Germany, Poland, or Italy. The old English and Scottish songs and ballads express community which, for an American, is his community (even if his ancestors are German). This expression later reverberates or echoes in a different setting. It reappears as the songs and ballads of the New World westward movement. The people are the same, and the community is the same. There is continuity, but what was celebrated amidst the rivers and hills of the British Isles now echoes in a different physical and social topography. The setting in this case is the abundant acreage of the Midwest and the prairies of the West. The people are not the settled villagers of the Old Country and New

England, but the isolated families who conquered the frontier and then set up villages and cities, doing so in constant interaction with the thrill-seeking and lonely individuals who gave the West so much of its character, both in fiction and in true story. The lines " . . . you take the high road and I'll take the low road, and I'll get to Scotland 'afore you" have as their echo songs such as "Shenandoah" and "Red River Valley." The story of the community has stages, just as does the biography of the individual.

Awareness of community also means cognizance of the community's variety. As an American, a person is aware of the calm and dignity of New England, the turbulence and romance of the Old South, the competence and vigor of the Midwest, and the rich imagery of ranching and cowboys in the West. Some of these generate more expressive life and therefore more memory than others. One can be sentimental about Alabama or Texas, but it is difficult to imagine an equivalent exuberance about Ohio or Wisconsin. A person can sing "Red River Valley," but could a man have loved a woman "so true" in New Hampshire? Still, these are all America, and they are all part of the memory.

Of special importance now are memories of time when American life was not as dominated by technology and industry as it is today. Certainly, there were technological developments that distinguished the 1800s from earlier eras. By mid-century the railroad and the telegraph were firmly in place, making both transportation and communication qualitatively different from anything known before. But compared to America today, technology did not so thoroughly dominate the scene. There was a life, both practical and expressive, that was America and had specific American personality without the overwhelming technological preoccupation of the present period. This is important because this technological focus, when it occurs, tends to absorb and obliterate other aspects of community life. The wonders of jet airplanes, televisions, and computers take over and do not allow other currents of life or thought to flow in their own channels. As Jacques Ellul argued in *The Technological Society,* when technological development reaches a certain point, it develops momentum which shapes all other aspects of social life.[51]

To be a patriot is to wish to identify with one's community, and this includes among its prime meanings that one wants to make contact and become familiar with the objective expressions of that community. These enable a person to join with others in being aware of the community's characteristic traits. The cultivation and cherishing of this awareness is fundamental to patriotism. The patriot may be willing to fight for his country. But if so, that is not all that he is, nor is that the essence of what it means to "love" one's country. It means that one wants to embrace his country through taking serious notice of its expressive life, particularly as embodied in art, song, and story. Doing so lifts a person out of his lonely individuality and his preoccupation with the projects that currently engage his attention and makes him part of a larger society. That community, like all communities, has to be particular. America may or may not be the greatest country on Earth, but it is still the individual's "own" country, and he embraces it as such.

Patriotism and Consideration for the Group

The second feature of patriotism is that the person comes to think of the community as a whole as the referent of his concern. It is the unit that, to him, "does well" or "does poorly." He does not abandon interest in whether he personally prospers. But parallel with his concern about his own condition is an equal fretting about whether people in general within his community are faring well or poorly.

This involves the willingness of the individual to make decisions in the interest of the community and not just in his own interests. The patriotic individual will do so in any decision he makes. He will reflect, that is, on whether his actions affect others within the community as well as himself. If it appears that others are affected, he will try to do what benefits them as well as himself. If water is in short supply, for example, he will not sprinkle his lawn, or will sprinkle it sparingly. There may be water enough in the reservoir for him to make his grass green, but he sees that he is taxing the supply, even if by himself he does so only a little bit. In leaving his lawn dry and perhaps even in letting the grass turn brown, he does something for others--for the community. He sees himself as making that herbal sacrifice alongside many others who do the same. In addition to making every decision in the light of its effects on others, he also seeks to make them explicitly community decisions by taking them up with organizations of various kinds, including government. He participates in the organs of community decision-making in order to act for the benefit of all. To cope with the water shortage, he confers with others, commonly in an organizational setting, in the hope that all can agree to act in a way that is good for all. The organizations can be formal or informal; they can be permanent or *ad hoc*. Regardless what their exact nature is, they enable people to act together.

Acting in the interest of the community is different from acting selfishly, in that it involves a sacrifice. There is an advantage or pleasure that a person could have, but which he forgoes in the interest of the community--that is, of other people. It costs him to act for the community, and for that reason his acting that way has an inevitable moral texture; he will do it only because it seems good and noble to him to act that way. The pleasure he gets from his actions, if he gets any, will be from its moral character. He will feel that he is acting as he should or that others are benefiting by what he does, and he will experience it as good for that reason, not because of what it does for him.

Part of the good feeling that comes from acting for the community derives from a belief that one is joined with others in such an endeavor. The person feels that he is part of something, that he belongs. This is a good feeling, as is evidenced by Americans having a nostalgia for the World War II period when there was a wide-spread feeling that "we are all in it together." It was a good feeling, one that people like to recall and celebrate, even if just briefly. In *Suicide*, Emile Durkheim noted that suicide rates generally go down in war time, and probably do so for this reason. People feel good about being part of something and therefore feel good about life and are more inclined to hang on to it. In this sense, the sacrifice involved in acting for the community is matched by a positive feeling of belonging.[52]

Whatever the value of belonging has been, Americans seem at this time in their history to emphasize it very little. Watching out for "Number One" is the order of the day. The 1980s were the "me" generation when everyone wanted to "get" for himself. Presently, decisions of all kinds, notably purchasing decisions, are made in the interest--and only in the interest--of the people who make them. That is, people both decide and act selfishly. It is not, however, only a matter of how people act overtly. It also has to do with how people think people are supposed to act. The person who buys automobiles and other items solely on the basis of what will serve him individually is assumed to be acting as people always do act and as people should act. If someone is not pleased with the purchasing decisions, he is supposed to see to it that the buyer is presented with a "deal" that would induce him to make one that is better. In the current mind-set, for example, if it is not desired that people buy Toyotas, let the Chevrolet manufacturers provide an automobile that is better, cheaper, or both. When American car makers fail to do this, they "should" not expect that any sense of obligation or any emotional identification with the community would move people to buy American products. Current thinking holds that it is a tough and manly world out there, and people should either measure up or quit complaining.

Behind these value judgments--against making value judgments--is the capitalist ideology to which allusion has been made more than once before in this present discussion. People should seek to become wealthy by producing fine products and offering them for sale at low prices. If all do this, the results will be good for all. Moreover, people often believe that this is a basic law of nature, and that when people pursue their interests entirely in market terms, they are tapping into the dynamics of the natural order and so assuring success in the long term. While this point of view has been battered mercilessly by events, it shows remarkable resilience and is very much in evidence today principally, as noted earlier, because it "fits" the power structure of society and not because of any intellectual virtue it can claim. It helps people to feel that their selfish decisions are legitimate and honorable.

Ideology, however, is not the only reason for the regnant selfishness of Americans. In an industrial society, people are separated from kinfolk and neighbors. They are set off by themselves, and they are seeking careers and otherwise trying to make life agreeable. They do this to a degree rarely found in other human societies. In their isolation, the acquisition of goods seems to be the only way to participate in community life. To have things is to be somebody; it is to have an identity and to be a person of worth in the eyes of any person who will take notice, and this is what is most important. Therefore, the effort is made to maximize income and to acquire an impressive assembly of goods. In this way, people validate themselves as worthy persons. The "consumer society," as it is often called, arises as the inevitable result of this kind of occurrence. Possession of consumer goods takes on a special importance because community itself is weak or missing. People do not act like members of a community because there is little in way of genuine and vibrant community to which they could belong.

Yet another explanation for the each-person-for-himself behavior of Americans is that it is a result of the efforts by corporate elites to gain control over society. The very successful battle against unions and unionism has left the workingman in the United States without any organization to promote his interests. He is on his own, and must contract with employers as the lone negotiator. In that state of affairs, he is all but helpless before the superior power of the employer. There is nothing he can do when that power is used to impoverish him, for the union movement is in disarray and is not able to act in defense of its members or of workers in general. The workers can do nothing that would force managers to take them seriously or to bargain with them as equals. This is exactly what the corporate elite want; "divided we fall" is rewritten as "divided *they* fall." With unions either destroyed or badly weakened, managers are free to do pretty much as they wish. The workingman has accepted this state of affairs with remarkably little complaining.

There is reason for his docility. In the series of events and changes taking place during the last two decades, it has become evident that managers tend to get what they want. Huff and puff as the middle and lower classes may, when all is said and done, the corporate elite seems always to come out on top. And while "might" does not truly "make right," it certainly has the appearance of doing so. Unconsciously, and step by step, people come to see that the elite is going to have its way, and they act quickly to join it lest they be left out in the cold. And their doing so enhances elite power even further. The fact that managers have power means that they can fragment the working classes and force people to act as individuals who stand alone as they face their employers. And when people act that way, they add to the power that forced them into that individualistic mode of behavior in the first place. With unions weak and always losing, it seems best for each person to run for cover as best he can. He tries to improvise solutions to his problems, but the solutions are only for himself. Community is gone. The loss of community is both effect and cause of corporate power. That power has engendered a general atmosphere of "each man for himself."

In addition to explaining the approval of selfishness, the weakness of ordinary Americans relative to the strength of the corporate owners and managers also explains poverty. It accounts for the progressive economic deterioration which besets poorer segments of the community over the last couple of decades. That such an economic decline should occur simultaneously with dramatic increases in ability to produce is remarkable and can be explained only by the growing power of the wealthy. To be sure, other explanations for the impoverishment suggest themselves. Even with technology advancing, deterioration of the resource base could account for the decline in levels of living. Whatever the technology is, it has to work with materials the planet provides. If technology advances but the materials decline, all could suffer. The reduction in the Earth's offering of soil, minerals, cooperative weather, and other resources may more than offset the benefits of improved technique. A knowledgeable world populace could be beaten down, so to speak, by the limited character of the planet which that populace has inherited. Also, American workers could experience loss of economic power because of having to share the world's largesse with workers in other countries. Prosperity could be more spread out and therefore less pronounced in the hitherto wealthier societies.

Despite the appeal of these explanations, it is clear that none of them is valid. The resource base has not declined that far yet. With the resources available, it is still possible for the human community to feed and otherwise care for all who are numbered within it. Workers in more prosperous nations could maintain the high levels of living attained twenty or so years ago while their counterparts in the poorer nations raise theirs. The pie, we might say, is not forced by a lack of resources to shrink, and it is not necessary to take pieces of it from one populace to give some to the others. What we must record, then, is that elites are armed with great and increasing power and that they have used this power in ways that impoverish the less affluent peoples of their nations and of the world.

It would not be correct, however, to attribute decline of the poorer classes to simple greed on the part of wealthier people. To do that would be to fall back on a too individualistic type of explanation. Lone persons have greed, but lone persons do not shape economic orders. Rather, corporate leaders act as individuals (individual companies) and have vigorously defended their right to act that way. Each buys, sells, and employs with an eye to maximizing profits or empire or both. And each does these things without regard for the consequences, that is, the aggregate effects. That is, corporate leaders do not concern themselves with what occurs as a result of their all doing the same thing at the same time. These effects, though not intended, nevertheless occur, and in due course come to shape events. One of these effects is that managers are put in a position in which they must, whether they like it or not, crush the working classes. Even the humane manager has to act that way, for his competitors are doing so, and if he fails to follow suit, he may lose out in the competition. His case is similar to that of the barber who opened his shop on Monday and so forced other barbers to do the same. Because one industrial manager minimizes the costs of production in various ways, all must similarly minimize theirs.

While it is denied here that greed explains managerial behavior (though it is not denied that many are greedy), it is *not* denied that they are unpatriotic. On the contrary, it has to be affirmed that business leaders are supremely *un*patriotic. The patriot, by definition, wishes to serve the community and not just himself. And the community, when all is said and done, is the people who comprise it. America is Americans; Peru is Peruvians, and Thailand is the Thai people. To serve the community, the patriot of necessity concerns himself with the welfare of its people. And he worries about how things are with all segments of the population, regardless how that population is divided into groups or strata. If he cannot act in their interest without risking the survival of the organization he manages, he seeks to engage others in making community decisions that will make it possible to both act in the larger interest and still survive. If necessary, he will appeal to government, as the major organ of community decision-making, to legislate such coordinated actions. He would, for example, favor a direct prohibition of "siting" operations outside the country. He would press for stronger, not weaker, labor unions (while insisting that they be properly democratic). These are the things that a patriotic manager would do. The fact that managers are behaving very differently leads one to conclude that they are not patriotic.

It is true that in the ideological syndromes that are at hand, capitalism and patriotism are coupled. Waving the flag and lauding the virtues of free enterprise seem to go together, as do presenting one's self as "all American" while enhancing one's income at the expense of the employees upon whom a person who is an owner or a manager of a business depends for his livelihood. It has to be concluded that the patriotism of corporate managers is an artifact of their public relations programs.

Also inescapable is the implication that there is little hope for ordinary Americans or for future Americans unless people wage battle against the corporate elite. That elite has shown itself to be uncompromising and intransigent on two fronts, the economic conditions of most Americans and the environment. They consistently insist on actions that promise only to impoverish ordinary people. They have already done so in great measure, and there is no reason to think that the condition of Strobel's "middle class" has bottomed out yet. They can become much poorer still. When it comes to protecting the environment, the corporate elite not only fail to show enthusiasm for preserving nature and for finding ways of fueling the industrial apparatus with sustainable and renewable resources, but they also seem determined to battle those who do display concern about these matters. Consistently, they define environmentalists as enemies to be opposed in every way possible. Of course, to change their behavior on any of these matters, they would have to do so together. Either all would have to agree to act in new ways, or some must agree while others are compelled by government to follow suit (thus making those who want to do right *free* to do as they wish). The trouble here is that they not only do not wish to act in the economic interest of other Americans or to preserve the environment, but they wage war against policies that would enable them to do so cooperatively and therefore survive the process. They use their abundant financial resources and personal corporate clout to preserve their right to act selfishly. This being the case, there is little reason to hope for any serious change without defining the corporate elite as enemies and waging battle against them. Just as Nazi sympathizers were an internal enemy (the Fifth Column) in World War II, so is the cadre of corporate managers today.

Confronted with a powerful adversary such as the elite, anyone has two strategies at hand for coping with it. These simply stated, are to fight them or to join them. Leaders in the United States have rather uniformly opted for the latter. Thus, Paul Tsongas, seeking the Democratic nomination for presidency for the 1992 election, spoke of himself as a "pro-business Democrat." He said that it makes little sense to oppose business when we all depend on business for the goods and services we need. In saying this, he was indulging in flawed logic. To oppose abuses by a group of people is not to oppose that group itself. One can, for example, set himself against police brutality without being opposed to the police. Similarly, in waging war against corporate managers and their antisocial actions, one is not opposing the manufacturing and distributing of goods and services. Nor is he necessarily taking up arms against generous salaries for managers, profits for the enterprise, or dividends for the owners of shares. He can, in fact, favor all of these while taking stern issue with managers who are determined to behave in ways that harm present and future generations of Americans and of human beings the world over. There is reason for the use of the word "strategy" above. A strategy, by its nature, involves a pattern of actions that rely on a certain dynamic or force for achieving a desired end. And in using a strategy, a person or group necessarily forgoes whatever force or advantage may be resident in an alternate strategy. For example, when confronted with a fierce dog, one can try to make friends with the dog or to best him in combat. To do either is to renounce all hope of doing the other. It is the same when dealing with the corporate elite. Political and intellectual leaders have determined that they will attain a best possible deal, considering the awesome power of the elite. Perhaps they will obtain an improvement in the medical care system, or establish a small bit of privilege for labor unions, or to tone down an abuse in the environment. By showing themselves to be friends to business, they will obtain some crumbs that might otherwise not fall from the table. Or, they may obtain some of the crumbs for their constituents so that those constituents will not suffer as badly as others.

At the level of the individual, this takes the form of coming to believe that one is "lucky to have a job." In an earlier era, the worker complained about his wages, his benefits, and his working conditions. He sought power, through the union, to defend and enhance his interests. But he now believes that all of that was based on a wrong estimate of his situation. He was being too generous with himself. He now thinks that in pressing for those "extras," he was putting the essentials in jeopardy. By trying to get more, he is risking what he has, like the bird that reaches for a bigger worm and loses the one he has already. So understanding that he is lucky to have a job--since he knows many who do not--he is prepared to make no demands. Instead, he will do what he is told and will accept what he is given.

Fundamentally, this strategy of placating the adversary holds out little promise of achieving even its limited goal. The adversary is too determined, and too ready to take advantage of every weakness. Indications are that he--the corporate elite--will continue to press his case until American workers are paid at third world levels and the social wage is all but eliminated. There may possibly be a bottom in this. There may be some feed-back mechanism whereby corporate leaders see that people have to have money if corporations are to have markets. If there is, there may be a level of privation above simple survival that will not be exceeded in the downward movement. But even if there is, the impoverishment that is taking place now and which seems destined to deepen in the future is not an appropriate lot for citizens of a democracy. The fact that the New Deal of the 1930s took place and that countries like Sweden and Costa Rica have had vigorous welfare states gives proof that such states can be established. Doing so is what Reinhold Niebuhr called a "possibility of history."[53] And that being the case, it can be asserted that sooner or later an alternate strategy will have to be adopted. That is, people will have to wage battle against the corporate elite and eventually tame it. The job is to make the elite take their place as part of the community and to force them to cease trying to dominate it.

More is wrong with corporate domination than just the fact that ordinary people are deprived economically. In addition, it tends to swallow all other aspects of society and culture. It recruits for its own purposes the divers forms of creativity which the community inherits from the past and carries on in the present. Art and music are absorbed by advertising and "public relations," and so lose their proper character as expressions of human existence and community life. Science comes to exist only for the sake of technology; the "what" of pure inquiry is surrendered to the "how to do" of engineering. And technology, in turn, has an exclusive contract with business. It is concerned only with "how to" make things that will sell and then with selling them. More specifically, its task is viewed as twofold, to contribute to cost-cutting and therefore to the competitive edge which each corporation seeks, and to devise products that are just new enough to render present equipment obsolete and make new purchases necessary.

Scholarship also has two purposes. It provides rationale and justification for corporate dominance (the free market system), and it facilitates business communications (technical writing). Literature, especially in its popular forms, serves in part to spotlight the entrepreneur as society's hero and in part to divert attention from society's ills. It does the former by telling "Horatio Alger" stories in which the person who is in business for himself or who climbs the managerial hierarchy of a large firm proves that he "has what it takes" to succeed. He thereby becomes the image of the ideal member of society. Commonly, he also finds happiness in romantic episodes and in so doing completes the picture of human life in its perfection. The literature achieves the latter, the withdrawal of attention from pain and suffering, by emphasizing sex and romance, and by directing all attention to the "who done it" issue in which violence and evil are seen as the work of individual malefactors. A person commits a murder for purely personal reasons or because of character flaws that are peculiarly his. This focus of attention on the individual as the source of evil diverts attention from the institutional orders from which the violence and heartlessness of our age proceed.

Further, with the preemption of art, music, science, scholarship, and literature, the institutions that house these activities are similarly taken over. Newspapers have abdicated their vocations as the media by which the truth reaches the public. Universities are increasingly organized to service the corporate-industrial apparatus. The prestige of each institution depends on the "research" carried on within it and the research, in turn, depends upon funding. Much of the funding is provided by corporations or by sources themselves beholden to corporations. When university faculties shape their activities to fit a "business" mold, therefore, they are simply recognizing the facts of life. In the context of these facts, the traditional liberal arts idea of free inquiry into all of life and existence becomes virtually unintelligible.[54] In general, the quest for truth, the search for beauty, and inquiry about the good and noble lose the independence which they must have to realize their true natures and to carry out their proper vocations.

To say that the patriot wishes to live a full life which enhances the ability of others to do the same--to serve the community--is to say a great deal. It is to expose America as a country in which patriotism is largely lacking. The people have been thrust into a situation in which each has to watch out for himself, and the dominant corporate leadership has elected to concentrate on maximizing its own power and wealth.

Patriotism and Law-Abidingness of Nations

The third meaning of patriotism is that a person wants his country to do what is right. The citizen of a country is in this regard like the parent of a child. Parents may want their child to be happy, but they also want him or her to be good, honest, and kind. The parents' desires are not only that their children enjoy life, but also that their offspring know the fulfillment that comes from doing what is right.

Similarly, a patriot may want his country to prosper and may be pleased if the country has a good position among the nations of the world. But he will not settle for wealth, glory, or power. In addition, he wants his nation to do what is right. He wants it to establish justice within its own borders, and he wants it to treat other nations with respect and compassion. This wish for his country to act in accordance with moral law and in a humane manner is integral to patriotism itself. Of necessity, to do what is right is to obey general and abstract principles that apply to all nations equally. The nation is not good just because it is a certain nation. America cannot be good by simply being America. It does not have an essence or a vitality that guarantees goodness when it is acted out. And it is not enough for the nation to be powerful, as Americans often think, since power is by its nature amoral and can be either good or bad, depending on how and to what ends it is used. Rather, the nation can be good if--and only if--it acts in accordance with abstract principles that are laid upon the whole human community and therefore on it in particular. In terms of method, this means that to be good, the nation has to act ethically by applying abstract principles to specific situations. It cannot rely on intuition and act out its own essence; the awareness of being "America" does not serve Americans as an ethical guide. The nation cannot, just because it is America--even a strong and powerful America--be assured that it is good. It can be good only by obeying the same abstract and universal laws that France, Russia, Iran, and Brazil must obey if they wish to be good.

Stated negatively, if the nation does what is wrong, it will not be rescued from its shame by the fact that it is the nation it is. America cannot do whatever it wishes and then find justification in the fact that it is America. There is no partiality when right and wrong are set against each other. The Book of Amos in the Bible, in words attributed to the Lord, put the matter this way:

> You only have I known
>   of all the families on earth;
> therefore I will punish you
>   for all your iniquities (3:2)

To be a special people is not to enjoy an immunity from the demands of abstract law or from the shame that descends on those who violate it. It is, if anything, just the opposite: *more* is demanded of it. There is an especially intense expectation that such a nation will obey a law which is above it, and a particularly bitter shame which is cast upon it if it does not. Has the United States been entrusted with the democratic ideal in special degree? If so, an especially harsh judgment will descend upon it if it violates that ideal, as it is now doing both at home and abroad.

When people utter patriotic slogans, someone often says, "That has a ring to it." He thereby registers his pleasure in the slogan. To say that a patriot wants his country to do *what is right* is to say something that does *not* "have a ring to it." It is flat and ring-free! As is commonly the case with statements of what is true and right, it has a certain drabness about it. Truth does not always present itself in glowing colors. Careful reasoning and attention to what is truly good do not announce themselves with trumpet-calls. But still, they are what is important.

The Dark Side of Patriotism

Patriotism has a dark side. Patriots spend almost all of their time in the company of other patriots. As they talk with one another, they construct images of reality. The reality they build together is inevitably one in which the group which they together comprise is exalted above all. It is exalted not only above all others, but above all limit. The nation becomes *ultimate reality*, and as such defines both what is good and what is true. This kind of patriot assumes that his nation can do no wrong. He thinks, in the first instance, that his country has a good essence and for that reason has a powerful impetus to do right. If his country performs any act, he therefore assumes that the act must be right, since it is in the nation's nature to act rightly. But his thought goes a step further than this. Under the force of this kind of group enthusiasm, the concept of right loses all independent content. There is no longer an idea of the good that can be distinguished from the nation itself so that it makes sense to say that the nation does or does not do what is right. That is, the very idea of good is absorbed into the nation so that what it does is right by definition: the "right" is what the nation does.

The same holds for truth. As ordinarily used, the term "true" means that there is correspondence between a statement and experience or logical consistency. An assertion that a certain car is blue is true if someone who looks at the car sees blue. But under the impact of patriotism on its dark side, the concept takes on a different meaning. To say a statement is true is to say that it enhances, exalts, and justifies the nation. And as with the good, the true becomes a matter of definition. If a statement justifies the nation, it is a true statement. It can no more be false than a square can be round. There is no need to investigate. If investigation is carried out, it is ceremonial. It is done to prove something, not to find out something.

Both perversions, that of goodness and that of truth, are illustrated in the June 1986 World Court decision which went in favor of Nicaragua against the United States mentioned in the previous chapter. The fact that Americans engaged in no soul searching is noteworthy. The World Court, the same court to which America made appeal in the case of the taking of American hostages by Iran in 1979, handed down a decision regarding Nicaragua's complaint. The decision was that the United States was guilty of aggression. Certainly it is conceivable that the World Court was wrong, for courts too are human. In extreme circumstances, a nation might think that it must "take the law into its own hands," as is said. But it certainly would not put itself above the Court and therefore above the law without considerable discussion and soul searching. It should not be able to take such a step easily. But easily is how the United States did take it, and the way to account for this is to note that in the eyes of Americans, it was simply unthinkable that their country's actions could be wrong. They believed that because America did it, it had to be right.

On the matter of truth, American journalism succeeded in erasing a Nicaraguan election from the pages of history. The election destined for oblivion was held in November of 1984. The Sandinista party won by approximately sixty-three percent, a figure high enough to establish that it was a victory over opposing parties, but small enough to suggest that it was a true election. Yet because the party that won was opposed by the American government, the election was declared to be a non-event. In 1990, newspapers even referred to the election of that year as being the "first" since the revolution of 1979 in Nicaragua. That the election of 1984 did not fit into American policy meant that the election did not take place. Truth is what serves policy.

Resources for use against "Dark" Patriotism

The cultural inheritance of our civilization does not leave us without resources against these dark side perversions of the good and the true. Such resources are to be found in rationalism and the enlightenment, in Catholicism and in Protestantism. As noted by John McKenzie, the rationalist tradition appeared first as the wisdom of the scribes in ancient civilizations. These were the first literate men who used knowledge of reading and writing to serve kings and nobility. In the course of time, they developed a special feeling of status and honor based on wisdom rather than rank in a political order. The emphasis on wisdom made them international. They shared their special position with colleagues in all nations, and they identified with other wise men (had them as "reference group") more than with the nobility of their own societies.[55] For this reason, they cultivated abstract concepts that were independent of specific nations, and they served to represent and exalt an internationalism that linked nation with nation. Through the abstract concept and the international connection, they softened the nationalist feeling of nations. Even kings began in due course to want some of their brand of prestige, as is illustrated by the notion that Solomon was singularly wise. The scribes were some of the first "intellectuals" who have appeared throughout history. These are people in all ages who identify with mankind rather than the nations, favor abstract concepts over the gods (foci of sacredness) of particular peoples, and exert pressure against the absorption of the "good" and the "true" by the spirit of nationalism. Whatever else one may think about them, there is little doubt that their philosophies soften fanaticism and serve to provide a platform from which to oppose the dark side of patriotism.

In his five volume *The Sociology of Religion*, Werner Stark indicates how Catholicism opposes this dark side of patriotism. He said that the focus on the Papacy gives Catholicism and its piety an international character lacking in other branches of Christianity, including both Protestantism and Eastern Orthodoxy. It allows rulers to exercise authority; indeed it regards their administrative labor as a work of God. It also respects social structures and orderly community life. But it does not allow either rulers or social structures to claim divinity. And it requires peoples to confirm that a person who is an outsider to a society is nevertheless fully human. To the extent that Catholicism does this, it stands in contrast to the tendency found in most religions and in most expressions of Christianity. This is a tendency to identify faith and society, and to view people outside of a particular society as neither fully human nor as candidates for salvation. Being Christian is identified with being British, German or the like. Because the Catholic looks outside of his particular society to see the human being who is head of his Church, the Pope, he does not identify religion and society and so sees all human beings as falling within the sphere of divine concern.

Additionally, there are, for Stark, two kinds of tension within the Catholic Church that help it oppose the dark side of patriotism. The first is tension between hierarchy and religious order. The hierarchy represents the element of order in human society. It affirms that it is good for relations between people to be patterned, regardless what the pattern is in a particular case. In the religious orders of monks and nuns by contrast, there are people who are in the grip of religious enthusiasm. To them, faith bursts the boundaries of established orders and criticizes those orders from standpoints outside of them. Justice and compassion form the major standpoints. The impulse is to seek good and fair relations among people, regardless whether they are orderly.

The second tension is similar. It is between priest and saint. The priest also represents societal order: he must be male, and he may be selected by church officials on any basis they choose. Most commonly they choose on the basis of competence in maintaining continuity in church tradition and practice. These selectees can be and often are men who are competent but uninspired and who want mainly to have a good job and living. Having been chosen, they can then be trained and can serve adequately. The saint, on the other hand, is elected and moved by the Holy Spirit. A human being of any ascriptive category (ethnicity, social rank or gender) can be saint. Notably, women can be elevated to this status, and many have. Sainthood is the work of the Holy Spirit and for this reason is not formed by officials acting in accordance with established social blueprints. It is not subject to the constraints of either "administration" or traditional rank-orders. The Holy Spirit, we might say, is a mischievous feature of the social scene; it is not subject to the dominant authorities. The Church recognizes saints, but it does not make them. Church officials can assure that there will be priests, and in so doing, guarantee continuity in the religious life. Saints, however, appear if and when they do; they cannot be produced deliberately. Here too, order and justice are held in tension.

The truth of the faith is not found in either the hierarchy or the priest on the one hand or in religious order or saint on the other. It is found, rather, in the tension between them. This tension affirms order, but does not allow that order to claim ultimacy for itself. It allows patriotism but does battle with its dark side.

The Protestant resource is found in two elements which this branch of Christianity shares with Catholicism, but to which it gives singular emphasis. The first is the doctrine of "justification by faith." According to this belief, every human being is so mired in sin that he cannot do anything to achieve his salvation. Being, as he is, separated from God, even his attempts at being moral can only dig him in more deeply. But salvation is, despite this, given him as a free gift. What he cannot even begin to earn is given to him in its fullness. Where this doctrine is taken seriously, the believer is required to take responsibility for applying values from a high level of abstraction. Because he cannot earn salvation, he cannot be good by obeying the rules of his particular society. He is, rather, saved by grace and so put in a position where he wants to do right. He must act on the basis of a wish to act with justice and kindness, and this means that he must discern what justice and kindness mean in particular situations. He is lifted up to a platform above the community in which he lives and is invited--compelled--to live by higher values. He cannot be a conformist, but must instead relate directly to the higher values.

The second feature of Protestantism is related to the first. It is the emphasis on the sermon. Preaching is found in all of Christianity (and Judaism) but became preeminent in the Reformed churches. Its exalted position gave Protestant worship a "wordy" character not found in the same degree elsewhere. Something is always being said, a message communicated. The intent is that religious life would take on intelligible form. Being a believer has structure to it that can be understood. This is unnecessary where religion is ceremonial and confirms traditional patterns of life. But where the faithful are saved by grace and put in a place where they apply high-level values, tradition is not a sure guide. That a value is of a high level means that it is above traditions and seeks to judge and reform them. The preacher, then, is what any believer is, saved by grace and invited to live by justice and kindness. He is different from others only in that it is his calling to give intelligible statement of the meaning of the higher values from within a specific situation. He addresses the question of how one lives by justice and kindness when he is in a certain place, surrounded by certain people and affected by certain pressures and dilemmas. He gives his answers to that question and so invites and lures others to answer it also. His is counselor leadership; no one is required to agree with what he says, but the obligation to hear it is a serious one. Protestantism, then, is re-form. That is, patterns of life are to be continually reshaped in response to values that are higher than those of particular times, places, and peoples.

So patriotism has its dark side. Patriotism is good when it affirms one's particularist belonging and its expressive life, when a person is community-minded rather than selfish, and when he insists that his nation do right. Its dark side appears when the nation is made ultimate, when it defines the good and the true. A genuine patriot will do battle with the dark side. Making use of resources, perhaps one of those just described, perhaps another (Judaism, Islam, Bahai, Buddhism, Marxism), he will try to put down the dark side and lift up the bright side.

Intellectualism and Morality

Also pertinent to doing basic thinking about social life is the matter of morality as it stands in contrast to immorality. Among the many forms of immorality, greed is of special importance, since a grasping for ever more wealth seems to lie behind the most serious anti-social actions. Greed, however, is not simply desire. It is, instead, a desire rooted in a basic and profound confusion. A person has taken the idea of "more," has pulled it from concrete situations, and has made it into a program for his life. Had he remained in life-as-it-is, he would not be in constant quest for more, for there are limits to what a person can receive and enjoy. Up to a point, he can enjoy more food, but that point is quickly reached, and adding to what he has will have no value for him. He must wait for his appetite to return. The same is true of sex and other pleasures. When the concept of "more" is abstracted, however, it is freed of all limit. A person thinks he can always add to what he has, no matter what it is.

In Chapter Two, money was seen as the basic form of the "more." It exhibits upward linearity. It, like numbers, rises in a steady progression to infinity. It is not what money buys that does this. What it buys is concrete and therefore limited. It is, rather, money itself--money as idea--that goes up to the sky. People then take the idea of indefinite ascent and see it as applying to their own welfare or state of being "well off." They mistakenly think that they can always be more well off than they are at the moment. This is the confusion.

Stating matters this way, one could think that confusion as such is the problem. To think this would be to adopt an intellectualist understanding of what people do. It would be to assume that ideas and opinions are primary, that people first hold opinions about the nature of reality and then act on the basis of them. And if they hold certain opinions because facts have been incorrectly gathered or fallacies committed in reasoning, they both believe and act as they do because of those errors. Using the term "confusion" to refer to all errors, both of fact and of logic, one could say that confusion would explain behavior. If this were the case, confusion would be the problem and clarification would be the solution. Education would be the means to improve both belief and action.

Unfortunately, confusion is *not* the problem. The person who pushes hard to add ever more to his estate certainly is confused. He wrongly thinks that the condition of being well off rises parallel with increased holdings of money, and that the former, like the latter, goes up to the skies. The fact that he has such an erroneous idea of being "well off" and its relation to money does not, however, fully explain why he acts as he does. It is an intellectual structure involving the person's actions, but it is not the engine that generates the actions. It is not confusion as such that does it.

Behind the confusion itself is another and more basic factor. This may be called the *quest for glory.* We human beings are never content to simply live, enjoy ourselves for a time, and then pass on, leaving others to do the same. Rather, we insist on laying hold of something that is not time-bound, to something that is beyond the ravages of the passing years. It does not come and go, as do other things, but is "always." One could, for example, be a champion at something. He wins the championship at a certain time, but once won, it is his forever. The next year, another may take it from him, or (as with Miss America) it may necessarily pass to another. But the fact that he was the champion at a certain time is eternal. He will always *have been* the champion. An aged football star or beauty pageant winner may no longer have athletic or erotic power, but he or she remains one who at a certain time *was* a winner. People can be impressed by what the person was "in his time."

We human beings are self-conscious. We are aware, not only of the world around us, but also of ourselves. We see ourselves as we think others see us. Without thinking about it, we jump, in imagination, out of ourselves and into the people around us, perhaps into one of them, perhaps into people-in-general. We then form an idea of who we are and what we are based on what we think people see when they look at us. This view of ourselves, attributed to others, consists of entities that are not time bound. A person is certain things, such as a nobleman or a peasant, or such as intelligent or stupid, or such as beautiful or ugly. These are entities of which he is an example, or they are Platonic forms in which he participates.

Human beings share with animals the instinct for survival. To live is to passionately wish to continue living. Every animal fights, flees, or evades in order to survive. People, however, are different from cats and aardvarks in that this passion for survival attaches to the self as image attributed to other people. It is what George Herbert Mead called a person's "me" (consisting of non-time-bound entities) that struggles to live.[56] The person who believes that people think that he is good or intelligent or handsome will fight for that image of himself with the same energy exhibited by a rabbit trying to avoid a carnivore.

Among the timeless images attributed to others' view of one's self is that of being "well off." A person sees himself--that is, he sees others as seeing him--as prosperous or wealthy. The view of himself is agreeable to him, just as being well-fed is agreeable to a cat. And as the cat will spare no effort to attain that condition, so the wealthy person exerts all his energy to become even more wealthy. The image of himself as rich--indeed, as richer than others--is the entity which he defends and seeks to enhance. It is, to be sure, an idea in his head. But it is an idea for which he will scratch, bite, and in general do everything he can. An image of himself, separated from bodily sensations such as hunger or being filled, is what is important.

Rather than confusion as an explanation for the acquisitiveness of the wealthy and the power-lust of the powerful, then, the answer lies in the quest for glory. It is the wish to be something that resides in calm repose above the flux of events and which is immune to the ravages of time. It is more a moral than an intellectual factor. The moral factor, not confusion, is the motor behind the struggle for "more."

The matter can be stated as follows: one can imagine one's ancestors reaching back into a dim and distant past. Each successive generation going backwards is denoted by an additional "great" in the prefix of grandfather and grandmother. To go back eleven generations, for example, one adds nine "greats" before "grandparent." Most people know very little about their ancestors going back that far. But all can know for certain that if they say "Grandmother"--referring specifically to their maternal grandmother--and prefix it with nine "greats," they are talking about a specific person. There definitely was such a person. And there is one thing that all can know absolutely--she lived long enough to bear a baby. At what age she bore it, how many more she bore and everything else about her life may be question marks, but there is no doubt that she bore at least one. Thinking about this little-known but very real ancestor, people are content to let her be what she was--someone who was born, grew up, bore a child, and in due course died. All sorts of other things were true of her, of course, but we do not know what they are. People are willing to let her be but one link in the ancestral chain.

It is another matter, however, when we think of ourselves. The time will eventually come when we will be no more than a link in a chain of ancestors. Even if we ourselves do not have descendants, our brothers, sisters, and cousins will. Unless the human community destroys itself or is destroyed by who-knows-what, there will be people for whom each of us will be nothing more than someone who was born, lived for a time, and died. Just this, as Reinhold Niebuhr said, is a condition with which we are not content.[57] All fibers of our being resist it. It is to us terribly important that there be something more. There must be a glory that is above the passing of time, the change of circumstance and the aging of the body. Possibly those in the future may not know about this glory. We could live with that. However, there must at least have been something that our descendants find interesting about us. Perhaps they find that we were champions at something. Perhaps we lived out a tumultuous love-and-sex affair, the kind about which operas are made. Perhaps we were good and noble--perhaps, in fact, anything that lifts us above the status of being just one link in a chain, We have had some kind of glory.

Peculiar about this desired glory is that it can derive from an exalted individuality or a suppression of it. One can be either "the" something, or "a" something. A person might want to have been the most beautiful, the most noble, the most skilled, or the most successful within a certain group. Or, he might prefer to be one of the troops, a Christian or an American. In the first case, beauty, skill, and success have to be entities. They have, that is, to be realities filled with glory. In the second case, "the troops," "Christians" and "Americans" are entities, also resplendent with glory, into which one can be absorbed. Glory can consist in standing out or in being embraced within. The quest for glory reveals much about human beings. It explains both things that people would call good and things they would call bad. But important to this discussion is that it explains the dark side of patriotism and the confusion about money and efforts to acquire ever greater amounts of it. In the case of patriotism, a person is resisting being someone who would be just one more link in a chain of ancestors to a descendant living three or four centuries in the future. To make his resistance successful, he must make his country into something that is much more than just his country. It must be "America" or "Britannia" or something else which is a fit object of songs, together with the waving of flags, blowing of bugles, and other actions. It must be a glorious nationhood that embraces an individual and bestows its glory upon him. In the interest of making it glorious, a person hoists it up above all limit. He makes it ultimate and therefore the definer of the good and the true, as explained earlier. For this reason, he feels that he does right in doing anything in its name (as stated in Psalm 137:9 and as evidenced in the Gulf War of 1991) and in holding any belief that justifies it. Even more than justified, he feels compelled to do anything which is at his country's bidding, since his own glory depends upon that of the nation.

Similarly, the desire to be more than just somebody who comes and goes helps us to understand why people always want more money. When people add to already bloated estates, they see themselves as achieving a generalized and timeless "more." They are going "up" in a way that is outside of time and is in that sense eternal. This is not wealth that satisfies specific desires. It does something much grander than that; it addresses a wish that is like a mountain-peak which reaches above the flux and change of the world. When people want ever more money, they are seeking a resolution to the basic problem of existence, not just some "things" that are nice to have.

The struggle for ever more wealth and the dark side of patriotism go together. The people who are winning in the race for more money and more things with money imprinted on them use patriotism to advance their causes. By insisting that the nation be ever more powerful, by assuming that no moral scruple can stand in the way of that project, and by believing that the nation defines morality, the wealthy prepare the ground for maintaining and improving their ability to acquire riches. The national interest comes to mean--to refer to--a world in which people and institutions are arranged to facilitate the wealth-getting activity. The dark side of patriotism adds force to the acquisitiveness of the wealthy and is in turn supported by it.

It is now possible to say what morality is. It consists in coming fully to terms with a basic fact about ourselves: that we are, in reality and in truth, no more than links in a chain of ancestors and descendants. We are destined to live, to enjoy life in greater or lesser degree, and then to die, leaving others to go through the same process. While doing so, we may call lands our own, as the Bible puts it, and we may claim all kinds of glory for ourselves. But when all is said and done, claims to glory will be merely that--claims. They exist in imagination and have no foundation in reality. They may be confirmed by groups of people who are authorities in the eyes of a very large audience. But groups, like individuals, are finite; they come and go, and their glory too is imaginary. Whatever its nature, the non-time-bound "more" which we seek is ultimately impotent against the ravages of time. People huff and puff, but they cannot stop the bulldozer of the passing years. Humans are creatures who are born, who do or do not enjoy life, and then who fly away.

Morality consists in accepting this fact and not fighting it. To be moral is to embrace finitude and the creature-like nature of existence. It is to face the devastations of time without blinking. It is to abandon hope of inheriting, building, or finding glory that will lift us above mortality and the condition of the creature. By giving up such a hope, we are pushed back into our creature-like nature and are forced to accept it. We are pushed back into a stark realism and made to walk in an uncompromising landscape consisting of things that are real, not imaginary. It is a realism we can accept and a landscape in which we can walk only by an act of choice. We choose to give up the magic wonderlands of wealth and glory and allow ourselves to settle into what we are. It is this choosing that makes our living moral.

Once we are in the stark realism and the landscape of realities, there is only one kind of glory remaining--the glory of being good and decent and kind. No one can make himself into something that is above time, or immune to time's ravages. However, he can affirm people. He can take community seriously and wish fulfillment and happiness for others just as he wishes them for himself. He can be a "real" person. Then we can ask, if eleven generations from now, around 2300 or 2400 A.D., his descendants discover something about him, what would he want them to know? Would he want them to know or believe that he was wealthy and lived a life of luxury? Would he want them to know that he did well in terms peculiar to his age, such as auto racing or bull fighting? Would he want them to know that crowds flocked to see him and cheered him? Or would he want them to know that he was a good person, one notable for his honesty and for the kindness he displayed towards people?

The issue, actually, is ontological. That is, it has to do with what is real--or really real--in contrast to what merely appears or to what people think. Commonly in our era we define the term "true" as referring to what people in general think about any matter. Of course we do not mean that merely some people think it. Rather, we have in mind that many, or most or all people think it. This multiplicity or unanimity of agreement is what carries, for us, the burden of the idea of "true." Somewhere below the surface, however, we sense that "true" has another and more basic meaning. It means that something is true or "so" whether or not people think it. Reality itself comes to the fore as "people" fade into the background. And with this primacy of reality comes a kind of assurance that "people" cannot give. It is an assurance that whether a person does one thing or another really is important. It is important in truth and not just in opinion. Whether he sought thrills or applause on the one hand, or undertook to be honest and kind on the other, now matters. It matters, as Paul Tillich said, ultimately or unconditionally. [58]

This was the point in asking the question about what a descendent centuries in the future would think. That descendent is a person, but he/she is a person who is not part of our current society and therefore not part of its prejudices, preoccupations, and enthusiasms. He is someone who is, so to speak, from outside of all that we know. His view of things, therefore, pertains more to the really real--the unconditional--than would the view of someone of our own era. So again, what would we like *that* person to know or think about us?

Notes

1.*The Christian Century*, January 20, 1993.

2.Galbraith, John Kenneth, *The Affluent Society* (Boston: Houghton Mifflin Company, 1976) 111.

3.Strobel, Frederick R., *Upward Dreams, Downward Mobility: The Economic Decline of the American Middle Class* (Lanham, Maryland: Rowman & Littlefield Publishers, Inc., 1993) 23.

4.Brown, J. Larry and H.F. Pizer, *Living Hungry in America*. (New York: Penguin Books), 1987.

5.Veblen, Thorstein, *The Theory of the Leisure Class*. New York: B.W. Huebsch, date unknown.

6.Simmel, Georg, *The Philosophy of Money*, 2nd Ed. (London and New York: Routledge), 1990, 259-260.

7.Simmel, Georg, *The Philosophy of Money*, 279.

8.Durkheim, Emile, *The Elementary Forms of the Religious Life*, (New York: The Free Press, 1915), 52.

9. Durkheim, Emile, *Suicide*, (New York: Macmillan, 1951), 246-248.

10.Bultmann, Rudolph, *Kerygma and Myth; A Theological Debate*, (New York: Harper, 1961), 1-44.

11. Durkheim, Emile, *The Division of Labor in Society*, (Glencoe, Ill.: The Free Press, 1947).

12.Durkheim, Emile, *The Division of Labor*, (New York: The Macmillan Company, 1933), 203-204.

13.Etzioni, Amitai, *The Moral Dimension,* (New York: The Free Press, 1988), 1-6.

14.Becker, Gary, *A Treatise on the Family,* (Cambridge Massachusetts: Harvard University Press, 1981).

15. Hobbes, Thomas, *Leviathan,* (New York: Penguin Books, 1968, originally published in 1651).

16.Ross, Robert J. S. and Kent C. Trachte, *Global Capitalism*: The New Leviathan, (State University of New York Press, 1990), 64-65.

17.Niebuhr, Reinhold, *The Children of Light and the Children of Darkness.* (New York: Scribner, 1944), 98-106.

18.Stark, Werner, *The Sociology of Religion,* Volume III. (Fordham University Press), 1967-72.

19. Packer, George, "Down in the Valley," *The Nation,* (June 27, 1994), 900-904.

20.Galbraith, John Kenneth, *The Affluent Society.* (Boston: Houghton-Mifflin, 1984), 110-111.

21.Berger, Peter, *The Capitalist Revolution,* (New York: Basic Books, 1986), 39-48, 132-139.

22.Arrington, Leonard J., and Davis Britton, *The Mormon Experience* (New York: Alfred A. Knopf, 1979), 109-126.

23.Murdoch, William W., *The Poverty of Nations,* (Baltimore: The Johns Hopkins University Press, 1980), 307-321.

24.Berger, Peter, *The Social Construction of Reality: A Treatise on the Sociology of Knowledge.* (Garden City, New York: Doubleday), 1966.

25.Strobel, Frederick, *Upward Dreams, Downward Mobility*, (Lanham, Maryland: Rowman and Littlefield Publishers, 1993), 14-17, 25-26.

26.Domhoff, William, *The Power Elite and the State*, (New York: Aldine de Gruyter, 1990), 259-264. The statement that people are willing to regulate business when business is prospering is attributed to David Vogel, *Fluctuating Fortunes*, 1989, page 228, 290

27.Ross, Robert J.S. and Kent C. Trachte, *Global Capitalism: The New Leviathan.* (State University of New York Press, 1990).

28.Bello, Walden, *People and Power in the Pacific*, (San Francisco, Pluto Press, 1992), 90-98.

29. Strobel, Frederick R., *Upward Dreams, Downward Mobility*, (Lanham, Maryland, Rowman and Littlefield Publishers, 1993) 61-62.

30. Strobel, Frederick, *Upward Dreams, Downward Mobility* (Lanham Maryland: Rowman and Littlefield, 1992), 13-17, 204-205.

31.Friedman, Milton, *Capitalism and Freedom*, (Chicago: The University of Chicago Press, 1962).

32.Mills, C. Wright, *The Power Elite*, (New York: Oxford University Press, 1956).

33.Chomsky, Noam, *Towards a New Cold War: Essays on the Current Crisis and How we Got there*, (New York: Pantheon Books, 1982), 5-6.

34.Domhoff, William, *The Power Elite and the State*, (New York: Aldine De Gruyter, 1990), 185-186.

35. Domhoff, *The Power Elite and the State.*

36.Berger, Peter, *The Capitalist Revolution*, (New York: Basic Books, 1986), 128-129, 138, 141 150-153.

37. *Ibid.*

38.Ortega y Gasset, Jose *The Revolt of the Masses*, (New York: W.W. Norton Publishers, 1932 and Notre Dame, Indiana: The University of Notre Dame Press, 1985).

39.Sussman, Barry, *What Americans Really Think and Why Our Politicians Pay No Attention.* (New York: Pantheon Books, 1988), 33-35.

40.Gerth, Hans, and C. Wright Mills, *From Max Weber*, (New York: Oxford University Press, 1958), 194.

41.Gerth and Mills, *From Max Weber*, 245-252.

42.James, William, *Varieties of Religious Experience*, (Cambridge University Press, Harvard University Press, 1902), 251.

43.Westoff, Charles F., and Norman Ryder, *The Contraceptive Revolution*, (Princeton, New Jersey: Princeton University Press, 1977), 28-29.

44. *The World Population Data Sheet* is published each year by the Population Reference Bureau, Inc.

45.See the first page inside of Jean Paul Sartre's *Anti-Semite and Jew* (New York: Grove Press, Inc., 1948) "The anti-Semite is a man who wants to be a pitiless stone, a furious torrent, a devastating thunderbolt--anything except a man."

46.Dorr, Donal, *Option for the Poor: A Hundred Years of Vatican Social Teaching.* (Dublin: Gill and Macmillan.   Maryknoll, New York: Orbis Books, 1958).

47.This adequacy of food production to take care of the five-plus billion people in the world could of course cease to be the case in the future.   If population continues to grow at its current rate of 1.6 percent per year (doubling in 43 years), and/or if changes in weather or loss of top soil of cultivatable land cause food production to drop, it could happen that food supplies would no longer be sufficient, even if distribution were perfect.

48.Hazlett, Thomas W., "Telecommunications, Starting the Future Early" in David Boaz and Edwin H. Crane, *Market Liberalism: A Paradigm for the Twenty-First Century*. (Washington, D.C.: The Cato Institute, 1993), 129-146.

49.Sherman, Amy, *Preferential Option: A Christian and Neo-liberal Strategy for Latin America's Poor*, (Grand Rapids, Michigan: William B. Eerdmans Publishing Company, 1992).

50. Bello, Walden, and Shea Cunningham, *The U.S., Structural Adjustment and Global Poverty*, cited in "Reign of Error," *Dollars and Sense*, September-October, 1994, on third-world debt and American Power.

51.Ellul, Jacques, *The Technological Society*. (New York: Knopf, Reprinted, 1964), 85-94.

52.Durkheim, Emile, *Suicide*. (New York: The Free Press, 1951), 228-239.

53.Niebuhr, Reinhold, *The Nature and Destiny of Man*. (New York: Charles Scribner's Sons, 1943), 81-90, 160-183.

54.For an Orwellian or "brave new world" image of higher education, see "The Learning Revolution" by Lewis J. Perelman in Boaz, David and Edward H. Crane, Eds., *Market Liberalism*, (Washington, D.C.: The Cato Institute, 1993), 159-173.

55.McKenzie, John, *The Two-Edged Sword: An Interpretation of the Old Testament*. (Milwaukee: Bruce Publishing Company, 1956), 213-214.

56.Mead, George Herbert, *Mind, Self and Society from the Standpoint of a Social Behaviorist*. (Chicago: The University of Chicago Press, 1934). A more frequently used term is "looking-glass self" proposed by Charles Horton Cooley in "The Social Self," in Talcott Parsons, *et* al eds., *Theories of Society* (New York: The Free Press, 1961) 822-828.

57.Niebuhr, Reinhold, *Moral Man and Immoral Society.* (New York: Charles Scribner's Sons, 1932), 42.

58.Tillich, Paul, *The Courage to Be.* (New Haven: Yale University Press. 1952). The theme of the "unconditional" or concern with that which is "of ultimate concern" runs throughout Tillich's writings.

Index

About the Author

Wilmer E. MacNair received his B.A. degree from Park College in Parkville, Missouri, his B.D. degree from Chicago Theological Seminary and the University of Chicago, and his M.S. and Ph.D. in sociology from the University of Wisconsin. After serving as pastor of the Congregational-Christian Church of Leaf River, Illinois, he taught sociology at Elmhurst College in Elmhurst, Illinois, Memphis State University and West Texas State University. He has been Associate professor of sociology at the University of Southwestern Louisiana in Lafayette since 1973. Between 1985 and 1992 he made five trips to Nicaragua, the last three of them with Witness for Peace.